C000027618

INTERNAT

LIBRARIANSHIP

Surveys of Recent Developments in Developing
Countries and in Advanced Librarianship submitted to the 1971 IFLA Pre-Session Seminar
for Developing Countries sponsored by Unesco

Liverpool City Libraries
August 24–September 1 1971

Edited by George Chandler

LONDON   THE LIBRARY ASSOCIATION   1972

A

© The Library Association and IFLA 1972

First published by The Library Association
7 Ridgmount Street, London, WC1E 7AE
1972

ISBN 0 85365 305 4

Printed by George Berridge & Co. Ltd., London & Thetford

Contents

Introduction

GEORGE CHANDLER

President, Library Association and Local Organiser, 1971 IFLA Council Liverpool and the IFLA Pre-Session Seminar for Developing Countries sponsored by Unesco

The Library Association was invited by IFLA (President, Dr. H. Liebaers) to organise the first IFLA Pre-Session Seminar for Developing Countries to be sponsored by Unesco. This preceded and overlapped with the 1971 IFLA Council in Liverpool for which an International Exhibition of Library Technology and an International Exhibition on the Services of Library Associations were organised.

All library associations throughout the world were invited to nominate participants for the Pre-Session Seminar and the IFLA Council and exhibitors for the Library Technology Exhibition, and also to forward material relating to their own work. As a result of support from Unesco, the Commonwealth Foundation and the British Council, many of these associations were represented for the first time at an IFLA Council. In all, 22 developing countries were represented by 32 participants at the Pre-Session Seminar, and 64 countries by some 750 participants at the IFLA Council—an increase of more than 50% over the previous record of 40 countries. The object was, however, not to obtain a numerical record, but a break through in world-wide library co-operation. This involved maximum participation from the developing countries themselves.

All participants from developing countries were accordingly invited by the local organiser to submit an account of recent developments in their countries in advance of the Seminar. No less than 10 did so and copies were forwarded to all participants and lecturers in advance. In all, 20 studies are printed in Part I of this publication. These studies constitute an important survey of conditions in developing countries. Hence, discussions during the Seminar took place against a reasonably adequate factual background. Naturally the studies varied greatly in treatment, length and value. Collectively they have an archive value and are printed in full as records of conditions in developing countries at the time of their first opportunity of collaboration with developed countries on a world-wide scale.

The theme of the Seminar was Recent Developments in Advanced Librarianship and was determined by Unesco. The lecturers were chosen from the presidents of international library associations or exhibitors who had indicated their intention of participating in the exhibition as a result of the circular to all library associations requesting them to nominate participants. Their papers constitute Part II of this publication.

1

Each lecturer was asked to survey the impact of recent developments on one type of library with particular reference to the growing need for co-ordination and co-operation between all types of libraries. H. C. Campbell, President of INTAMEL (International Association of Metropolitan City Libraries), spoke on INTAMEL. K. W. Humphreys, President of the Universities Sub-section of IFLA, discussed university libraries. G. Marco, chairman of the International Library School Committee of the American Library Association, surveyed education for librarianship. D. J. Urquhart, who mounted an impressive exhibit in the International Library Technology Exhibition and invited IFLA delegates to visit the National Lending Library for Science and Technology, spoke on national technical libraries. H. Liebaers, President of IFLA, spoke on national libraries and was supported by Mrs. D. Anderson. Miss W. E. S. Coops spoke for P. Lazar of Unesco on international library co-operation and was supported by P. Havard-Williams, on international librarianship. D. H. Varley arranged for the case study of Liverpool University Library.

The local organiser arranged for various participants from developing countries to report on the papers and the discussion, as an illustration of the kind of impact that outstanding librarians from developed countries made on their colleagues from developing countries. Their reports are also printed in Part II. The local organiser also gave an introductory talk and presided at the last session.

Participants were also requested to attend the various meetings in connection with the 1971 IFLA Council whose general theme was the Organisation of the Library Profession, and to report on them. The object was not only to find out whether the proceedings were relevant to their needs, but also to record reactions from developing countries when they were for the first time represented in good numbers at an international library conference. The comments of the participants are understandably critical and should do something to help IFLA to secure the resources to become truly international. They are also published in Part II.

Participants were given guided tours of the International Exhibition of Library Technology and were asked to report on their reactions. The exhibition included 27 exhibitors from five countries, but mainly from the United Kingdom and the United States. It was organised by Liverpool City Libraries and the local organiser on behalf of the Library Association. Most of the exhibitors were concerned with library technology and library automation. The American Library Association mounted an extensive exhibition on its Technology Programme. The British Library Association's interest in library technology was reflected in the exhibits of the first two winners of its new Robinson Medal for innovation—Mansell Information/Publishing Ltd., publishers of the National Union Catalog for the Library of Congress and other important bibliographical works; and Automated Library Systems Limited which gave practical examples of the use of automation in library housekeeping and other procedures. Important examples of technical innovation were exhibited by the Automata Corporation Limited, the National Lending

Library for Science and Technology, Oriel Computer Services Limited, the Plessey Company Limited and Xerox Bibliographics. Electronic security devices were demonstrated by Diver Detection Devices and 3M Company.

Innovations in micropublishing and reprints were exhibited by Kraus Reprint, Library Resources Inc., National Cash Register Co. Ltd. and Scolar Press.

A contrasting range of library furniture and equipment was illustrated in the exhibits of the Einkaufszentrale für Offentliche Büchereien, the Scandinavian Library Centre, B. Serota Ltd. and the Werner Kullmann Organisation.

Publishers of library literature and reference books and library binders who were represented in the exhibition included Academic Press, Clive Bingley Ltd., Cedric Chivers Ltd., Blackwell's, Crosby Lockwood Ltd., André Deutsch Limited, Dunn and Wilson, Swets and Zeitlinger, and F. A. Thorpe (Publishers) Limited.

A practical demonstration of the international use of computers was arranged by Kent State University and Liverpool City Libraries. Telephone requests were sent from Liverpool to the computer data bank in Columbus, Ohio, into which a set of Marc tapes had been fed. Participants in the Seminar suggested authors and titles of works for which they required the classification number. The information was displayed on the American cathode ray tube terminal within a few seconds and was transmitted to Liverpool by telephone. There was no hitch.

Participants were also invited to visit the exhibition relating to the services of library associations. The contributions from the developing countries had revealed that most of these had recently established or were developing library associations which play a key part in the organisation of libraries in the democratic world. The exhibition had a section on international co-operation through Unesco, IFLA, FID, the International Association of Music Libraries and INTAMEL, which booked the largest accommodation in this section. In all, INTAMEL displayed some 400 publications illustrating the work of 55 city libraries in 15 countries.

Material was also exhibited from 31 national library associations in 20 countries, totalling approximately 600 items, and arranged by continent. Africa was represented by the Zambia Library Association, Asia by the Indian, Iranian, Pakistani, Saudi Arabian and South Korean Library Associations. The Australian, Canadian and American Library Associations were well represented, the ALA's exhibition being particularly comprehensive and impressive. It was by far the largest. European library associations were the most numerous and exhibits came from Austria, Finland, France, Federal Republic of Germany, the German Democratic Republic, Great Britain, Holland, Malta, Norway, Poland, Rumania and Spain.

The exhibition brought out forcibly the tremendous differences in the types of library associations. It was regretted that so many had not the resources to exhibit. However, the participants from the developing countries were no doubt pleased to see that, in spite of differences in size, there was a common thread. At the start of the alphabet, the American Library Association demonstrated its great resources in organising co-operation, while at the other end, the Zambia Library Association showed that, in spite of its small size, it too was able to send significant material on co-operation for the exhibition.

PART I

Surveys of Recent Developments in Developing Countries

1 AFRICA

(a) The Library Scene in Ethiopia: Problems and Prospects

RITA PANKHURST

University Librarian, Haile Selassie I University, Addis Ababa

Ethiopians possessed a script already in the first, pre-Christian days of the Aksumite Empire. The literary tradition is therefore an ancient one, continuing without interruption to the present day, despite changes in language and alphabet. Christianity dominated this tradition from the time of the conversion of King Ezana in the fourth century, when religious texts began to be translated into Ethiopic (Geez), the literary language of Northern Ethiopia of early times, until the beginning of printing in Ethiopia in the late nineteenth century.

1 Manuscripts

It was the custom of rulers and noblemen to endow churches and monasteries with manuscripts. Over the centuries religious institutions became the main repositories of manuscripts, the librarian being one of the more learned priests or monks. Despite the pillaging of churches which reached a climax during the Muslim invasions of the early sixteenth century, some churches, purposely located in inaccessible places, survived with their manuscripts the worse only for wear, damp, insects and neglect.

Ethiopia thus has a priceless written heritage mainly, but not exclusively, religious in character. There is as yet no complete register of manuscripts in Ethiopian churches, though Church officials have made inventories in a few provinces. There are estimated to be over 12,500 churches and some 800 monasteries in the country. More than 2,000 manuscripts are preserved in libraries outside Ethiopia. An important collection of 359 volumes was purchased by the British Museum in 1868 at an auction of plunder taken from the mountain fortress of Magdala where Emperor Tewodros II (1855–68) had assembled about 1,000 manuscripts for the endowment of a church.

A complete inventory of Ethiopian manuscripts at home and abroad will require priority in the programme of Ethiopian bibliography. Equally important is the crusade to preserve the manuscripts for posterity, in microtext form if not in the original. A pilot project was carried out by the Unesco Mobile Microfilming Unit which operated in Ethiopia September 1969– January 1970 and succeeded in filming 368 manuscripts, 177 of which were from monasteries and churches in the eastern part of Gojjam Province. The University Library and the Ministry of Education have acquired microfilming equipment and have technicians partially trained by Unesco.

7

It is hoped that, in co-operation with the Ethiopian Orthodox Church and the Antiquities Administration, full-scale manuscript microfilming will soon begin.

2 The beginnings of modern libraries

After the coronation of Emperor Haile Selassie in 1930 a few libraries of printed books began to make their appearance, partly in response to the needs of modern education, which the Emperor was encouraging, and partly under the stimulus of growing foreign communities in Addis Ababa. The Emperor, whilst still Regent, had established the Berhanena Salam Printing Press in the capital in 1923. This press was an important factor in encouraging the growth of printed Amharic literature.

During the Italian occupation the Italians established a central government library for Italian East Africa and built up a good library in Asmara, the capital of Eritrea.

Libraries as a public service began to make some impact in post-war Ethiopia largely through the establishment of the National Library.

3 The National Library and public libraries

The National Library, now holding some 100,000 volumes, was inaugurated by the Emperor in 1944 and serves both as a reference and a public library. The Research Division inherited the East African Collection of the Italian Library and developed strong holdings of material published in or about the country. A catalogue of the 272 manuscripts in the possession of the Library was published in Amharic in 1970, the first bibliographical publication of the Library. Understaffing and inadequate funds have prevented the development of national bibliographic and exchange services and there is little prospect of their developing in the near future.

On the public library side the Library has, from the beginning, offered its clientèle, consisting largely of students, reading and, later, lending facilities. This service has been very popular, especially as there is no other government library in Addis Ababa lending books to the public.

In October 1968, Mr. William Paton, a library consultant, visited Ethiopia at the request of the Ethiopian Government, under the Unesco participation programme and stayed for three months; he had been asked to prepare a long-term plan for nation-wide development of public and school library services and to make recommendations concerning the future of the National Library. His recommendations on school library development are discussed in the section on school libraries. With regard to the National Library, he recommended that it should leave to the University Library and its Institute of Ethiopian Studies branch the responsibility for 'national' and reference functions, which these libraries were fulfilling to some extent already, and should concentrate its resources on the public library functions, becoming in effect the headquarters of the central public library in a country-wide public library system.

Recently there have been encouraging signs that the National Library is seeing its role as the initiator and co-ordinator of public library services throughout Ethiopia along the lines envisaged by Mr. Paton. A small community library at Debre Zeit was absorbed in 1968 and small branches were opened at Yirgalem in 1969 and Harrar in 1971. There are plans to open another branch in the province of Beghemder this year. At the moment the intention is to open a total of 10 branch libraries.

The only other public library financed from government funds is the Education Department Library in Asmara, though a few municipal authorities have sponsored local libraries in co-operation with groups of enthusiasts.

Community libraries have been springing up under local initiative in Addis Ababa, provincial capitals and other towns. Enthusiasm is widespread, specially among the school-age population. The Addis Ababa Municipality is planning to open a library in the Town Hall in 1972; books and staff are being selected, with technical assistance from the British Council and other agencies.

Mr. Paton made the following major recommendations about public libraries in Ethiopia:

(a) Public library service in the provinces should be linked with nation-wide efforts to increase literacy.

(b) Libraries in rural areas and small towns should provide simple books in Amharic specially written to cater for the practical interests of the newly literate adults; in general more Amharic literature must be stocked for students and adults who have completed their schooling.

(c) In these areas public library service would be best provided by extending the scope of the school library service to include the general public in the surrounding area.

(d) Public library development in the larger provincial towns and in the capital should be placed on a sound organisational basis under one central governing body.

(e) A Public Libraries Board should be set up by legal enactment with representatives from the Ministries of Education, Community Development, Finance and Interior, the National Library, the University, etc., on the patterns of successful schemes operating in Kenya and Tanzania. It should be responsible for public library services throughout the country.

(f) The director of the Public Library Service should be a fully qualified and widely experienced librarian.

The above recommendations await implementation as soon as there has been a government decision to co-ordinate and develop existing public library services, and to create a single authority to direct and administer them.

4 School libraries

From his survey of school libraries in Ethiopia, Mr. Paton gained a general impression of 'hopefulness for the future, tempered by frustrations in the present'. Below are listed his main recommendations with comments on their implementation:

(a) 'A school libraries department should be set up within the Ministry of Education under the control of a director who must be a qualified and experienced librarian to organise and supervise the school library service and select and allocate the book stock.'

In 1970 the Department of Cultural Affairs and External Aid of the Ministry appointed its first expert librarian. Although the expert was a graduate with only a minor in library science, this first step was significant as a particular person in the Ministry was henceforth assigned the general responsibility for following up all matters concerning school libraries. Recently a Division of Libraries, Museums and Antiquities was established and headed by a Director-General. The Department of Cultural Affairs devised a questionnaire on existing library services in schools throughout the country and circulated it to provincial education officers. The result was as follows:

Number of schools	1,329
Number of libraries	139
Number of librarians	83
Number of trained librarians	8

(b) 'Greatly increased provision of library books is essential, both by purchase and by gifts.'

With a USAID grant of Eth.$50,000, books have been purchased and distributed to secondary schools in the country. With World Bank International Development Association assistance, the project to provide 61 new junior and senior secondary schools with 100,000 volumes is well under way. Library books are being selected for a second IDA project.

(c) 'An annual allocation of funds from the Ministry for the purchase of school library books is essential for the future development of the service.'

This allocation does not appear to have been made.

(d) 'A central book store or depot should be established in Addis Ababa where library books would be received, processed and distributed. Books should be classified and catalogued centrally before distribution.'

The book store of the Ministry in Addis Ababa, where thousands of volumes intended for school libraries have been accumulating, is now serving as the centre Mr. Paton envisaged. A large number of books in the store have been catalogued and are soon to be distributed, though no additional permanent staff have been appointed.

(e) 'Books should be distributed regularly and systematically. Due regard must be paid to the suitability of the books sent.'

Such a regular distribution system has not yet been devised.

(f) 'A pamphlet should be prepared and distributed to all schools given simple instructions in the organisation and effective use of school libraries.'

Such a pamphlet, which should be in Amharic, has not yet appeared in print, although a mimeographed brochure was apparently produced for limited distribution.

(g) 'School directors should be officially notified that the person in charge of a school library is no longer financially responsible for lost books.'

It is the writer's understanding that such a directive from the Ministry exists but is not widely known to exist.

(h) 'All senior secondary schools should have a full-time librarian with some background of library training.'

As was seen from the Ministry survey, there is an urgent need for trained librarians. The courses offered by the Faculty of Education of the University are presently under review and are to be adjusted to meet the immediate need.

(i) 'Courses of training in library methods should be given to students in the teacher training colleges, so that teachers should have practical knowledge in the effective use of libraries.'

Recommendations were made that librarianship courses should be taught at all teacher training institutes in Ethiopia by university graduates with a minor in library science but these recommendations could not easily be fitted into the existing teacher training programme and have not so far been put into effect.

(j) 'Vacation courses in librarianship should also be organised in the summer months, so that teachers already qualified can gain basic knowledge of library techniques.'

This suggestion was implemented in July 1971, when more than 30 teachers working in school libraries began to attend the first of three six-week summer vacation courses held in the towns of Gondar and Nazareth. The courses were organised by the library expert of the Ministry of Education. They are being held on: the school curriculum and the library; the administration and organisation of school libraries; and library activities and practical training. The courses are being given by American school librarians with the assistance of the National Education Association of the United States and the United States Agency for International Development and will be completed by August 1973. This programme should be greatly expanded so that interim teacher librarians can begin to develop school libraries until such time as higher-level manpower can be trained.

The school library situation, it will be seen, is on the threshold of major improvement, especially if the University can organise courses in librarianship fitted to the needs of the embryonic school library system.

5 The University libraries

(a) *Haile Selassie I University*

As in many developing countries, university libraries have had more opportunities for growth than did public or other types of library. Being a part of the university, academic libraries are able to attract a larger share of government funds as well as considerable external assistance.

The Haile Selassie I University was created in December 1961 out of a number of previously autonomous institutions of higher learning, each with its own book collection; additional faculties and institutes developed and sprouted libraries almost overnight. However, a degree of centralisation was gradually introduced so that a more homogeneous library system began to take shape. A statute on the Library, incorporated in the University legislation in 1965, defines the role of the librarian, the library committee and the relation between the central library and other libraries in the system.

By 1971 there were some 221,000 volumes in the University libraries. The largest and oldest library in the system was that of the University College of Addis Ababa, an institution founded in 1950. Ever since the establishment of that library, it had been the policy of the Librarian to develop Ethiopian collections to serve the research needs of scholars and the requirements of the general readers, as well as the needs of the staff and students of the College. This policy still prevails. The responsibility of the University Library, now the largest library in Ethiopia, is increasingly seen as exceeding that of a library serving the needs of the University alone. External readers, some 1,000 in number, are encouraged to avail themselves of all library facilities.

The Central University Library moved into a new building in August 1969, given by the United States Agency for International Development: it was dedicated to John F. Kennedy and was inaugurated on 23 July 1970 by the Emperor Haile Selassie and Mrs. Rose Kennedy.

The Library is a two-storey concrete, aluminium and glass structure covering an area of 5,000 square metres and capable of housing 200,000 books and 700 students. The basement, excavated but not finished, will house another 200,000 volumes.

The University Library has collections of foreign government documents and enjoys the depository privilege for United Nations and most UN agency materials. It exchanges publications with several hundred institutions abroad and an interlibrary loan scheme operates for most libraries in the city. Because of the cost of sending books by airmail and because of the time taken for books to reach Ethiopia by sea from foreign centres of learning, prospects for extensive international loans—or even inter-African loans—are remote.

All libraries in the University contribute to an author union catalogue housed in the Kennedy Library. Ordering and cataloguing for sub-libraries in Addis Ababa is done centrally at the Kennedy Library. The process of recataloguing from the Dewey Decimal to the Library of Congress classification is almost complete in all libraries which are scheduled for reclassification. The annual list of some 4,000 current serials in the University libraries has since 1967 been incorporated in *Periodicals in East African Libraries,* a union list produced by computer at West Virginia University.

The Institute of Ethiopian Studies (18,300 volumes) was created in 1969 to act as a centre for research on Ethiopia. Its library incorporated in the University Library System in 1967, and with university resources behind it has built up by 1971 a fine Ethiopiana collection including 8,000 volumes in Ethiopian languages; there are 634 microfilm units and 555 manuscripts and scrolls. The Institute publishes a series of bibliographies which make it in effect the centre of national bibliographic activity. These are the annual *Register of Current Research on Ethiopia and the Horn of Africa*, 1963—; the biennial *List of Current Periodical Publications in Ethiopia*, 1964—; and the annual *Ethiopian Publications*, 1965—. The latter publication lists and classifies books, pamphlets and periodical articles published in Ethiopia but the list is not exhaustive as efforts to obtain a law of deposit have not yet been successful.

The monthly acquisitions list of the University Library lists separately the acquisitions of the Institute and is the nearest approach to a current national bibliography. A retrospective card index of Ethiopian periodicals is in preparation by the Reference Department.

The following divisional libraries are administratively centralised: Law Library (17,500 volumes), Medical Library (7,600), Science-Technology Library (27,000), Technology Reading Room (3,000), Theology Library (4,800).

The Faculties of Science and Technology (previously Engineering) are served by a joint library, but the Reading Room presently on the new Faculty of Technology Campus is to be replaced by a full-scale Technology Library. The Law Library possesses a fine collection of African legal materials, completed where necessary on microfiche.

Other libraries in the system, though not under the financial control of the University Library, are:

Addis Ababa

Laboratory School Library (8,000 volumes): a school library administered by the Faculty of Education.

Technology Southern Campus Library (5,700 volumes): a library on building technology and related subjects which receives Swedish Government assistance.

Alemaya (548 km east of Addis Ababa)

College of Agriculture Library (21,100 volumes).

Gondar (748 km north of Addis Ababa)

College of Public Health Library (8,900 volumes).

The Colleges outside Addis Ababa will in due course develop into branch universities. Their collections are presently being supplemented by a USAID loan which extends to all libraries in the system.

The University libraries have benefited immeasurably from Ford Foundation assistance which is being followed by the aforementioned USAID loan. However, because of this assistance, the University book budget has received a lower priority in the apportionment of University funds than it might otherwise have done. Though the total library expenditure is over 6% of the university budget (Government funds), more than half of the Library budget is expended on salaries; the main reason for this is the fragmented nature of the University itself, which spreads over five campuses in Addis Ababa and two campuses hundreds of kilometers from the capital. Inevitably this fragmentation is reflected in the library system which employs over 100 persons in its 11 libraries. This multiple library system is expensive not only in terms of staff

13

but also in the need to duplicate reference and other materials. From the student's point of view, on the other hand, the system offers several advantages: the library is close at hand; the collections are more appropriate to his needs; the catalogue is smaller and less terrifying and the library staff are not so remote.

The professional staff of 14 is largely expatriate. Ethiopian graduates are selected every year and are mostly sent abroad after a two-year period of in-service training to obtain masters' degrees in librarianship. By the end of academic year 1971–2, five Ethiopians are expected to have taken up professional positions in university libraries.

Librarians in the University have been working towards a development plan by producing projections of staff and book needs in the coming years, which are appended to annual reports. Special attention will have to be paid to the out-of-town campuses and to areas to be selected for post-graduate study.

Mr. Paton suggested that 'in the interest of efficiency and economy, consideration should be given to a proposal to merge the research department of the National Library with the University Library (i.e. the Kennedy Library) and the Ethiopian collection with the Institute of Ethiopian Studies'.

In several African countries it has been decided not to duplicate expensive library services by developing research and reference collections both at a national library and at a university library; instead research workers are to be served by a single university and reference collection and the savings are to be invested in developing extensive public library services radiating from a large central public library. This pattern has emerged in Uganda, which does not have, or plan to have, a national library, and in Zambia, where the University Library was designated the National Reference Library in 1969.

Such a division of resources would appear to be a rational one for Ethiopia where public library services have not yet received the attention they deserve.

(b) *University of Asmara*
The private University of Asmara was founded by an Italian order of nuns, the Pie Madri della Nigrizzia, and was granted university status in 1967. Its library, in spacious new premises, has a book stock of some 40,000 volumes, consisting mainly of donated books in Italian. The collection is not yet organised.

6 Government libraries

In government ministries and agencies there has been a growing realisation of the importance of library and information services, though budgets to develop these have often been small. Among the largest and most active libraries may be counted that of the Institute of Public Administration, the Abba Dina Police College and the Imperial Air Force at Debre Zeit. Most important departments now have some library provision. The Emperor's private library has collections of books donated by Ethiopian and foreign writers, as well as manuscripts of great interest.

7 Special and foreign libraries

Of the special libraries in Ethiopia the most important is that of the United Nations Economic Commission for Africa, founded in 1958. Its strength is mainly in African government and agency documents and in an excellent serials section containing a large number of periodicals not easily obtained by purchase. There is also a fine collection of bank reports as well as a section of the United Nations documents. The Library has over 50,000 volumes, excluding documents, and is manned by a staff of 20.

The most active among libraries supported by foreign governments is the American Library founded in 1952. It is a public library sponsored by the United States Information Service and it pioneered library service in the provinces. In the '60s, reading rooms were opened, often in co-operation with the Ministry of Education, in Dessie, Dire Dawa, Gondar, Harar, Jimma, Lekemt and Mekele, though the Harar library had subsequently to be closed. The Library of the British Council contains a fine collection of 15,000 volumes from and about Britain. This Library is well organised and is open at useful times of the day. The German and Italian cultural institutes, the Russian Exhibition, the Alliance Française and a number of other foreign cultural institutions maintain small libraries in the capital.

8 Library Studies in Ethiopia

Traditionally little prestige accrued to the keeper of the books. In the late 1950s and early '60s, however, courses in elementary librarianship organised by the Ministry of Education, the National Library and the Extension Department of the University opened the way for a recognition of librarianship as a profession.

The Department of Library Science, Faculty of Education, Haile Selassie I University, began in 1966 as a programme in Library Science—part of a Secondary Teachers' Training Project of the United Nations Development Programme which was executed by Unesco.

The first Chairman of the programme, Dr. C. P. Shukla, a Unesco expert, was succeeded by Miss Ruby Martz, who became first Head of the Department of Library Science when this was established in October 1969. An Ethiopian graduate received a Unesco fellowship. He joined the Department in March 1971, and is now in charge. Other teaching is contributed voluntarily by University Library staff, five of whom held courses in 1969–70.

The Department offers a Minor in Library Science to secondary education students working for BA or BSc(Ed) degrees and is oriented towards school librarianship. Eleven students graduated in 1969, 16 in 1970 and 17 in 1971— 44 graduates in all. As of 1969–70 enrolment was restricted to 20 students a year.

As part of their academic requirement, all degree students at Haile Selassie I

15

University spend one year on Ethiopian University Service in the provinces. This year of service is most useful in providing students with the opportunity of working in small school or community libraries.

A second course, designed to train library assistants, consisted of 32 semester hours and could at first be taken either as a full-time one-year course or as two-and-a-half-year part-time course in University Extension. Seventy-two students have so far been awarded the diploma.

The Faculty of Education, in consultation with the Ministry of Education, is considering the possibility of lengthening the diploma course to two years in order to meet a more selective demand for better-trained library personnel, but as yet there are no library manpower projections for Ethiopia and a survey is being undertaken. The diploma course was suspended in 1970–1 and will not be held in 1971–2.

At a Conference of Head Librarians of Eastern African Universities held in Addis Ababa in 1971 (see paragraph 10b below), it was recommended that graduate studies programmes in librarianship should be established to serve the needs of Eastern Africa. To this end, and for purposes of co-ordinating existing training programmes, curricula and standards, the heads of the three existing programmes of library studies (i.e. those of Makerere University; University of Zambia; and Haile Selassie I University) have been asked to form a permanent committee. It is hoped that this welcome step in the direction of co-operation will soon be taken.

9 Library organisations

(a) *The Ethiopian Library Association* was founded in 1967 and achieved official status as a registered society in 1969. At present there are over 60 members. High on its programme of action is a campaign to obtain a law of deposit for Ethiopia, the lack of which is a serious obstacle to library development. The Association has been pressing for adequate librarianship education in Ethiopia and has set up committees to study school, special and government libraries. A seminar for officials in charge of such libraries is being organised.

(b) *SCAULEA*. The University Librarian is a member of SCAUL—Standing Conference of African University Librarians—and the Library organised the inaugural conference of the Eastern Area branch of the parent organisation, at which 10 East African university libraries were represented. SCAULEA's aims are, broadly, closer co-ordination and co-operation between university libraries in Eastern Africa. The Conference, held in February 1971, was the first move in this direction.

10 The next steps

The above survey has indicated that, very recently, there have been considerable developments on the Ethiopian library scene. However, these developments have been unco-ordinated and sometimes competitive rather than co-operative in spirit. Authorities interested in library development in Ethiopia face a great opportunity to unite their efforts. From these there should arise a comprehensive national plan envisaging:

(a) Library legislation setting up a national authority for planning and co-ordinating library services.

(b) An ordinance establishing legal deposit.

(c) A plan for the preservation and registration of Ethiopian manuscripts.

(d) A plan for a comprehensive national bibliography.

(e) A plan for school library services.

(f) A plan for national public library services.

(g) A programme of library science education at all levels from elementary school librarian to full professional librarian.

When these plans and programmes are drawn up and set in motion, Ethiopia's library services will make a more effective impact on national development.

REFERENCES

Belcher, Sheila. 'Libraries in Ethiopia.' *PNLA Quarterly,* v. 35, 1971.

Haile Selassie I University. Library. *Annual report, 1970–1.* Addis Ababa, 1971.

Paton, W. B. *Ethiopia: development of public and school libraries.* Paris, 1969. (Unesco serial no. 1110/BMS.RD/DBA. Limited Distribution.)

Pankhurst, Richard. 'The foundations of education, printing, newspapers, book production, libraries and literacy in Ethiopia.' *Ethiopia Observer,* v. 6, no. 3, 1962.

Pankhurst, Rita. 'Ethiopia, Libraries in.' (Provisional title of article to be published in *Encyclopedia of library and information science,* A. Kent and H. Lancour, eds., New York, 1968—.)

Pankhurst, Rita. The history of the Emperor Tewodros II at Mägdala; paper presented at the Interdisciplinary Seminar of the Faculties of Arts and Education, Haile Selassie I University, Addis Ababa, 1971.

Pankhurst, Rita. *National and regional library organisations in Eastern Africa, with special reference to Ethiopia and SCAULEA.* (Paper submitted to IFLA General Council Meeting, Liverpool, 1971.)

Paton, William B. 'Libraries in Ethiopia.' *Unesco Bulletin for Libraries,* v. 24, no. 1, 1970.

Standing Conference of African University Librarians. *SCAUL Newsletter,* no. 6, July 1971.

Standing Conference of African University Librarians. Eastern Area Conference, Addis Ababa, 1971. *Preliminary report.* Addis Ababa, 1971.

Wright, S. 'Book and manuscript collection in Ethiopia.' In *Journal of Ethiopian Studies,* v. 2, no. 2, 1964.

(b)   Possible impact of past, present and future developments of Library Services in Ghana

DAVID CORNELIUS
Principal Librarian, Accra Central Library

The development of libraries, in particular the spectacular growth of public libraries in Ghana, is too well known to require repetition here. So much has been written on it. However, it might be worthwhile to outline some of the salient features which have had impact on the systems of other countries and which I hope could well be noted with respect to those countries which are just about to develop their library services.

1   Planning and co-ordination at national level

The Ghana (Gold Coast) Library Board ordinance of 1950 was the first of its kind in tropical Africa and perhaps in most developing countries. It was remarkable for its departure from responsibility by local authorities for public libraries as in other countries to a central government responsibility. The circumstances in developing countries in Africa were different. The Ghana Library Board, with full government support backed by legislation and financial means, set out to establish, equip and maintain libraries throughout the country. *This departure set the model for many developing countries throughout Africa and other parts of the world,* and was responsible for the rapid growth and development of public library services in Ghana.

It was obvious from the start that, with the slow pace of development of local government in Ghana and generally in most newly independent countries, support for public libraries by local authorities was likely to be very slow, if at all.

A central government body with legislation and the financial means was needed. This would take account of the needs of the entire nation and plan accordingly. Again, with this departure initially from local authority responsibility for public libraries, it was possible to provide a uniform service throughout the country, in addition to other supporting services which otherwise would have been expensive because of obvious duplication of effort. A centralised book purchasing, classification and cataloguing service proved more economical and efficient and generally the experiment has been successful. As a future policy, and until the time when local authorities would be sufficiently strong financially and when the service would have expanded sufficiently, local authorities were initially called upon to agree to a small financial contribution wherever libraries were established in their areas. The contribution was rather small but the whole idea was one of foresight to make for more financial support for the libraries at a future date and to create local support for a service which in many ways is a local service anyway.

Though the Ghana Library Board at a later stage established the Research Library on African Affairs as part of its services, its main area of concentration has been with public libraries. At a later stage it took over responsibility for middle-school libraries throughout the country by offering a mobile library service specially for schools. But the underlining idea was, of course, to cater for the vast majority of school children in the rural areas who did not have access to the children's libraries offered by the public libraries in the larger towns. Very shortly, the Ghana Library Board may take over libraries in secondary schools and teacher training colleges.

Here again, the Ghana Library Board is concerned with creating the readership for its public libraries quite apart from other motives.

Other types of libraries have, of course, developed independently, notably university libraries of which there are at present three. Several specialised libraries have also sprung up in support of scientific and technical research, the majority being under the aegis of the Council for Scientific and Industrial Research. With respect to public libraries, the present pattern of growth of local government particularly regional administration following the government's policy of decentralisation, and the expansion of the library service itself would seem to call for a greater decentralisation of the library service so that the small grant-in-aid by local or regional administrative authorities might develop into a substantial source of income for the library. As a matter of policy, it seems that, in future, regional or local administrative authorities would be made responsible for providing buildings whereas the central government through the Ghana Library Board would be responsible for books, staff and other ancillary services.

All these developments apart, it has become obvious in all quarters that further development at this stage must now take place within an agreed framework of a national library service. This was realised quite early on in 1964, when a Technical Advisory Committee to advise the Ghana Library Board on a National Library recommended instead a Council for the coordination of library services to attain the objective of a national library service. It became then quite obvious that any talk of an adequate book provision or library service for the entire Ghana must first be based on a rational organisation of the existing libraries themselves.

This would seem to call for a National Planning body for all types of libraries throughout the country. Such a body is likely to have considerable impact on the further development of libraries throughout the country, as it will be in a position to consider the library needs of the country as a whole and not from the point of view of individual types of libraries. This is yet to be achieved in Ghana.

2 Secondary schools and training college libraries
Although libraries in secondary schools and teacher training colleges have remained the responsibility of the Ministry of Education, the new move to entrust such responsibility to the Ghana Library Board seems a step in the right direction. Initially, and at the request of the Ministry of Education, the Board conducted a survey of the situation of libraries in secondary schools and training colleges. A positive move has now been made by the Government in

its 1971–2 budget by the allocation of a large sum of money to start off a number of these school libraries. Further funds are to be made from year to year until all secondary schools and training colleges have been covered. These are, of course, capital grants but recurrent grants are also to be made. Because of this, the Ghana Library Board, in conjunction with the British Council, have mounted several courses for teacher/librarians in anticipation of this move towards improvement of libraries in secondary schools and teacher training colleges throughout the country.

The possible impact of this type of development would mean that the output of secondary schools and training colleges would already be library users. This is important from the point of view of the public library and its use and also the whole economy of Ghana. It is realised that the greatest manpower resources of the country would come from these institutions. There is also the possibility of more openings for professional librarians and its consequent effect on the library schools.

3 Ghana Library Association

The Ghana Library Association, like other professional associations in Ghana, is fully recognised by the Government but a new development is just about taking place. The new Constitution of Ghana expressly calls for the registration of all professional bodies in the country by the President. The conditions for acceptance for registration are very stringent and, amongst others, require such a professional body to be so registered to show that it has in fact been engaged in research for the furtherance of professional knowledge in its field, has a code of ethics for its members to observe, and can enforce discipline amongst its members. There are fees to be paid by the Association itself and by members. The article in the constitution forbids anyone not so registered to practise the profession in the country.

The possible impact of this move will be in the strengthening of the Ghana Library Association, thus giving it a greater say in government circles. It should also lead to the Association being in a position to have more say in the development of library services in the country. Again, it would place the Association on equal footing with the other professional bodies in the country. Another move which might augur well for the profession is the formation of the Commonwealth Library Association which is at present under discussion.

4 Library education

The education of librarians in Ghana was put on firm footing in 1962 with the establishment of the Ghana library school.

The school later moved to the University of Ghana and became the Department of Library Studies. The earlier British Library Association examinations and an undergraduate course has given way to a postgraduate diploma in library studies.

With the nature of the service, in particular public libraries, it was realised that the very nature of the service, with its numerous small service points, etc., required another type of staff who did not need to be highly qualified professional people. Although the training of this type of staff was initially undertaken by the individual libraries, it has now been put on a firm foundation by the mounting of a sub-professional course as part of the Department of Library Studies at the University of Ghana.

(c) Books for a Growing Kenya

FRANCIS OTIENO PALA
Chief Librarian, Kenya National Library Services

In a developing country like Kenya, there is a very close relation between economic development and the spreading of knowledge. Books are the main agent for the spreading of knowledge in a literate society.

To get an idea of how rapidly Kenya is becoming a fully literate society, let us look at school enrolment figures. The number of pupils in primary schools increased from 781,000 in 1960 to 1,427,000 in 1970. The number of pupils in secondary schools increased over the same period *sixfold,* from 20,000 to 127,000.

Not only does formal education increase literacy; there are also ambitious programmes of adult education.

Books are required in order to produce literacy and spread knowledge. But as soon as literacy and knowledge have been acquired, this in itself generates new demand for books. As a matter of fact books, as more or less continuous exposition to the written word, are necessary to keep up a newly acquired reading habit. If the new literate is left in a vacuum without access to reading material, he will soon lapse back into illiteracy.

If we assume that the population of Kenya will continue to grow by 3.3% per year, the population in 1980 will be 15,600,000. There are many rough methods by which we could estimate the need for libraries by that year. Let us, for example, look at the actual situation today in a country like Denmark. In that country there are, in public libraries, 3,295 books per 1,000 literates. In schools there are 8,000 books per 1,000 students. In Africa as a whole there are in public libraries 100 books per 1,000 literates, and in schools 100 books per 1,000 students. Even if the situation in Kenya is better than in Africa as a whole, these figures illustrate the magnitude of the task of providing books to a rapidly growing number of literates. If Kenya were to attain the Danish ratio of books to people by 1980, she would need about 22,000,000 books in public libraries. The figure today is a mere 200,000 volumes.

In 1965 Parliament passed the Kenya National Library Service Board Act. As a result of this Act the library service was established in 1965 with powers 'to promote, establish, equip, maintain and develop libraries in Kenya'. The Library Service became fully operative in 1967. In this short time the service has achieved some good results.

The Library Service's Development Plan for the five financial years 1969–70 to 1973–4 is incorporated in Kenya Government's Second Development Plan. The goals of the library plan, to be attained by 1974, can be summarised as follows:

1 headquarters building in Nairobi
5 area libraries

5 book mobiles

purchase of books to an amount of K£56,062

So far the plan has been implemented as follows:

At Kisumu the construction of one area library financed by British Council is complete. The building will be occupied in August 1971. Temporary lending facilities are already available in a room provided by the Municipal Council of Kisumu.

At Embu, an area library was recently inaugurated. Temporary but inadequate facilities are currently being offered in a rather makeshift accommodation belonging to the Embu County Council. A centrally located site has been allocated for a new building and preliminary drawings have already been prepared.

One book mobile has been secured by British loan. This mobile will arrive by August this year.

K.£15,000 worth of new books have been purchased.

Still to be financed and implemented are then the following projects:

1   Headquarters library (1971–2)

A site has already been allocated for this building on Ngong Road in Nairobi, close to the Ministry of Works Headquarters.

This building is intended to create room for the following:

(i)   large storage space for books being processed awaiting being forwarded to the provinces

(ii)   lending and study space for Nairobi residents

(iii)   restricted areas for the storage and use of rare material, particularly about Kenya

(iv)   individual study space fitted with carrels

(v)   lectures, exhibitions, etc.

(vi)   office space and staff welfare facilities such as a common room.

(vii)   a canteen which, if rented, should result in revenue for the Board apart from offering mess facilities for the staff and people in neighbouring offices.

The estimated cost for this building was first attempted on a rough basis in 1966 as £150,000. However, even as far back as 1967, the Government Architect remarked that the figure was conservative. Further, it is now known that since 1966, the cost of buildings per square foot has more than doubled itself having risen from 30/– to 80/–. A realistic figure to date would be £318,550, which includes a contingency sum of £11,000 calculated on a standard rate of 5%. The full sketch design of the building is under preparation.

It is appropriate to add that the present library headquarters are wooden barracks constructed more than 30 years ago and therefore constitute a serious fire risk. Second, it is hardly possible to accommodate all the office and professional staff (who are only 22) in these buildings without serious overcrowding. Third, it is nearly impossible already to find adequate room for the present stock of books.

2 Four area libraries

At Embu, Eldoret, Nyeri and Wajir. The plan schedules one area library each financial year, so that the last one in this period, at Wajir, should be started in 1973–4. Eventually, there will be one area library in each Province. The area libraries will be expected to serve the people by way of mobile libraries, postal lending and small, local branch libraries.

A site has already been allocated for an area library in Embu Town. The total cost of that library will be approximately K£35,000. It is to be added that this library, which will be typical of the rest of the area libraries, is not designed purely to meet the requirements of Embu Town. It is considered that this building should be capable of housing an excess stock of books which will enable the service to supply the needs of schools and other institutions in the whole of the Eastern Province by means of a mobile library vehicle.

Eldoret, Nyeri and Wajir area libraries are to be built on the same pattern and estimated costs. These costs may be revised accordingly at the time of construction, taking into consideration all relevant factors prevailing in the particular province. It is at the moment estimated that a sum of £35,000×4– £140,000 will be required for the four libraries.

3 Four mobile library vehicles

Each area library will be serving regions with populations ranging from about 3,000,000 to 1,000,000. Some of the regions served are extremely large in area. Access to the towns from the rural areas still leaves much to be desired. In order therefore to reach the majority of the rural public, mobile libraries will be essential to carry books to the people, particularly to secondary schools, community centres, etc. Apart from the obvious value of bringing books to distant places, book mobiles are likely to make a big impact on the ordinary man, who in some cases has still to be persuaded to value the book as a source of knowledge. One book mobile will be attached to each of the area libraries.

Each mobile has been designed to contain up to 2,000 volumes and to allow for a collapsible counter plus a seat for an assistant librarian, a wash basin and wardrobe. It was estimated that each vehicle would cost £4,000 ex-works, if bought from the United Kingdom. Even in that country, vehicle prices have risen by about 10% since the estimates were made and, if a further 10% is allowed for freight, the realistic total cost of each vehicle to date would stand at £5,000. It is not known yet what the corresponding cost would be if the vehicle were to be obtained from elsewhere, say, a Scandinavian country. It is therefore to be expected that these figures would be adjusted according to the prices prevailing in the donor country or other agreed country. Based on UK prices, however, the total estimate for mobile library vehicles would be £20,000. It has been mentioned earlier that each vehicle is designed to contain

2,000 volumes but it is reasonable to estimate that an initial reserve stock of 1,000 volumes is desirable if the vehicle is to operate continuously while some books are on loan. Estimating the cost of each book at the rate of £2, the initial bookstock for each vehicle would amount to a sum of £6,000, which results in a total of £24,000 for the four mobile library vehicles.

4   Purchase of books apart from mobile library bookstock

Books will also be needed to stock area libraries and branch libraries apart from K£15,000 already financed and K£24,000 required to stock the mobile, and another K£17,000 will be required to reach the target of K£35,000 set in the Government's Development Plan.

The Kenya Library Service development programme was off to a very promising start. It is important that the strong forward momentum be carried on. The library services are now provided to the people free of cost. It is essential that the services be geographically expanded as quickly as possible, to avoid misgivings that we are only providing something for a few.

To illustrate the growing popularity of the library services, I wish to mention that when the obligatory borrowers' deposit of £1 was recently discontinued, the number of registered borrowers increased in one month by 500 in the capital. In the same month 300 borrowers registered at one provincial library and 200 at another. In primary and secondary schools there is an obvious and grossly under-supplied need for books. Among adult pupils, the eagerness and the strong will to increase one's knowledge, even after a full day's labour in the fields, workshop and kitchen, cannot be overemphasised. What we lack can therefore be summarised simply as follows:

(a)   books and,
(b)   qualified staff.

What has been said above about books may suffice for the time being but a few more words on the subject of qualified staff is still desirable.

It has been estimated that Kenya needs to train at least 80 professional librarians during the five-year period covering 1978–83. This number is considered the minimum which is necessary for the expansion of library services in the University of Nairobi, Kenya National Library Services, Nairobi City Libraries and the various government libraries. At the time of writing, only 12 professional librarians have been produced, including about seven who were already qualified before the beginning of the quinquennium. This shows that, for a little under three years, only five librarians have been trained—which is seriously below the target.

The delay can be attributed to one cause and one cause alone, namely, limited facilities for training within East Africa.

East African School of Librarianship

This library school was started in 1963 with the aid of the Rockefeller Foundation and Unesco. Its purpose was to train library assistants as well as professional librarians at the undergraduate level. While the Directors of the

School have worked hard in very difficult circumstances, the fact still remains that the School cannot be relied on yet to produce large numbers of librarians quickly—which is what East Africa is crying out for at the present moment. As evidence one may cite the fact that the highest number of trainees for the diploma in librarianship that has ever been admitted to the School is 15 for the entire Eastern Africa, which includes not only Uganda, Tanzania and Kenya but also Mauritius and other neighbouring islands in the Indian Ocean. We therefore hold that while we wish to have the East African School of Librarianship improved and enlarged, and while we would sincerely welcome help for its development from friendly countries in the form of teaching staff, books, building funds, scholarships, etc., we would also submit that for an interim period of up to about three years or so, we would not be doing injustice to libraries and librarianship in East Africa if older and friendly countries were to accord us training facilities especially at the postgraduate level. Any support would enable each country in East Africa to produce quickly a fairly large supply of professional librarians which could be added to gradually by the East African School of Librarianship in the future.

(d)   Past, Present and Possible Future Developments of Librarianship in the Sudan

IZZEL DIN MAMOUN

Secretary General, Sudan Library Association

Introduction

The Sudan is a vast country of about 1,000,000 square miles. It is surrounded by Egypt from the north, Ethiopia and the Red Sea from the east, Kenya and Uganda from the south and the Republic of Chad from the west. It is the largest country in Africa. It had its independence from British rule in 1956. From 1898, date of the British re-occupation, the country was known as the Anglo-Egyptian-Sudan. After independence in 1956 it was called the Republic of the Sudan. In 1969 after the May revolution its name has been changed to 'The Democratic Republic of the Sudan'. The country's name is very much tied with the Great River Nile, the second longest river in the world after the Mississipi. The confluence of the Blue Nile that comes from Ethiopia with the White Nile, coming down from Uganda and the south, in Khartoum the capital, makes a very beautiful and fantastic appearance for everyone to admire. The River Nile goes through to Egypt and ends in the Mediterranean.

The Sudan depends heavily, particularly at present, on agricultural products, mainly cotton as a cash crop. It has also a rich animal wealth making a big proportion of the population a nomadic people moving from place to place for pasture and water. Settlement of nomads is being conditioned by agricultural projects and livestock fattening projects. A sort of planning is also taking place for the introduction of light industries, e.g. sugar production, textile, carton paper, wine, plastic, glass, oil, etc., and some of these industries are functioning. Such light industries are added every now and then. Excavation for mineral resources, e.g. petrol, copper, zinc, tin, etc., is running in some parts of the country.

The Sudan has a population of about 14,000,000 people with about 80% engaged in agricultural work. The large majority of the population is illiterate. Many schools have been opened in the last few years to make elementary education compulsory. Adult education schools are functioning under the supervision of the Ministry of Education in almost all parts of the country with deep concentration on heavily populated areas.

Library history in the Sudan

1 *Before the Condominium Rule*

Libraries in the Sudan, in the past, used to be small collections of books and manuscripts owned by individuals mostly of a religious nature. Most of the past religious chiefs used to own these small collections for their own reference and for their followers and students. They used to contact these books to seek relevant verdicts for solving social, economic and other problems on a religious basis. Marriage, divorce, trade, taxes, family relations, jurisdiction, industry and other aspects of life were run according to Islamic religion in most cases, particularly in Islamic families.

2 During the British Occupation

The Sudan did not have big collections of books in the form of libraries to serve the public or any general groups of people except at the beginning of the present century. The establishment of higher schools in the country at the dawn of the twentieth century was followed by establishing small collections of books on the subjects taught, e.g. medicine, engineering, education, etc. Some other small libraries were attached to the office of the British senior administrators and other centres of social activities devoted more or less to the British officers and administrators. Other scientific libraries were established to back original research in the Sudan, e.g. Wellcome Chemical Research Laboratories, founded in 1903, Stack Medical Research Laboratories, established in 1927, the Agricultural Research Library founded in 1931 and other libraries with fairly good collections in other Ministries and Departments in the country (Nasri, 1964 and Mamoun 1965 and 1970).

Library development after independence

Many libraries since independence (1956) have been established; many more are now in the process of establishment. Many old libraries have been greatly developed. Universities, higher institutes, ministries and departments, research centres, public libraries, cultural centres, clubs, etc., have established libraries that really back research and create cultured generations to undertake full responsibility for the development of the country. As mentioned on many relevant occasions, libraries can play a leading role in maintaining literacy and in pushing the pace of development particularly in developing countries. The Sudan started planning on a scientific and technical basis, as planning without a scientific and technical base proved to be wasteful of money and time. On the other hand most scientists and technologists undertaking responsibility for planning in the Sudan have had higher and postgraduate education and training in European countries, where they have used great centres of learning and libraries for their studies. They have, moreover, noticed the role of libraries in development and the great facilities that they render to scientists. It is now quite apparent that there is a high demand everywhere in the country for books and journals to lead the country on the right lines.

Libraries

The leading and biggest library, at present in the country, is the University of Khartoum Library which was established in 1945 with a collection of about

3,000 volumes handed over by the higher schools available at that time in the country. Another addition of 3,000 volumes was donated by the administrative secretariat of the Sudan Government at that time. The library has now a collection of more than 200,000 volumes and about 4,200 current journals. The Library has a good bindery and a small photographic unit. It has also a very rich Sudan collection containing literature pertaining to almost all subjects discussed in the Sudan in writing. This is a great help to scholars in Sudan studies and research. The Library adds 8,000–10,000 volumes per year to its collection.

This Library works, on one hand, as a university library and, on the other hand, as a national library. It extends its services to the whole public. It supplies photographed literature to the public according to need and according to availability of literature in the Library.

The Library is a legal depository institution for every work published in the Sudan by the Government officers or by individual authors.

Public libraries
In towns there are several public libraries, e.g. Omdurman Central Library, the British Council Libraries in Khartoum and Omdurman, the American Cultural Centre Library, the Soviet Cultural Centre Library and other small libraries opened by friendly countries attached to their embassies in Khartoum. There are also other public libraries in big towns of the country as well as other regional libraries of the British Council.

Other special libraries
Many other special libraries are attached to Ministries and Departments as mentioned earlier. Some of these libraries are in good condition and could offer good services to their readers. Those attached to research centres and educational institutions, besides the University Library mentioned earlier, are well organised, e.g. the Khartoum Polytechnic, the Teachers' Higher Institute, the Agricultural Research Library, the Ministry of Foreign Affairs Library, the Institute of Public Administration, the Ministry of Youth, Sports, Social and Religious Affairs. The Ministry of Youth is supposed now to look after establishing public libraries for the youth in the whole country. The newly founded National Council for Research is establishing its library with the help of the United Nations. The Food Processing Research Centre in Khartoum North is in the process of establishing a Regional Documentation Centre for Food Sciences for the Arab countries, which is establishing its documentation with the assistance of the FAO.

The central archives
The central archives was established in 1920 for the purpose of collecting records of historical events for reference by research workers, students, government officials and other scholars. It is also responsible for government records and it should arrange these records in a systematic order for easy

29

c

reference. It has now more than 2,000,000 records, but the space problem hinders badly the progress of the centre. A solution to the space problem is now being sought. According to law, all documents and records more than 50 years old could be made accessible to readers; other documents may be inspected on application. The centre is a legal depository unit for publications and other literature published in the Sudan.

Library schools and training

Some of the senior staff in big libraries are university graduates who were sent abroad for diploma and higher degrees in librarianship. Others were locally trained and sent abroad for further training. The first organised course in librarianship in the country was a six months' course held in 1961 by the Unesco expert to the Sudan, Mr. Sewell. The first university level course in the country was at the Omdurman College for Arabic and Islamic Studies which graduated 12 students in 1969–70 and another batch of 12 in 1970–, but the course has since ceased. The University of Khartoum Library established two library courses in librarianship, e.g. a junior course for six months, established in 1963 which has graduated about 150 library staff. Students admitted to this course should have a higher secondary education. Subjects taught in the course are general knowledge, classification and cataloguing. A higher-level course for six months was started in 1969 and takes about 20 students per year. Students admitted to this course should have passed the junior-level course. Subjects taught at the higher level are: general knowledge, classification, cataloguing and technical services. The University of Khartoum Library with its branches is also functioning as a practical training centre for librarians.

Conclusion

There is at present an active movement for establishing organised libraries in all teaching institutions, government ministries and departments, research centres, etc. Authorities are looking forward to appointing trained and qualified staff to run these libraries adequately according to modern library techniques. On the other hand, there is not enough qualified staff to run these libraries including the old libraries that need restocking and technical reorganisation. Most of the existing libraries in the country are being run by unqualified personnel. This is one of the most harmful problems that hamper the development and the organisation of libraries.

It is advisable that the present two courses taking place in the University Library should be extended to meet the requirements of the country. The two courses could solve the need for assistants. The problem of senior staff will exist until a university level course is founded. By upgrading one of the existing two courses to a higher level, the problem of staff might be solved.

Planning for the establishment of new public, regional and research libraries might go hand in hand with the planning which is expected to take place in the country in the next few years.

The help of the United Nations and its affiliated agents in establishing a higher-level library course and in advising on the establishment of libraries is certainly greatly appreciated by the Sudan Library Association and welcomed by the Sudan Government.

Bibliographical situation in the country

There are a good number of bibliographies published about the Sudan. Many of them are of a general nature comprising almost all literature published about the Sudan according to chronological eras. (1) R. L. Hill, *Bibliography of the Anglo-Egyptian Sudan from the earliest times to 1937*, Oxford University Press, is the first general bibliography on the Sudan. It is arranged by subject with an author index. It was followed by: (2) Abdel Rahman el Nasri, *A bibliography of the Sudan, 1939–58*. This bibliography is a continuation of Hill's work with author and subject indexes. Nasri and Asma Ibrahim are compiling *The Sudan Bibliography* as a continuation to Hill's and Nasri's previous works. Their work is published in *Sudan Notes and Records*—a well-known Sudanese journal founded in 1918. So far two supplements of the bibliography have appeared covering the years 1959–62 and 1962–5. A. R. C. Bolton's work *Soviet Middle East Studies: an analysis and bibliography*, Volume 7: *The Sudan* was published by the Institute of International Affairs in 1959, 23 pp. This bibliography includes 30 articles on the history, geography and sociology of the Sudan in Soviet publications.

There are other special bibliographies covering agriculture, geology and geography, law, medicine, and social sciences. A bibliography of Arabic works about the Sudan, 1874–1961 in Arabic under the Arabic title *Masadir al-dirasa al-Sudaniya* is in print. A very great work in the field of bibliographies in the country is the *Sudan Bibliography* which is in the final stages of publication. It is a record of publications about the Sudan since 1959. It is also worthy of mentioning that the *Sudanese Union Catalogue of Periodicals,* published by the University of Khartoum Library, is playing a fundamental role in facilitating exchanges between libraries in the Sudan. The University Library also published in 1969 the *List of periodicals in the Main and Branch libraries* which is considered valuable in locating journals in the University Library and its branches, as this is the leading library in the country. Another success in the field of bibliographies is the *Agricultural Research Index* on punched cards (Mamoun, 1970).

REFERENCES

Ahmed, M. I. (1964). 'The central archives and possibilities of research.' *Proceedings of the 12th annual conference of the Philosophical Society of the Sudan,* Khartoum, 1964, pt. 2, pp. 1–6. Published in 1969.
Mamoun, I. D. (1965). 'The role of libraries and documentation centres in agricultural development in the Sudan.' *Proceedings of the 13th annual conference of the Philosophical Society of the Sudan* on agricultural development in the Sudan, Khartoum, 1965.

Mamoun, I. D. (1970). 'Agricultural libraries and documentation centres in Africa with particular reference to the Democratic Republic of the Sudan.' *Proceedings of the 4th congress of the International Association of Agricultural Librarians and Documentalists,* Paris, 1970 (in print).

Nasri, A. R. (1964). 'Research libraries in the Sudan with a note on general and subject bibliographies. *Proceedings of the 12th annual conference of the Philosophical Society of the Sudan on research in the Sudan,* Khartoum, 1964, pt. 2, pp. 135–143. Published in 1969.

(e) Development of Libraries in Tanzania

F. K. TAWETE

Librarian, College of National Education Library, Dar es Salaam

In Tanzania, libraries can, in general, be divided into the following types:
(a) Public libraries which are organised by the Tanganyika Library Service.
(b) Special libraries.
(c) University and other educational libraries.

Tanganyika Library Service—background
The Tanganyika Library Service started with the East African Literature Bureau. In 1947–8 the East African Literature Bureau was set up as a result of the investigations undertaken between the years 1945–7 by the East African High Commission, now the East African Community. The aims of the Literature Bureau were:
(a) To meet and foster the ever-increasing demand for books.
(b) To encourage local authorship.
(c) To publish books in the local language and in English.
(d) To set up large libraries in the three capital towns of East Africa, i.e. Kenya, Tanzania and Uganda with branches elsewhere in these countries.

Libraries were set up mainly through the generosity of individuals or charitable trusts. This is not very different from the way libraries were set up in some developed countries in the mid-nineteenth century.

The original plan of the East Africa Literature Bureau to set up large libraries failed due to expenses involved. Two alternatives were then sought:
(a) Postal library service for isolated individuals who wanted to increase their knowledge through books.
(b) Book boxes sent to community centres, schools, prisons and other organised groups.

These also failed for the following reasons:
(a) Fewer books could be circulated due to long distances.
(b) Lack of staff and no proper supervision.

In 1961, static libraries were considered. These were intended to serve a community in a town, e.g. where people were dense and were interested in what was being done. The Bureau therefore succeeded in the following major areas:

32

(a) It pioneered the library service in East Africa.
(b) It extended the provision of literature to a wider community.
(c) It managed to publish some books in both English and a few local languages—especially in Swahili.

However, the Bureau failed to supply editorial and advisory assistance to local authors on a really large scale or to develop bookselling by local book-sellers.

Library legislation in Tanganyika

Though the East Africa Literature Bureau failed in its attempts to establish library services in East Africa, it still aroused an interest for libraries in the minds of the East Africans.

Thus in 1959, on the request of the East African High Commission, Mr. S. W. Hockey, British Council Library Organiser, was appointed for East Africa. After a study of the library situation in the East African countries, he drew up a programme of plans for the development of libraries in East Africa and his document, *The Hockey Report,* is very important in the history of libraries and librarianship in Tanzania and East Africa as a whole. This report was handed to the three respective governments, recommending that each government set up a Library Service Board by Act of Parliament to run the library service of the country as a whole. Tanzania (then Tanganyika) was the first to accept and implement this major recommendation.

On 1 July 1963, the Tanganyika Library Service Board was established by the Act of Parliament. The terms of the Act are: 'to establish the Tanganyika Library Service Board, and to provide for matters incidental hereto and connected herewith'. This was the culmination of long persuasion to obtain a library service. The Act provided for:
(a) A Board of nine members appointed by the Minister of Education, charged with the duty of promoting, establishing, equipping, managing, maintaining and developing libraries in Tanganyika.
(b) Finance to come from the Treasury, on the vote of the Ministry of Education.
(c) Municipalities to have powers to establish libraries inside and outside the boundaries.
(d) Reinforcement of the Deposit of Books Act of 1962 which provided for printers to deposit a copy of all material published in Tanganyika in the University College Dar es Salaam. In this reinforcement the Tanganyika Library Service also became a legal depository library.

Actual development of the public libraries

The Board appointed Mr. E. M. Broome, FLA (now serving as a library advisor in the British Department of Education and Science in London), as Director of the Tanganyika Library on 1 August 1963. As things were at that time, Mr. Broome had to start the service from scratch. Between 1963 and 1964, 15 new libraries were projected at an estimated cost of Sh.500,000/-

(East African currency). Provision was made in the National Plan by Parliament in 1964. Unfortunately only five libraries were started.

In 1964, the first branch library up-country was opened in Iringa (a town about 300 miles away from Dar es Salaam, the capital of Tanzania) through the efforts of a Resident Tutor of the University College for Extra-mural Studies. In 1965, in Bukoba (another town near the border of Uganda and Tanzania), three organisations providing library services in that area formed a committee and transferred their powers to the Tanganyika Library Service Board. A new building, Bukoba Branch is now in full operation. In July 1965 two subscription libraries in Moshi and Tanga (northern and north-east of Tanzania respectively) handed over their services and assets to the Tanganyika Library Service Board, bringing up the total number of libraries owned by the Board to four. Then in 1969 a branch library at Mwanza (another town outside D'Salaam), built purely from funds raised by the Board, became functional. And now, apart from the Dar es Salaam central library, the Board has seven library branches.

Other services

In addition to its many activities, the Library Service at the National Central Library, Dar es Salaam, organises a Postal Library Service whereby readers enrol themselves with the library service and subscribe a deposit of Sh.10/- per book. With this service, readers residing far from any library premise are able to borrow books of their own choice for eight weeks. These books are selected by a member of the library staff responsible for the service and posted to the reader at the library's expense.

Mobile libraries

According to Mr. Hockey's report, it was suggested that Book Mobile services should be organised sooner or later, so that books can be circulated throughout the country even to the remote places where branches have not been established. A survey was carried out and it was estimated that a cost to run one such Book Mobile would be at least not less than Sh.25,000/-. Early this year (1971), however, the West German Government donated two Book Mobiles to the Board. The Board has now purchased two other mobiles (one for schools and one for adults) making a total number of four Book Mobiles.

Academic libraries

The University Library

The University Library was established at the same time as its parent institution in 1961 to serve the teaching and research needs of the University. Since then the growth of total library stock has been substantial: from 9,304 volumes in 1961, to 91,480 volumes in 1967. According to a statement by the University Librarian which appeared in a local newspaper in July 1970, the library had about 120,000 volumes, including some 8,000 serial titles. There were about 1,718 serial titles received on subscription, and well over 6,000 titles received by the library through the University's exchange and gift programme.

Technical college libraries
Very little development has been done along this line.

Teacher training college libraries
A great effort has been done to improve libraries in the teacher training colleges. Separate library buildings have been provided within the campus of each teacher training college (there are about 10 teacher training colleges— all admitting ex-Form IV students and one of them, the Dar es Salaam Teacher Training College which admits ex-Form VI students also). In addition to this, the Dar es Salaam Teacher Training College Library acts as a central library for the other colleges. Its functions are:
(a) To classify and catalogue books for other colleges.
(b) To advise on the running of college libraries.
(c) To train library assistants (library clerks) for college libraries.
(d) To train teacher-librarians for secondary school and college libraries.

Special and other libraries
As one might expect, many of the government departments have their own excellent specialist collections, particularly in the field of agriculture, veterinary research, law, and geology. These serve the special groups of the Ministries or Departments to which they are attached. Then, of course, there are the libraries of the cultural and information services of the many countries now represented in Tanzania. The largest of these are those of the British Council and the USIS (United States Information Service) and both of these organisations engage in a limited programme of book presentations to schools and educational institutions. The only main weakness of both these organisations is that their collections are for propaganda. They are intended to reflect the publications of their respective countries.

Unesco
The activities of Unesco in the development of libraries and literacy in Tanzania cannot be left without mentioning. Apart from providing a library expert to make a survey of the position of school libraries in Tanzania, Unesco is currently running a literacy programme in one of the regions in Tanzania. In this programme, Unesco organises adult education for various groups in the region as well as producing literature both in Kiswahili (the national language) and English for the different groups. Attached to this programme are one local librarian and some Research Fellows who are expected to carry on the programme once Unesco hands it over to the Tanzania Government. This is a very commendable programme as it supplements the work of the public library service as well as that of the Tanzania Ministry of National Education, Adult Education Section.

Problems in the development of libraries

One of the most critical problems in the development of libraries in Tanzania is that of illiteracy. Of the 12,000,000 people of Tanzania, it is estimated that only about 25% are literate. This accounts for the slow economic, educational and cultural development of the country. There is, at present, a great campaign against 'ignorance, poverty and diseases' which are an integral part of a vicious circle caused by lack of a sufficiently educated population. Adult education classes are conducted all over the country and libraries are asked to supplement these programmes.

The lack of enough literature in the local vernaculars contributes also to the problems of library development in Tanzania. A strikingly noticeable feature on the shelves of libraries is the predominance of Western literature. Only about 8% of all books published are in Swahili, the national language and lingua franca of East Africa. The cause for this problem is the absence of indigenous writing and publishing houses. There are very few African writers in Tanzania. Almost all books about Tanzania are written and published by foreign firms such as Longmans, Nelson, Oxford, etc. Only recently (in 1966) the Tanzania Publishing House was established.

On the side of the academic libraries there is a psychological problem. Students and teachers tend to use only a few prescribed books as sources of information. This problem seems to have been caused by the colonial educational system which, unfortunately, stressed more the importance of passing examinations than reading for information and knowledge. It is very encouraging to note that the government has now taken a drastic step to revolutionise the formerly British-oriented educational system. President Julius Nyerere has issued his policy paper, *Education for self-reliance*, which calls for reforms in the present system so that it aims at fulfilling the country's needs. All the subjects and the local examinations are geared to the country's requirements.

Lack of adequate funds for libraries is also a major problem in a developing country like Tanzania struggling to meet, apart from libraries, several other important national programmes. Tanzania, like many other countries, would like to have as many Book Mobiles as possible so as to extend her library services to even remote villages. Limited funds, however, do not permit of such services.

Last but not least, lack of a formally established system of co-operation among different types of libraries in the way of inter-library loans is another problem in the development of a country's library service. Each library system in Tanzania tends to be self-sufficient in its resources. A poor country such as Tanzania (or any rich country for that matter) cannot afford to duplicate expensive books which can easily be made available to users through the inter-library loan system.

Finally, the development of libraries in Tanzania is also hindered by lack of sufficient professional librarians and a powerful professional association whose function, among other things, should be to catalyse the library development. The Tanzania Library Association is a new creation (founded in 1965) and it will, therefore, take some time before its influence can be strongly felt.

With all these problems, the government and the people of Tanzania are, however, very much encouraged by the interest which is being displayed in our work by the organisations responsible for library services overseas, particularly in Great Britain, United States of America and, of course, not forgetting Unesco. It is up to the Tanzania Library Association and to all Tanzanians to translate this goodwill into practical terms. We can assure our many friends that any aid provided in any way will be used to the full.

REFERENCES

Resuick, Idrian N. *Tanzania: Revolution by education*. Arusha: Longmans, 1968.
Nyerere, Julius K. *Education for self-reliance*.
Hockey, S. W. *Public libraries in the developing Commonwealth: Librarianship Overseas*. London: The Library Association, 1964.
Hockey, S. W. *Development of library services in East Africa: A report submitted to the Governments of East Africa*. December, 1960.
Tanganyika Library Services Board: *An Act to establish the Tanganyika Library Services Board and to provide for matters incidental thereto and connected therewith*. November 1963.
Kaungamno, E. E. *Library conditions and library training in Tanzania*. Paper presented at a Unesco course for Teachers of Librarianship. Copenhagen, 1968.
Tanganyika Library Service Reports: 1964–5, 1965–6 and 1966–7.

(f) Trends of Library Development in Uganda since 1962

T. K. LWANGA

University Librarian, Makerere University, Kampala

The Local Organiser of this Seminar asked me to submit 'a short paper on the past, present or future impact of recent developments on some aspect of libraries in your country . . .'. I must admit that I was at first baffled by what was required of me. The task before me seemed even more overwhelming when I read the theme of the Seminar 'Recent Developments in Advanced Librarianship'. My problem was that on our library scene we do not have many recent or advanced developments; and no research has been carried out to measure the impact of such developments. Let us, however, look at some of these developments and their deducible impact on librarianship in 'independent' Uganda, i.e. since 1962.

1 Public Libraries Act 1964

The history of the development of public libraries in Colonial Uganda is well documented in a number of publications, the most important one, perhaps, being the Hockey Report of 1960. After attainment of independence the Government of Uganda took a decisive step to implement some of the recommendations of the Hockey Report, by enacting the Public Libraries Act of 1964.

The Act authorised the setting up of a Public Libraries Board whose responsibilities were laid down as follows: 'It shall be the duty of the Board to establish, equip, manage, and maintain libraries in Uganda, and take all such steps as may be necessary to carry out its functions under the Act.'

In spite of this definite commitment to the development of a country-wide network of public libraries, the Board has faced a number of problems in its short life. The most outstanding problems have been:
(a) Lack of adequate headquarters.
(b) Lack of administrative stability including unclear relationship with local authorities.
(c) Lack of books.
(d) Lack of funds.
(e) Lack of professional staff.

There have been already two searching reports on these problems. The 'Report of the Special Commission' set up by Board itself in 1968, and the 'Report of the Committee of Inquiry into the Affairs of Public Libraries Board' by A. A. Nekyon on the authority of the Minister of Culture and Community Development, in 1970.

The enacting of the Public Libraries Board saw the establishment of a free library service open to all. The result has been the rapid growth of undirected readership, as the service points (branch libraries) expanded to the present figure of 17, plus postal lending book boxes, and mobile library services. Ten years ago if you mentioned the need for public libraries as one of the national priorities, you would only manage, perhaps, to raise laughter. Now, the development of public libraries in Uganda forms part of the National Development plan.

We are very much still at the beginning of a journey where it has been important to justify the necessity of taking the journey at all. I therefore think that the most important impact of the start so far made in establishing public libraries in Uganda is to show that such libraries are important in the Community and that the demand for the service is far greater than anticipated at this stage of our country's development. One reader wrote recently in a local newspaper saying: 'I have read all the books in my local library; please can we have some more.' This simple plea sums up correctly the enormous demand for library services in Uganda today.

2 Libraries in colleges and schools

In Uganda we believe that one of the most important types of library in any country is the school library; and the recent development in this field is the tremendous effort taken—at very great financial costs—to establish good libraries in all our secondary schools. One of the major problems here is the need for the services of professional librarians. Most of the people responsible for the libraries are teachers with no library training whatsoever. The same is true of libraries in a number of teacher training colleges and technical schools. Headmasters and Principals all over the country are crying out for professional help in organising their school and college library collections. Research has yet to be carried out to investigate the impact of the establishment of libraries in schools and colleges on the pupils' and students' ability to learn. It is also assumed that pupils who have good libraries at school, and use them, form the future readership of the public library system—having acquired at school the love for books and a habit of reading. I have doubts about this theory, because I know that in a developing country the man who receives formal education has, on leaving a school, so many pressures of one kind or another that he hardly has time for undirected reading.

3 The university library

There is only one university in Uganda—Makerere University Kampala, which reached full university status in the academic year 1970–1.

This academic year, the University has reached the size of nine faculties: Agriculture, Arts, Social Sciences, Law, Education, Science, Technology, Medicine, and Veterinary Science. The University also has a School of Fine Art, the East African School of Librarianship, Makerere Institute of Social Research, the Centre for Continuing Education and the Institute of Statistics and Applied Economics. Makerere provides courses leading to about 17 awards of diplomas and degrees including PhDs.

The total enrolment in the current year 1971–2 is about 3,330 including some 250 postgraduate degree and diploma students. The number of academic and senior administrative staff is about 410. Makerere students and staff, and many scholars from other parts of the world, carry out vigorous research programmes. Thus the campus Library clientele is very complex; and yet still, by its very nature, as the only important and large general library in Uganda, *the University Library serves many people outside the University. The advanced serious students have nowhere else to turn but to the University Library.* The same is true of public officials, teachers, doctors, librarians, civil servants, commercial men, etc., who are officially recognised by the University as people whom the University Libraries have to serve. Through its photographic services and inter-library loans, it provides materials to researchers and scholars throughout East Africa.

Serving this complex and rapidly expanding clientele at Makerere is a system of four related libraries, consisting of: The Main Library, Education Library, Medical Library, The Makerere Institute of Social Research Library, plus a rapidly expanding small library at Kabanyolo experimental research farm, and a number of departmental libraries.

The University Library Service has grown, since 1940, from a small collection of department textbooks to the largest general library system in the country, and possibly in East and Central Africa.

The library materials acquired so far include largely books and periodicals: and the total estimated number of volumes in the library system is 200,000 books, and 150,000 bound periodicals and documents. Throughout the library system we subscribe, approximately, to 4,000 titles of periodicals. The library service at Makerere forms the largest concentrated collection of library materials in East and Central Africa. We have also a rapidly expanding volume of reading materials on microfilms, microfiche and microcards. *The University Library by virtue of 'the Makerere University College (deposit library) Act 1958', became a legal depository for Uganda publications.* It is also a depository library for Uganda for the publications of major international organisations such as the United Nations Organisation. The World Health Organisation, the International Labour Office, and the Food and Agriculture Organisation. It is the largest general reference and research library in the country and by its very nature is likely to remain so. The Library is proud of its large and unique East Africana collections which have been built up over the years. This collection comprises all publications relating to East Africa, i.e. Kenya Tanzania and Uganda; all publications in African languages held in the library and a large variety of important publications about Africa and Africans generally. Also included in this collection are a number of special collections of official documents of various countries, archives and manuscripts.

In a developing country, like Uganda, the university library has to play a national role, in addition to its normal function of providing adequate reader services for undergraduate and postgraduate students, research scholars, and faculty members. We are, more or less convinced in Uganda that the university library should also be designated to serve as a National Reference and Research Library. This is also the view held by many librarians and scholars in East Africa, and in many other developing countries; that this is the role university libraries should play in the development of library services.

In Uganda, we visualise three main streams of development of library services: the public library, serving the general population in cities, towns and rural areas; special libraries, including government departmental and research libraries; and college libraries and the university library; the latter acting also as the National Reference Library with a wide range of research collections.

There are sound reasons for this kind of thinking and planning, both in terms of finance, professional staff, and availability of rare material. We find that inevitably much of the material necessary for all aspects of research (which should be in a national reference collection) is basic also to university research needs; also the academic core of the country is largely to be found centred upon the university.

By its very nature, content and organisation, and in the absence of a strong public library service or national library, the Makerere library finds itself obliged to assume responsibilities of a National Reference Library. What do we mean by a National Reference Library? We mean not only a library which collects material published within the country and material about the country published elsewhere, but also a library in which there is a large concentration of research materials covering a wide range of subjects. Its collections are at once both extensive and intensive in the subject coverage, and not intended to be a substitute for research, government or public libraries, but rather a comprehensive collection that will supplement these libraries when their requirements go beyond normal needs.

Plans for the official recognition of the Makerere Library as the National Reference Library have been put to the Government for legislation. Once this role is granted then the logical consequence of the library's operation would be for it also to be designated the Centre for the International Exchange of Official publications. The exchange programme would enable the library to send official material to other overseas institutions, particularly universities, and in turn the library would receive material issued by them. This systematic exchange arrangement would enrich the holdings of the university library.

We also feel that with the status of a national reference library should come the right to microfilm and distribute film copies of official publications which are out of print to enable the library to meet the many overseas requests for out-of-print titles, and at the same time to extend its international exchange programme through the use of film copies as exchange media.

The university library, as a national reference library, will have to be responsible for producing a National Bibliography. There is at the moment no institution in Uganda—let alone East Africa—which produces a comprehensive National Bibliography. We have, at Makerere, already recognised the great need in this field. An attempt at compiling a Uganda Bibliography was started at the beginning of 1965. A 'Uganda Bibliography' section appeared for the first time in the Makerere University Library Bulletin and Accessions List, No. 55, January–February 1965. The Bibliography includes material published in Uganda (including Government Publications) received under Legal Deposit; and books, etc., about Uganda published outside the country.

4 Special libraries

There are quite a number of special libraries covering the fields of agriculture, mining, commerce and industry, education, law, banking, etc. However, their usefulness and size differ greatly, depending on whether or not they are run by a full-time qualified librarian. Although the main concentration of these libraries is in and around the capital city, Kampala, there are a number of them scattered all over the country.

The main concern of librarians, over the years, in regard to special libraries, has been the complete lack of co-operation among them—especially where there is similar related subject coverage. The problem is still with us, but the spirit of co-operation is slowly beginning to emerge. A *'Union list of scientific and technical periodicals . . .'*, published by Makerere University Library has greatly enhanced the inter-library use of the special libraries' periodicals collections. Another publication which has also had similar effect is the *Directory of East African libraries.*

The biggest problem facing many of the special libraries in Uganda is the lack of trained librarians and documentalists.

5 Library training

The local training of librarians is one of the recent key events in the development of library services in East Africa. A School of Librarianship was founded in 1964 to provide common specialised facilities for training library personnel for the development of all types of libraries, principally in East African countries. The East African School of Librarianship is one of the constituent faculties and schools of Makerere University, Kampala. The School is independent of any faculty, but it is governed by the Council for Library Training in East Africa which is responsible to the Senate.

To train the library personnel required at different levels for various types of libraries, the School of Librarianship conducts three types of programmes: a two-year course of professional studies for non-graduates leading to a Diploma in Librarianship; a six-month Library Assistant's Certificate; and a course in School Librarianship given as part of their syllabus to the students for degrees with education content. The School is also expected to conduct occasional non-residential courses in School Librarianship for practising teacher-librarians in association with the National Institute of Education.

The work of the School has been seen both by the University community and Uganda Government to fulfil the real needs of providing the libraries with much needed trained library personnel. This has resulted in complete integration of the School into the academic and financial structure of Makerere University. What is more, Uganda Government's concern for proper functioning of the East African School of Librarianship and for securing its future has resulted in the construction of a permanent building which is nearing completion. This favourable development is yet another proof of the impact which the work of the School has made in improving library services in East Africa, and its future plans for expanding its functions.

Although the School has been in existence since 1964. It is, however, only from 1968–9 that the School was able to implement all its three training programmes envisaged at the time of its foundation. All its programmes are at undergraduate level. During the last few years demand for graduate librarians has been reflected in the recruitment policies of the libraries. It is interesting to record that growing recognition of the School has led to the suggestion being made recently by the University Council of its own volition that the School should embark upon a programme for training of graduates so that the need for this category of personnel could also be met within East Africa.

The School has also helped to propagate the idea, through the medium of its Introductory Library Studies Course conducted at the Faculty of Education that one of the most effective ways of raising the standard of secondary education in the country is to employ qualified teacher librarians. Plans are now under way to organise a full-fledged course in theory and practice of librarianship for teachers in charge of secondary schools and colleges of education libraries.

The School of Librarianship has made an important contribution to the salary structure now enjoyed by library workers at different levels. It has now been generally accepted that salaries of library workers should be equated with those engaged in the teaching profession, with which the library profession can be compared in terms of academic qualifications and length of professional training.

The School has thus played a significant part in giving enhanced status to the library profession. It has also underlined the role which the libraries placed under the charge of qualified personnel can play in research and educational development in East Africa.

Librarianship is a new discipline in East Africa as in other developing countries. It was therefore inevitable that in the first few years of its work the School had to depend entirely on the libraries to sponsor their personnel for training at the School of Librarianship. In the current academic year, fresh school-leavers have been admitted to provide the trained manpower badly needed by the libraries. They account for 50% of the total 1970–1 intake of the two-year Diploma in Librarianship.

What is equally significant is that, for the first time since 1968 when the School started to operate effectively, the School has experienced little difficulty in securing bursaries, for all of its 46 new students, from the governments of the three East African countries.

The School of Librarianship at Makerere University has reached the take-off point. This is so because those in authority have recognised the claim of the School that libraries need to be placed under the charge of professional librarians and that such libraries play an essential role in the developmental programme of the new nations.

6 A library development plan

All libraries in Uganda are financed by government, with the exception of a few special research libraries of East African Community. But, in spite of this very important common base, libraries have developed independently of each other. There is now a very strong view that we ought to evolve a national plan for development of library and documentation services for the whole country. We feel we should not just copy the pattern of services and organisation of other countries. A developing country, like Uganda, must, on economic grounds, work out well co-ordinated plans of development in all fields, including the provision of library services.

In December 1970, at a Unesco Experts' Meeting on National Planning of Documentation and Library Services in Africa, an effort was made to work out a 'Draft Plan for Uganda'. Many participants spoke of the urgent need to create a satisfactory framework for the co-ordination of library development. It was felt that, if co-ordination were achieved, then co-operation between libraries would be automatic. Most librarians and planners in Uganda would like to see a plan co-ordinating the development of all types of libraries in the country under one national body.

7 The library profession

Librarianship as a reputable profession is now well established in Uganda, with a growing demand for qualified personnel to run libraries. More and more young men and women at all levels are now showing keen interest in training as librarians. Five years ago, when the Makerere University advertised for graduates for posts of Trainee Assistant Librarians, there were only three applications from people who had failed to get satisfactory employment elsewhere. This year we had well over 30 applicants, many of them with very good degrees and with librarianship as their first choice for a career. This is so because library work is competitively well remunerated at all levels, with extremely good prospects.

The profession is strengthened by the existence of a regional association: the East African Library Association with branches in Uganda, Kenya, and Tanzania. The Association holds conferences every two years in each of the three East African countries. The last conference, which was held in Uganda in September 1970, helped tremendously to focus everybody's attention, through press, radio, and television, on the problems of library service development. These conferences are a very useful forum for discussing our problems and learning from each other.

The Association publishes a Bulletin as often as circumstances permit; and every two years there is a special issue of the conference proceedings.

The future

The take-off period of development of library services in Uganda is not very far off. There is a general feeling that, possibly very soon, there will be established an overall planning body to co-ordinate the development of all libraries in the country. If this is done, then the future of library development in Uganda will be very bright indeed.

REFERENCES

Hockey, S. W. *Development of Library Services in East Africa: a report submitted to the Governments of East Africa.* Nairobi, 1960. 42 p.

The Public Libraries Act; an act to provide for the establishment of a Public Libraries Board and for other purposes connected therewith. Laws of Uganda, 1964, vol. IV, Act 28 of 1964, Chapter 121.

Directory of East African Libraries, edited by Makerere University College Library Reference Section. 2nd ed. Kampala, 1969.

Lwanga, T. K. *Union list of scientific and technical periodicals held in East African libraries.* Revised edition. Makerere University Library, 1970.

(g) Recent Developments in Libraries in Zambia

L. Z. CHEELO
Librarian, Lusaka City Library

Two aspects of library development have had notable impact in this country, and these are (1) Voluntary Co-operation, and (2) Library Training.

1 Voluntary co-operation

(a) *Zambia Library Association*

This body, which is a split off from the Library Association of Central Africa, was established in 1967, with the following objects:

(i) to unite all persons engaged in library work or interested in libraries in Zambia;

(ii) to encourage the establishment and development of libraries and library co-operation in Zambia;

(iii) to improve the standards in all aspects of librarianship, bibliography and documentation in Zambia;

(iv) to act as an advisory body in all matters pertaining to libraries, bibliography and documentation in Zambia;

(v) to stimulate an awareness among central and local government bodies and other institutions of their responsibilities in providing adequate library services and facilities;

(vi) to promote whatever may tend to the improvement of the position and the qualifications of librarians;

(vii) to undertake all such activities (e.g. meetings, conferences, publications, etc.), which will further the above objects.

Since the Association was formed, it has held regular meetings. It has also met government representatives with a view to influencing considerations for the need of a proper Civil Service Cadre of Librarians. It has also taken up with the government such matters as price-control on books and internal book-post costs.

(b) *Lusaka Libraries Liaison Committee*

This was formed in 1966 to develop co-operation between libraries in Lusaka. It has developed standardised inter-library loan procedures, co-operation in acquisition, co-ordinated plans for exhibitions, and has formed a sub-committee to develop co-operation in cataloguing and classification.

(c) *Standing Conference of Head Librarians of Zambia*

The inaugural meeting of this body was held in March 1971. Although its terms of reference have not been finalised yet, it is hoped that they will be similar to those of the Lusaka Libraries Liaison Committee ((b) above), but on a national level. It is proposed that Working Parties will be set up in selected parts of the Country.

D

(d) *National Council for Scientific Research Documentation Centre*
The Council is an officially constituted para-statal body set up in 1967 with the following objects:
  (i) to advise the Government of the Republic of Zambia on national scientific policy and its implementation;
 (ii) to ensure the maximum utilisation of the results of such research;
(iii) to initiate and co-ordinate scientific research and activities within Zambia;
(iv) to maintain liaison and the exchange of mutually beneficial information with other scientific organisations throughout the world.

The Centre provides technical information to researchers in the form of abstracts, indexes and original publications.

Hence, co-operation is achieved in all forms of library work through the workings of the above organisations.

2 Library training
University of Zambia Professional Board of Library Studies
This body was formerly the Ministry of Education Library Advisory Council Professional Board on Library Studies formed in 1967. The Board organised and administered courses of training at the Professional non-graduate and Sub-professional (Intermediate) levels.

In 1971, the Board was absorbed in the University of Zambia, and is responsible to Senate, and all library training in the country has become the total responsibility of the University.

The Board is, however, fully representative of all library institutions and bodies.

The above two aspects have been singled out as of particular significance, though there are several activities throughout the country.

2 ASIA: MIDDLE EAST

(a) Library Trends in Ceylon

T. G. PIYADASA

Acting Librarian, Vidyalankara University, Kelaniya

The island of Ceylon has been an important centre of literary activity from very early times. Historical sources refer to books and libraries as far back as the pre-Christian era. Among the great seats of Buddhist learning were the famous monasteries, Mahavihara and Abhayagiri vihara. Practically every temple had its own library—'potgula'. Kings and chieftains were large-hearted patrons of culture and many of them encouraged learning. They are referred to in the island's chronicles as builders of libraries for the dissemination of knowledge and the preservation of books. Our heroic ancestors had to fight many a battle against a horde of foreign invaders to safeguard their independence. These sometimes caused a set-back to their literary activities. But the literary revival that started during the time of Kirti Sri Rajasinghe (A.D. 1747–82) of Kandy, continued until it merged into the modern period and restored the balance. At the head of this literary movement was Welivita Sangharaja.

The first public library opened during the British period was the Government Oriental Library, in 1870. A little later the Colombo Museum Library was opened. In the early twentieth century, Kandy and Colombo municipalities started their own public libraries. Gradually this idea was followed up by many other local authorities. In addition to these were the libraries of learned societies such as the Royal Asiatic Society Library.

The establishment of the University College in 1924 and subsequently of the Universities was a further step in the cause of organised libraries in Ceylon. These libraries were started and nurtured not according to any plan or programme but according to the individual bent of the particular institution. The expansion of libraries did not go hand in hand with the growth of the literate public.

In 1956 a Department of Cultural Affairs was started which inaugurated the Ceylon Book Trust. This department took an interest in libraries and librarianship. The then Director of Cultural Affairs was responsible for getting together the handful of librarians in Ceylon to serve a common interest. The Ceylon Library Association was thus formed in 1960. From its inception this organisation was active and took various steps to promote the cause of librarianship, to develop a library consciousness in the people, and to provide a better organised system of libraries. Bibliographical activities soon became the responsibility of the Ceylon Library Associaton. The Assocation became very sensitive to the demands of the country in this field. The Association organised courses, seminars on topics of bibliographic interest, workshops, etc. The Ceylon National Bibliography was started during this period. At about the same time Unesco enhanced activities in this field for South and South East Asia. A number of Unesco Library Experts visited Ceylon. In 1960 Mr. Harold Bonny, Unesco Library Adviser, submitted to the Government of Ceylon a plan for the development of libraries in Ceylon. A Conference of the South East Asian Library Experts was held in Colombo in 1968. At this conference, too, a special report was prepared on the planning of library services in Ceylon.

The Ceylon Library Association continued to agitate about the need for planned action. In response to this in 1970, Parliament passed the Ceylon Library Services Act. Following this, a Ceylon Library Services Board has been set up.

A well-planned library system to a great extent depends on the professionally qualified librarian. In his report Harold V. Bonny, Unesco Library Adviser, said: 'It is perhaps an over-simplification to say that the largest single fact retarding Library Development in Ceylon is the shortage of trained librarians.'

In 1961 Ceylon University started a post-graduate course in Librarianship of one year's duration. Simultaneously the Ceylon Library Association started its part-time courses. After one or two years of work the Ceylon University abandoned its course, which action proved rather detrimental to the cause of librarianship in the country. But the Library Association continued to organise its courses on a wider basis. It conducted courses in Colombo, Kandy and Jaffna, and started a course in the Sinhala medium too. These courses continue to be very popular.

The effects of free education, together with the introduction of the Swabhasha as the medium of instruction and of Sinhala as the official language of the country, opened avenues for a greater percentage of the rural child population to enter the portals of higher education institutions. Literacy in Ceylon has achieved perhaps the highest rate in South and South East Asia, being well over 80%. As a result the production of textbooks in Swabhasha has increased appreciably. An increased taste for good reading is felt amongst the Swabhasha educated. All this has promoted the production of secondary reading material in Swabhasha.

We know that the growth of population, and the increased number of educated youths, have resulted in the demand for more and better jobs. But the slow progress of the economy and the foreign exchange crisis have made matters difficult for different governments. The era after 1956 saw some industrial development in Ceylon. This trend continues to date. New problems have to be tackled with new methods. Hence programming and planning have become vital for the government. Recently a Planning Ministry under the care of the Prime Minister herself was created. The idea of planning and programming in different areas of activity has again brought up the need for organised, well-equipped libraries. As a result of the new planning and programming, each industry or profession is compelled to be acquainted with data and information in their respective fields of study. Bureaucrats who were generally in the habit of depending mainly on their basic education and general intelligence have had to change their attitude too. Officials are to be acquainted with the best traditions of programming and planning. Hence the study of literature on different subjects has become indispensable. Research has become the need of the day. The library and the trained librarians have had a difficult role to play in this set up. Apart from the demand for public libraries by the vast majority of the educated, this may be regarded as the most visible modern library trend in Ceylon.

One could hardly say that the library profession in Ceylon is still prepared to face this situation. The need for more and more professionally trained librarians is keenly felt. The supply is not at all in keeping with the demand.

The Government started library courses in two of its new Junior Universities. But these, too, have now been abandoned. The burden of training librarians once again has fallen on the Library Association. It is too much of a burden for the Ceylon LA with its handful of fully qualified librarians who are also burdened with their own institutional obligations. There is a popular demand for more and better libraries. The 10,000 schools with a student population of over 2,600,000, over 600 local bodies and several technical institutes need the services of professionally qualified librarians. A plan for the development of the libraries in Ceylon, in the first instance, requires the services of the professionally qualified librarian to organise the different bibliographical activities.

The report of the Library Experts on the National Planning of Library Services in Asia says: 'The Ceylon Library Association has done pioneer work in Staff Training and much of the credit for improved standards must go to the Association.' But the need for international co-operation and support is a matter that can hardly be over-stressed, so that the functions of the Ceylon Library Association and the cause of librarianship in Ceylon could be more richly served.

(b)   The Impact of Recent Developments on Indian Libraries

D. R. KALIA, *Director, Central Secretariat Library, New Delhi*
and
J. C. MEHTA, *Director, Delhi Public Library, Delhi*

As is well known, the first Convention of Librarians was held in 1853 at New York and the first body of working Librarians called 'The American Library Association (ALA)' was founded in 1876—a long-delayed outcome of the Convention. It was followed by the formation of The (British) Library Association in 1878. The persons who attended the first Convention and founded ALA and LA were librarians only by virtue of their holding charge of libraries. They had not received any formal professional training as no Library School had been founded by then. The first Library School, called the School of Library Economy, was founded at Columbia in 1887 where, for the first time, a systematic body of knowledge in library science began to develop out of the art of librarianship practised in the past.

Let us now review similar early developments in India in the context of this global situation before we discuss the impact of recent developments on Indian libraries.

The first stimulating influence on Indian libraries came from abroad as early as 1910 when the Maharaja of Baroda appointed William Alanson Borden—an eminent American Librarian—as Director of the State Department of Libraries, Baroda. Mr. Borden laid the foundation of a State-wide Public Library system in the State of Baroda, perhaps unheard of in those days in the eastern part of the world. He introduced systematic classification and cataloguing, free library service, open access, children's library and book mobiles. He also conducted library training classes for the staff working under him. His work at Baroda had an abiding influence on several libraries in the country and created a demand for the establishment of a Library School on the lines of the Columbia School.

Another, even more stimulating, influence came to India from abroad in 1915 when Asa Don Dickinson—an eminent library expert of Pennsylvania University—was appointed as Librarian of the Punjab University Library, Lahore (now in Pakistan). Mr. Dickinson organised the Library and established the first Library School in India. The training course was known as a course in 'Library Science' instead of 'Librarianship'. The Lahore Library School was the forerunner of all the subsequent training courses and Library Schools established in India. It held for a long time a place of pride among the library training institutions in India, and has contributed two National Librarians, namely, K. M. Asudullah and D. R. Kalia.

As a result of the influence of these American library advisers, India decided in favour of educating her librarians through a professional school in preference to the system of apprenticeship then obtaining in the UK. This policy has throughout been maintained in the history of library development in India. The first Library School at university level was established in the UK only in 1919. The Lahore Library School is, therefore, considered to be the second in the world, the first being the Columbia School.

The indigenous know-how in library science began to develop in the 1930s. By that time, about half-a-dozen Indians had received their library training abroad. Dr. S. R. Ranganathan—a product of the University of London School of Librarianship—published his scheme of Colon classification in 1933 and has since played a prominent role in the development of libraries and library science in India along with other senior librarians.

Impact of recent developments

As a consequence of India's long contact with developments in the library field abroad, India has evolved a national library system suited to local requirements and has made a substantial contribution to the growth of library science, especially in the field of depth classification, cataloguing, documentation techniques and bibliographical devices. Some of the techniques developed in India have been adopted abroad by several institutions. We shall now review the recent developments in India in various fields.

1 *Public libraries*

During the British rule the provision of the public library service was entrusted through legislation to the local governments or the municipal administration. There was no statutory obligation on the part of local bodies to provide a library service. By 1947, when India attained Independence, hardly any local government had established a public library worth the name. In 1948, the Madras State—now known as the State of Tamil Nadu—adopted library legislation. Having been disappointed with the performance of the local bodies, it was decided to constitute a statutory autonomous library authority for each District and one for the city of Madras to provide a free public library service. A State Library Advisory Council was instituted to lay down policies and coordinate the working of the various District Library Authorities, assisted by a Directorate of Libraries. In order to ensure a stable source of library finance, library cess was imposed on property tax. Since 1948, three other States, i.e. the States of Andhra Pradesh, Mysore and Maharashtra, have adopted library legislation. While the States of Andhra Pradesh and Mysore have levied library cess, necessary funds for library development in the State of Maharashtra are provided out of State revenues. As a result of library legislation and the national development plans, the national library structure that has emerged is: a National Library at the apex, a State Central Library in each State and a District Central Library in each District, which will provide service both to the urban and the rural population. So far, only about 10% of the total population has been covered by this system. India has yet to go a long way in the provision of universal free library service.

2 *Academic libraries*

At the time of Independence in 1947, there were 21 universities, 533 affiliated colleges and about 200,000 students on their rolls, whereas today there are 104 universities, 3,500 affiliated colleges and 3,000,000 students on their rolls. This phenomenal growth of facilities for higher education in India has spurred the development of academic libraries. With the establishment of the University Grants Commission in 1956, the university and college libraries received greater attention. The UGC has made very liberal grants for the construction of new buildings, development of book resources and has accorded librarians the status and salaries of faculty members. Some of the university libraries would compare very favourably with the best anywhere in terms of buildings, book resources, staff allocation and services. The school libraries have not yet received much attention and are the most neglected component of the national library system.

3 Special libraries

At the time of Independence, India had only limited facilities for scientific and industrial research. Since Independence, numerous scientific and industrial research institutes have been established, and today there is hardly any branch of knowledge which does not have a research institute supporting it. Every research institute has a library of its own and some of them are very well organised.

4 Library training

India today has 34 post-graduate library schools—the second largest number among all the countries of the world after USA with 43. The first degree awarded is Bachelor in Library Science—a one-year course after university graduation—ten of them award Master's degree in Library Science (one year after the Bachelor's) and two of them awards Doctorate degree in Library Science. This includes Associate Degrees (equivalent to Master's) awarded by the Documentation Research and Training Centre, Bangalore, and Indian National Scientific Documentation Centre, Delhi—the former in Documentation and the latter in Documentation and Reprography. The total annual output of all the schools is about 1,000. The medium of instruction at all the schools is English. In addition to these schools, several State Library Associations and Women's Polytechnics run Diploma and Certificate courses and their total output is about 500. The library training facilities in the country today are quite adequate. A number of Indian librarians have emigrated to other countries and at present as many as seven of them are working abroad as library experts with Unesco and other agencies.

5 Library technology

Until computers began to be applied to library programmes, library techniques in India, barring automation, were almost at par with the rest of the world. Photo-charging and punch-card system introduced in the West in the 1950s could not be adopted in India for various reasons. The equipment was not locally manufactured nor did the stringent foreign exchange position permit any imports. But in the field of computer technology, India is not very much behind the rest of the world today so far as 'know-how' is concerned. The first Digital computer was imported in India in 1956. The second computer was installed in 1960 and today there are as many as 130 computers in the country. According to a recent UN survey, the number of computers in India is the highest among the developing countries. The IBM and the ICL computers are now being assembled and progressively manufactured in India. The Bharat Electronics Corporation of India, Hyderabad, a Public Sector Undertaking, has already manufactured a small computer called the TDC-12 using indigenously developed technology. Medium and medium-large computers namely, TDC-16 and TDC-32, using third generation technology, i.e. integrated circuits, etc., based on completely indigenous know-how are also in the process of development. Assorted soft-ware for these computers is also under development. The Electronics Department of the Government of India is planning to establish Regional Computer Centres all over the country where the entire governmental work would be concentrated. At present the Indian National Scientific Documentation Centre in Delhi, the Indian Institute of Technology, New Delhi, the Indian Statistical Institute, Calcutta, the Tata Institute of Fundamental Research, Bombay, the Central Secretariat Library, New Delhi, and the Atomic Energy Institute Library, Bombay, are experimenting with the application of computer to library programmes and INSDOC has already brought out a few fascicules of computerised listings. One of the authors of this article (D. R. Kalia) prepared a computerised fascicule of the Indian National Bibliography in 1969 at the National Library, Calcutta. The Punjab Agricultural University, Ludhiana, and the Petroleum Research Institute, Dehradun (UP) have since long adopted the punch-card system for cataloguing and circulation respectively. The know-how about the use of computers for the library programme is yet to be fully developed in India. Only a handful of librarians are toying with the idea of developing library technology but they are learning the hard way in the absence of technical assistance from abroad. The results so far achieved have been quite encouraging and it is hoped that India will not lag behind in this field.

(c) Library Situation in India—A Brief Survey

M. N. NAGARAJ
Assistant Librarian, National Library, Calcutta

India through its five-year plans is making efforts for the all-round development of the country. It is an obvious and well-recognised fact that libraries help to preserve the culture of the country and to promote the advancement of the education of the people. One of the important requirements at this stage is the assessment of the needs of the country in terms of library service at various levels of educational and cultural activities. Once this assessment is completed, efforts should be made to get the programmes of development integrated with those of educational and cultural development. The major areas, for such a purpose, are:

1 Public libraries and library associations;
2 School and children's libraries;
3 College and university libraries;
4 Special libraries;
5 Documentation centres and bibliographical centres;
6 Library schools.

1 Public libraries and library associations

In India the tradition of learning existed since ancient times and libraries were just appendages to institutions of learning. Since these libraries were not agencies for mass education, they did not form a structure of a public library system. By the middle of the nineteenth century Bombay, Calcutta and Madras had 'Public libraries', the use of which was restricted only to certain people. During the next 50 to 60 years there was a total absence of public libraries in the sense of an open collection of general materials designed for use by anyone who sought information, recreation, self-education or aesthetic pleasure. There were so-called public libraries in some places, meaning that admission was not denied to anyone who wished to enter, but they seldom attempted to collect and to organise their materials to meet the needs or the interests of the average man. There was total absence of service to children in either public libraries or in schools. Libraries as social agencies, reflecting the needs and objectives of societies in which they operate, did not exist.

Baroda libraries
The concept of free public libraries for the masses was carried to India by Sayaji Rao Gaekwad who visited the United States of America at the turn of the century. Newton Mohan Dutta, in his presidential address at the first All Asia Educational Conference Library Section (1930), said that the Gaekwad was the pioneer not only of free and compulsory education but also of the free public library in India. He chose the free public library as the agency that should take charge of enlightenment of masses after their formal education. There was a comprehensive library development programme in Baroda which included training of librarians and publication of a library journal. In 1915 the Punjab University reorganised its library on a functional basis and a training class was begun and a textbook on librarianship published.

Library associations
As an appendage to the Indian Science Congress of 1918, a conference of librarians was convened by the Government of India, for the first time wherein was discussed problems including library co-operation, training of library assistants, compilation of catalogues, etc. This conference served a useful purpose in informing the delegates about the existing library facilities in the country and drawing up a plan for future development. Andhra Desa Library Association which was formed in 1914, published journals in Telugu and in English and held conferences regularly. The first All India Public Library Conference was held at Madras in 1919. This was a regular feature of the Indian National Congress and was the inspiration behind the formation of Library Associations in Maharashtra (1921), Bengal (1925), Madras (1928) and Punjab (1929).

Under the aegis of the first All Asia Educational Conference, the Library service section organised a conference in 1930. For the first time in India a Library Bill was brought before the Bengal Legislative Council in 1932 and before the Madras Legislative Assembly in 1933. Both failed to become law but in 1948 the Madras Public Library Bill was passed. The Punjab Library Association started publishing the *Modern Librarian* in 1930. The Government of India librarians met in Simla in 1933 and formed the Government of India Libraries Association, to co-ordinate and stimulate the work done by many state library associations and for the promotion and furtherance of a library movement. The Indian Library Association was formed in 1933. The other library associations that exist today are Bihar Rajya Pustakalaya Sangh (1936), Assam (1939), Utkal (1944), Kerala (1945), Delhi (1953), Gujarat (1953), UP (1956), MP (1957), Maharastra State Libraries Association (1961), Mysore (1962), Rajasthan (1962), and Jammu and Kashmir (1966).

Library Acts
A Public Libraries Act is now functioning in the following four states:
Madras (1948);
Andhra Pradesh (1960);
Mysore (1965);
Maharashtra (1968).

Fyzee Committee Report
The first worth-while and realistic assessment of the requirements of public library services for a particular region was made by a committee under the chairmanship of A. A. A. Fyzee, appointed by the government of Bombay in 1938–9. Having surveyed the existing conditions of the libraries in Bombay province, it examined the possibilities of future development. It suggested a scheme for the progressive building up of a library movement which would encourage and keep pace with the spread of education and literacy. The scheme outlined envisaged a network of libraries spread over the whole province with three regional libraries and a central library at the apex. It was a realistic report containing recommendations based on feasible financial expenditure and attainable targets.

Sinha Committee Report
The next important attempt made to study the state of public library services, to assess the requirements as well as to recommend measures to implement a practicable scheme of development on an All-India basis, was under the aegis of the Union Ministry of Education by a committee under the chairmanship of K. P. Sinha. The report of the committee was comprehensive and it contained many useful recommendations regarding programmes of development for a span spread over a period of 25 years. It was a highly ambitious plan. The report recommended a structure for the library system of India, based on library legislation at state level. Little was done to implement the recommendations of the committees.

The latest effort to draw up a public library development plan was by the Working Group on Libraries appointed by the Government of India Planning Commission (1963). Realising the need for promoting an integrated plan of library development for the country, the Government of India set up a Working Group to work out the details of the library development programme with special reference to the administrative set-up required, personnel training, library legislation, the public library system and children's libraries. The intention was not only to give an opportunity to our young people to get acquainted with the vast field of knowledge but also for promoting the utilisation of literacy among the general population, thus helping them in intelligent public participation in the social, economic and political development of the country. The Working Group suggested a programme of balanced development of public library services for five years during the fourth five-year plan. Another important recommendation of the group is as follows:

'whatever method of financing public libraries is adopted, financing entirely out of general revenues or out of funds collected from general revenues, the group feels it necessary to emphasise that the Central Government must share in a generous manner the financial burden of providing adequate public library services in the country and that the provision for public libraries should be such that the annual expenditure thereon is in no case less than 1.5% of the total annual expenditure on education'.

This may be interpreted as that the central and state governments should accept the responsibility of financing public library services in the same manner as they have accepted responsibility for free and compulsory primary education. To make people literate through primary education is one thing and to make them functionally literate is another. For the latter, library services are essential and are the only means. A decision should be taken at the national level to determine the priority and quantum of resources to be earmarked for public library services. A specific percentage of total budget should be earmarked for the purpose.

An outline of the public library system is that the village library forms the base over which is laid the next layer of Block or Panchayat library reaching directly or through sub-divisional or Taluka Library, the District Central Library from where the State Central Library is reached, completing the system at the state level. Co-ordination of the state systems will be affected by a National Library which will also provide leadership and guidance at the national level.

According to the survey made by the Working Group on libraries in 1966, it is estimated that on 1 January 1965, only 12 out of 16 states or 75% had State central libraries. Five union territories out of nine, or 55% had central libraries; 205 out of 327 districts or 63% had district central libraries; 1,394 blocks out of 5,223 or 27% had block development libraries and only 28,317 villages out of 566,878 or 5% had village libraries. These figures may seem to be impressive but the study of the actual working of these libraries would reveal that in most cases the situation is appalling.

It is paradoxical that India as a whole utterly lacks free public library service but, wherever public libraries exist, they are coping with a lot of difficulties. The library authorities resort to so many restrictive measures in the name of preventing any loss of books that the very purpose of establishing a library is defeated. They refuse to admit that certain losses in the use of library facilities are inevitable with all the best security measures that a human mind can devise and that losses are to be treated as part of the cost of service. In their attempt to prevent unavoidable losses through restrictive measures, they actually discourage the genuine readers from the use of the library. In spite of such restrictive measures and the librarian being penalised, losses still do occur. Unless progressive and imaginative steps are taken in the running of these libraries, the use of existing facilities would continue to be limited. The Delhi Public Library service is a living example in India to prove that free public library service is appreciated and used by the common people when adequately provided and that free access to books on open shelves is the *sine qua non* of a free public library service.

It is true that libraries are the exclusive responsibility of the state governments and Parliament cannot legislate on this subject. The union government can take initiative in the matter of library development while so much is being done by way of centrally sponsored projects in other fields of education. The first practical detail to be tackled is how the Ministry of Education should be geared to accomplish the plan for the development of libraries, bearing in mind that the development of the libraries is largely a matter for state initiative. A national forum in the form of the National Library Advisory Board can be instituted so that through that forum the state governments can be persuaded to do something about it. If a Library Bureau is established in the Union Ministry of Education and Social Welfare, the decisions of the Board could be followed up for action. Free public library service is a direct contributor to economic and social growth. The growth of libraries in the country has been spasmodic and that, too, in an uneven manner. Fortunately there has been lately a greater awareness among planners in India with regard to the wisdom of investment in human resources. A great amount of money has been kept apart for educational development. Emphasis is being laid on school and children's libraries. If there is no school or children's library of the right sort, there will be no effective demand for public library service.

2 School libraries and children's libraries

We have nearly 400,000 primary schools, 70,000 middle schools and 25,000 high/higher secondary schools in the country. At this stage it would be unrealistic to think in terms of providing library services in primary schools and middle schools. The Working Group suggests that the public library's children's section should take care of the former while a selected number of middle schools should be taken up for providing library services. At the high/

higher secondary school, state libraries should be provided. The under-utilisation of library services at the university stage is partly because of a lack of the library habit at the school stage.

There is total absence of service to children in either public libraries or schools. Most of the public libraries that do exist are essentially adult institutions. Children's services, which are very few, are housed and administered separately and specifically for children and mainly as study areas rather than general libraries. There is seldom any attempt to make the children's library an attractive foyer which will lead eventually to the adult collection.

3 University and college libraries

At present we have nearly 85 universities, including institutions of higher studies deemed to be universities under the UGC Act 1956. By and large, the older universities have a good stock of books and, thanks to the generous dispensations from the UGC, they have new buildings, though a good number of them are not functionally well built. The pay scale and status of librarians have also been improved. In spite of all this, it is felt that 'librarianship in India has not risen to the needs of modern learning and research, despite the recognition it has received as an academic discipline'. The UGC appointed a Committee in 1957 under the chairmanship of S. R. Ranganathan to advise the UGC about development of libraries and their organisation so as to strengthen library facilities in the universities and colleges and to administer them more efficiently. The Committee has made a set of recommendations which the UGC followed for some years when, to its dismay, it found that the resources made available to the university libraries were not, perhaps, being fully utilised, and appointed a Committee under the chairmanship of Professor A. R. Wadia to review the entire situation. The report of the Committee is still awaited.

The condition of the 2,400 college libraries, with a few exceptions, is very unsatisfactory. The UGC has taken up this issue and is doing its best to improve the situation.

4 Special libraries

The tremendous emphasis on technological development obliges us to keep pace with the demand created by the needs of laboratories, research institutions and universities in the way of periodical and book materials. Since Independence great emphasis is being laid on economic, scientific and technological development. Acceptance of overall planning as an agency for national development in all spheres by the central as well as state governments has brought in its wake the growth and establishment of a large number of specialised institutions in all spheres of national life. The central as well as state governments have under their control a number of specialised departments. The Council of Scientific and Industrial Research, the Indian Council of Agricultural Research maintain national laboratories, institutes, etc. All such agencies have a library to support their programmes. It is only in this sector that a fairly well-geared library service exists today. The Government of India is planning to develop the National Medical Library, the National Science Library and the National Agricultural Library. An effort is being made to strengthen the existing specialised libraries as well as to build up grids of special libraries in major subject fields to effect economy and efficiency.

5 Documentation centres and bibliographical centres

The Indian National Scientific Documentation Centre, established in 1952 by the Government of India in collaboration with the Unesco, has made a meaningful progress during the last decade. A number of bibliographies, union catalogues, *ad hoc* reading lists, etc., have been published in addition to the *Indian Science Abstracts* and a new-look periodical *Annals of Library Science*. The translation and abstracting services and some pioneering efforts in informing the Indian scientific world about existing and proposed services through exhibitions, seminars, conferences, etc., have earned the respect of the profession as well as of scientists. The documentation wings of a number of specialised libraries are doing good work in so far as their own field of activity is concerned. The Unesco publication *Bibliographical services throughout the world* includes a large number of specialised bibliographies published in India. *The Indian National Bibliography*, which started publication in 1958, lists all the publications received in the National Library, Calcutta, under the Delivery of Books Act.

6 Library schools

Nearly 25 universities run a post-graduate Bachelor course in Library Science. Four universities impart a Master's degree training. Two women's polytechnics offer Diploma courses. The DRTC, Bangalore, INSDOC, New Delhi and IASLIC, Calcutta, have specialised advanced courses in Documentation and Reprography. A number of State Library Associations offer a certificate course in Library Science.

The National Library

The National Library in India occupies a special place in the professional map. The Library has made great progress since Independence. In view of the need for personnel with adequate language competence coupled with professional education, and its limited terms of reference and limited budget, the progress made has been spectacular. A Reviewing Committee set up in 1968, to go into the working and to suggest improvements, has submitted a report and the Government of India have already taken steps to implement the recommendations.

The Delhi Public Library

The Delhi Public Library, sponsored by Unesco in 1950, has established itself as an active public library. The Library's potential as a centre for demonstration and training has not yet been exploited fully. This Library holds a promise, which if not exploited suitably may even affect its own efficiency and progress.

Book production

The most important fact to bear in mind is that, in our country at the present moment, there are not enough books published to go round. The planning of book publication for a country like ours has to be dealt with in a wholehearted manner. Our standard of book production has a long way to go to reach basic standards. The highest priority is for the publication of books at all stages of education. Human and material resources should be given to the National Book Trust, Children's Book Trust, Sahitya Akademi at the national level and similar organisations at the state level. The implications of finding the vast amount of paper for this purpose should not be lost sight of. The problem is not solely a matter of illiteracy. Obviously there can be no readers if the ability to read is lacking. It is odd that it is not equally obvious that there can be no readers, if there is nothing to read.

The types of books that are needed by different types of readers for different purposes may be classified as: (a) basic textbooks for the elementary, secondary, college and university students and books for supplementary reading bearing on the curriculum; (b) books for general reading (non-textbooks); and (c) scholarly works for use by advanced students and researchers.

(a)(i) Elementary, secondary school textbooks

All over the country the mother tongue of the student has been introduced as the medium of instruction. The quality of education depends not so much on the textbooks themselves as on the quality of books used by the students for supplementary reading. Supplementary reading can be encouraged only if the method of instruction and the system of examination make allowance for it. A survey of the supplementary reading material available in the Indian languages would show that there are wide lacunae in subject coverage, and the quality of the books that exist is far from satisfactory. Greater attention is to be paid to this aspect of book production. A carefully selected catalogue of such books should be compiled in each Indian language. This will help to identify the lacunae and show the deficiencies in the existing material.

(a)(ii) College and university textbooks

The Government of India has sponsored, in collaboration with foreign governments and agencies, the reprinting of textbooks for college and university students and so far over a 1,000 titles under the scheme have been brought out. These are the low-priced reprints of the titles published in the English language primarily in the UK, the USA and the USSR. List of books brought out under this scheme by each agency are no doubt available, but it would be helpful to all concerned if a combined list of such titles could be issued regularly by an agency of the central government and made available at a nominal cost.

A catalogue of books for supplementary reading at the college and university levels bearing on the curricula in various subject fields should be compiled, so that the college and university libraries will have a basic book selection tool. The Government of India has recently adopted a scheme to produce college and university textbooks in Indian languages. With the changeover to Indian languages as the medium of instruction at college and university levels, the need for supplementary reading material bearing on the curriculum has become paramount. It is, therefore, necessary to take up the production of supplementary reading material in the Indian languages.

(b) *Books for general reading*
Standard catalogues for public libraries should be compiled in all the Indian languages. This will not only help in the use of the already existing material, but will also help to map out the lacunae.

(c) *Scholarly work*
Books of lasting value, the Government of India's select publications and the other state publications, should be translated into all the Indian languages so that these basic items of research are available to scholars all over India, irrespective of the language group to which they belong.

Promotion of reading habit
The reading habit is best formed at an early age when the mind is most impressionable. Every school must have a well-equipped library and every public library must have a children's section so that children are exposed to books at an early age. Once the reading habit is well formed at the school level, it is carried through the rest of life provided reading facilities are available free of cost at public libraries. Talking about promotion of the reading habit without first providing facilities for reading to all citizens is like putting the cart before the horse.

A national library week and other promotional activities should be undertaken at national as well as state level.

(d)   The Impact of Recent Developments on Iranian Librarianship

A. SINAI
Director, Iranian Documentation Centre

Recent developments in Iranian librarianship have been discussed in another paper.[1]

The return of a few enthusiastic foreign-educated Iranian librarians during the first half of the last decade, and their active participation in professional activities, caused an awakening of professional library conscience in Iran. Their

E

own activities and the assistance of foreign librarians residing in Iran led to three major events which had, in their turn, a great impact on other developments in Iranian professional librarianship. These major events were the (a) founding of the Iranian Library Association in the Winter 1966, (b) establishment of the Department of Library Science at the Faculty of Education, University of Tehran, in September 1966, and (c) founding of IRANDOC/ TEBROC in September 1968.

The Iranian Library Association
The Iranian Library Association was founded in the Winter 1966 by a group of eight enthusiastic librarians, all women, and most of them educated professionally in the USA or UK. The Association was successful in awakening professional conscience and in bringing new ideas to Iranian librarianship. Its most important means of disseminating new ideas is its *Bulletin* which began publication in the Winter 1966. After a period of decay, it became a regular quarterly publication in the Winter 1970. The *Bulletin* contains articles on various professional and technical matters which are summarised in English. It is widely circulated to Iranian librarians and also to Afghan librarians who have recently formed their own professional association. Since Winter 1971, the news section of the Bulletin has been published in a separate monthly newsletter.

Organising lecture series and meetings is another means of promoting librarianship in Iran. The lectures are either organised by ILA independently, or in co-operation with the Department of Library Science and IRANDOC/ TEBROC.

Although the Association has always had members in the provinces, only in 1970 was it successful in extending its influence to one provincial capital, Tabriz, in north-west Iran, where it has now an organised activity. This activity owes much to the establishment of a library school there.

ILA appeared on the international scene by joining IFLA in 1970 and by sending three representatives to the 1970 Moscow conference. Six ILA members are expected to participate in the 1971 Liverpool conference.

Department of Library Science
The same group of enthusiastic librarians who founded ILA submitted a report to the University of Tehran in early 1966 to state the need for establishing a Department of Library Science in the new Faculty of Education. The report was accepted and a provisional curriculum drafted. The US Fulbright Commission agreed to provide the Department with an American professor each year. The first Fulbright professor, Miss Alice Lohrer, Professor of Library Science, University of Illinois, USA, arrived in September 1966. She organised course work at the Master's degree level. In 1968 the Department started offering courses at the undergraduate level leading to a minor in library science for Bachelor's degree students, also.

The Iranian professional librarians who first assisted the American profes-

62

sors gradually took over most of the teaching load and all of the administration. The language of teaching, English at the beginning, changed into Persian. However, strong knowledge of English was required of graduate students since nearly all reading assignments were given from English language sources and their American instructors still taught in English. Now, the Department has three full-time and several part-time Iranian instructors.

The Department has had a great impact on Iran's understanding of modern librarianship and has created a demand for professional librarians. Students of the Department, if not already employed by a library, are employed immediately after they are admitted to the Department. However, this does not mean that all library positions are filled. Due to the civil service laws, it is very difficult for teachers to get transferred from the Ministry of Education. Therefore, teachers admitted to the Department have difficulty getting transferred to library positions after graduation. This problem causes 40% of the library school graduates to remain in non-library positions after graduation.

IRANDOC/TEBROC

The Iranian Documentation Centre (IRANDOC) and Tehran Book Processing Centre (TEBROC) were founded in September 1968 as the result of two proposals written by Dr. John F. Harvey and submitted to the then Minister of Science and Higher Education, Dr. Majid Rahnema. Both organisations are part of the Institute for Research and Planning in Science and Education. The Institute is responsible for planning research, determining national scientific and research policies, and drawing up educational plans at all levels.

While functionally separate, the two sister organisations, IRANDOC and TEBROC, co-operate very closely in all aspects of library and information work. IRANDOC has several basic functions:

(a) To collect, organise, develop, and service the national research library in science and social science.

(b) To provide modern, quick and intensive literature analysis service for Iranian scientists and professors.

(c) To publish bibliographic and reference material useful to the scholarly world.

(d) To serve as the Iranian link in a future Middle Eastern information network as well as in the world scientific information system (UNISIST).

(e) To encourage co-operation and co-ordination among Iran's research and special libraries and information centres.

TEBROC's basic functions are:

(a) To provide central processing services for libraries, including book acquisition and cataloguing. As a result of this function, TEBROC provides printed catalogue card service.

(b) To advise institutions in planning all aspects of library design and work.

(c) To provide in-service training facilities for practising librarians and for students of the Department of Library Science.

(d) To do research on the expansion of the Dewey and LC classifications to fit Iranian materials. Also, to make a list of Persian subject headings.

(e) To publish library science books useful to students and librarians.

IRANDOC/TEBROC, as government agencies, have had a major impact on the development of modern librarianship in Iran. Much pioneering work has been done by the two centres. The first *Abstract Bulletin and Contents Pages Bulletin* were published by IRANDOC in September 1969. The most comprehensive *Directory of Iranian Periodicals and Directory of Iranian Newspapers* were published by IRANDOC and portions of the most comprehensive *Directory of Iranian Libraries* have been published. The first bibliographies of Persian printed books in economics and law have been published. The Iranian National Union List of Serials has been prepared and is now in press. Also, IRANDOC has prepared a list of Iranian *Technical Journals for Industry* under the supervision of FID. Bibliographies of theses in Iranian universities and of government publications are being prepared. TEBROC is preparing the Iranian National Union Catalogue. In agreement with the publisher of the Dewey Decimal Classification and the Library of Congress, TEBROC is expanding these classifications to fit Iranian materials. So far the 'Iranian Languages' section has been expanded and the Persian Edition has been published. Other books have been published by TEBROC for use by Iranian librarians. These include books such as *Farsi Author Numbers to be used with the Library of Congress Classification Schedules and Explanation of the Cutter-Sanborn Author-Marks, Three-Figure Tables.*

TEBROC, through its advisory function, has spread many new ideas. Its central cataloguing service and printed cards are increasingly useful.

Other developments

The work of ILA, the Department of Library Science and IRANDOC/TEBROC have motivated other agencies to seek better library service and to improve conditions in their libraries. Such other developments have occurred in Iranian librarianship as the following:

The Institute for Intellectual Growth of Children and Young Adults has established a national system of children's libraries. All of these are open access libraries and are heavily used by children. Modern means are used to attract children, such as story-telling hours and exhibits of children's paintings.

Tabriz University has established a Department of Library Science offering courses leading to bachelor's and master's degrees in library science. However, the teaching staff is all, except one, composed of foreign librarians. Iranians must be educated to take over the Department when the foreign instructors leave. No one has yet graduated from these courses and it is expected that for some time all graduates will be absorbed in the libraries of Azerbaijan Province.

The Iranzamin Junior College has established a two-year course to train people with high-school diplomas as library technicians.

A proposal for a national library plan was prepared in 1969 by a committee of Iranian and foreign librarians and submitted to government authorities.[2] Although the proposal has not yet been accepted, it is hoped that it will be accepted soon and carried out, probably with some changes.

The Institute of Standards and Industrial Research of Iran has established a Committee on Library Standards. This committee is in charge of preparing standards for library equipment and supplies. So far, several standards have been prepared. On the other hand, TEBROC is preparing standards for various types of libraries in terms of personnel, budget, space, collection, etc. If accepted by government authorities, the two sets of standards will greatly influence library progress.

An inter-library loan code was prepared for the first time by IRANDOC and launched in October 1969 to encourage co-operation among special and academic libraries. It was warmly accepted and inter-library loan is now increasing.

The impact of modern ideas has been less on public libraries than on other kinds of libraries. Although $1\frac{1}{2}\%$ of each province's tax money is allocated for library purposes by law, lack of professional librarians in public libraries slows down their progress. Closed stacks are still very common, but the Board of Trustees for Public Libraries has agreed that open access should be introduced to public libraries. Proper cataloguing and classification have been introduced to a few libraries, but they are not common. The impact of recent developments on Iranian public libraries will increase when these libraries can employ professional librarians.

REFERENCES

1. Sinai, Ali and John Harvey. 'The Iranian Library Scene.' *Int. Lib. Rev.* (1969) *1*, 107–17.
2. Proposal for a National Library Plan for Iran, *Int. Lib. Rev.* (1970) *2*, 253–61.

(e) Developments in Pakistan Librarianship

SYED JALALUDDIN HAIDER

Assistant Professor, Department of Library Science, University of Karachi

Pakistan, no doubt, as a new nation was born on 14 August 1947, but the history of modern librarianship in the territories now constituting the country dates back from 1915, when Don Dickinson, an American librarian, was invited by the authorities of the University of the Panjab (Lahore) to organise the university library on modern lines and to start a training programme for the librarians of the Panjab. Thus the subject of Library Science, for the first

65

time, was incorporated in the curriculum of a university in the East. The course was of short duration leading to a Certificate in Library Science, and included all the core courses supplemented by practical training in the university library. In reorganising the university library, several new practices were introduced by Dickinson. These included: introduction of Dewey Decimal Classification, use of author entry over title as main entry, and adoption of dictionary catalogue on cards instead of author catalogue in the form of register. Also, the first book on librarianship, *Panjab library primer,* was written by Dickinson for the use of students as textbook.

The University of the Panjab (Lahore) through its Library School and Library exercised a great influence on future development of libraries and librarianship in British India. From now on librarianship was regarded as an independent discipline. Libraries all over British India started organising their collections on modern lines. The librarians educated by the University took an active part in the organisation of this profession in British India.

Soon after Independence, the Government of Pakistan, being conscious of the importance of the libraries, appointed Khan Bahadur Asadullah, the former librarian of the Imperial Library, Calcutta, and founder-Secretary of the Indian Library Association, as Officer on Special Duty in the Ministry of Education. On the recommendation of Asadullah, the Directorate of Libraries and Archives was set up as early as 1949 as a central authority for library development in the country. Another significant move in this direction, on the part of the Government, was the mission of Mr. L. C. Key, a library consultant to the Government from Australia, during the period 1955-6, under the Colombo Plan. His assignment included 'the preparation of development plans for the Liaquat National Library (now Liaquat Memorial Library), other reference and public libraries in each province, university and college libraries and research libraries'. The Report, submitted by Key in 1956, proposed an integrated scheme for library development, involving 36 libraries and two library schools to be developed over a period of four years. The scheme could not be implemented because it was unrealistic at the time.

Besides the Government and its agencies, working librarians were also conscious of the need for library development and their activities included: writing articles in professional magazines to draw the attention of the Government; formation of associations at regional and provincial level for joint efforts; and organisation of short-term courses in librarianship to meet the immediate need for qualified manpower in this field. Similarly, the universities have contributed their share by instituting graduate training programme in librarianship. In 1956, the University of Karachi established its Post-Graduate Diploma in Library Science, which was followed by the Universities of Dacca (1959) and Panjab (1959).

In the following I shall try to describe the developments which have taken place in academic, public and special libraries during the last 10 years, or likely to take place in near future as a result of national or international forces.

Academic libraries

At the time of Independence there were three universities and few colleges in the country. At present, there are 14 universities and 381 colleges. All the universities, with the exception of the University of Baluchistan, have libraries. Excluding Islamabad, they contained approximately 1,000,000 volumes in 1968 to serve 25,000 students and 2,500 faculty members. The largest library had 238,000 volumes and the smallest had 5,000 volumes; the average, after excluding the universities of Islamabad and Chittagong, was approximately 87,000 volumes.

Besides books, the existing libraries are acquiring rare items on microfilms and microfiche, etc., from the great libraries of the world. Special facilities for the housing and use of these have been provided. Photographic services, such as microfilming, photostating, etc., have also been started.

None of the existing libraries, because of budgetary limitation and control of foreign exchange, can build resources either in scope or depth. The current trend is therefore towards co-ordinated purchase.

The libraries are no more considered a luxury item but rather as a resource centre on the campus. This is evident from the various documents of the Provincial and Central Governments. The report of the Commission on National Education (1959), Scientific Commission of Pakistan (1960) and various developmental plans have regarded the library as essential for quality education at all levels.

Another significant development has been the accord of faculty status to some qualified staff.

These developments have also affected university libraries in terms of organisational structure. The university libraries are now thinking of adopting a Centralised Subject Divisional Plan, to meet the problem of interdependent disciplines. This system is already in practice in Karachi University.

Public libraries

There is no organised system of public libraries, although there are a number of so-called public libraries, mostly subscription libraries, under the charge of municipalities and local bodies. In 1965, there existed 317 such libraries with a total book collection of 1,194,000 for 14,500,000 readers (literate population) in the country, according to a Unesco source. The Panjab Public Library, established in 1884, is the largest public library.

The modern concept of public library service, as outlined in Unesco's Manifesto and reaffirmed in Unesco's Seminar at Delhi in 1955, is gaining ground both in the governmental and private circles. The importance of libraries was also recognised under the Basic Democracy System, introduced by a former government. The provision and maintenance of public libraries was laid down as one of the function of Union Councils and District Councils in Basic Democracies Ordinance 1959. Hence, the union councils maintain some kind of libraries and reading rooms. Such libraries receive grants from municipalities and local bodies, and are run by the secretaries of the councils under the guidance of their chairman. In Karachi alone, there are 84 such libraries, having a collection of about 50,000 volumes with an annual addition of 2,000 volumes.

Various library associations took an active part in promotion of public library service in the country. Inspired by the services of Unesco's Library Project at Delhi, the PLA (Pakistan Library Association) on the eve of its Second Annual Conference (1959) urged the establishment of a similar project, under the auspices of the Government and Unesco in Pakistan with a view to providing a model for public library development in the country. The Project was developed by a committee, formed by the Association in 1960, and it was submitted to the Government but it could not achieve approval for reasons not known.

Another organisation, the Society for the Promotion and Improvement of Libraries, formed in 1960, has been striving hard to promote the development of a public library service in Karachi. For this purpose, a scheme was prepared by the Society but it met the same fate as the previous one. It was, in fact, much too ambitious. The Society, however, succeeded in convincing the authorities of Karachi Municipal Corporation so far as the creation of a Library Board was concerned. The Board was created on 11 April 1967. A number of small libraries are functioning in Karachi under the Board. The Karachi Municipal Corporation is also planning to have a central library for the city with separate sections for various groups of population.

The East Pakistan Library Association, founded in 1955, is also active as far as the promotion of the idea of public library service is concerned. A seminar on the need for the public library was organised by the Association, in 1966, with the co-operation of the British Council, Dacca. The impetus for the seminar came from the British Public Libraries and Museum Act 1964. The seminar also discussed draft legislation, but enactment of such legislation is still awaited.

The All Pakistan Women's Association, popularly called APWA, has been very active in the promotion and establishment of children's libraries. The first children's library has been set up at Karachi, under the auspices of the Association, and a similar establishment has been projected for Dacca in East Pakistan.

A number of Government-supported organisations, e.g. the Pakistan Council for National Integration and the Bureau of National Reconstruction, have established libraries at various places with modern public library facilities and provision for children's services. These libraries have been opened at Lahore, Rawalpindi, Dacca, Chittagong, Rajshahi, Hyderabad and Quetta. These libraries are open to the public free of charge, but for reading on the premises. For borrowing books, one has to become a member of the Council.

The fourth Five-Year Plan (1970–5) laid emphasis on the development of libraries, particularly public libraries as a popular weapon against illiteracy. The Plan suggested the establishment of a chain of libraries. It also suggested the introduction of a book mobile service for villages and rural areas.

68

Science-Technology libraries

The role of science-technology in solving the national problems of vital interest is being increasingly recognised. The four successive developmental plans, launched by the Government, laid more and more emphasis on research by allocating increased finances for promotion of research in scientific and technological fields. The emphasis on research resulted in the establishment of a number of agencies for research, investigation and analysis of the problems. There are more than 150 such agencies, owned by departments of provincial and central governments, autonomous research councils, research institutions and universities of the country.

Information on science-technology libraries, like other types of libraries, is obscure because no census of the library resources available in the country has been made. According to a rough estimate, there are 60 such libraries in the country. They were originated to meet the needs of individual organisations in a single subject field or in a group of subjects. To a large extent they are located in urban areas where industrial and technical developments have been greatest. The libraries, with the exception of agricultural and technical universities, vary in size from 5,000 to 50,000 volumes. Almost all the libraries are headed by professionally qualified librarians. The common services offered by most of the libraries include answering quick reference questions, literature searching, indexing journals of interest, and preparation of subject bibliographies. In some libraries, translation and photocopying services are offered.

PANSDOC, established with the assistance of Unesco in 1957, is helping scientists through its procurement, translating, microfilming, and bibliography compiling services. The Centre issues *Pakistan Science Abstracts*. A *Union catalogue of scientific periodicals* held by the libraries of Pakistan has been brought out recently.

Since 1960, after the report of the Scientific Commission of Pakistan, a new force in the development of libraries was evident. The report expressed its dissatisfaction with the present resources and suggested numerous measures to improve the situation. Realising the poor condition of science-technology libraries, PANSDOC organised a Symposium on the Development of Scientific and Technical Libraries from 14–16 March 1963, at Karachi. The recommendations included the development of two Central Science Libraries at Karachi and Dacca. A detailed project to this effect was prepared by PANSDOC, and Unesco was requested to sponsor it through the Government. To examine the feasibility of the Project, Dr. Herman H. Henkle was deputed by Unesco in 1966. Mr. Henkle, in his report, recommended the establishment of Central Science Libraries as autonomous agencies. He also recommended the creation of an agency called the National Science Libraries and Information Centres to govern these libraries, and the formation of an Advisory Board for providing advisory service to the agency.

Bibliographical control

As a result of the world-wide bibliographical survey initiated under the auspices of Unesco and Library of Congress, a group was formed in 1950 to prepare a report on Pakistan. Later on, it was named the Pakistan Bibliographical Working Group. It has greatly contributed towards development of bibliographical sources and has initiated the work of compilation of bibliographies on an organised basis. Its greatest contribution has been the compilation of retrospective national bibliography of Pakistan, covering the period from 1947–61, with the financial assistance of Unesco. The bibliography is under publication.

Efforts on government level to compile a national bibliography began in 1962, with the establishment of the National Bibliographical Unit by the Directorate of Libraries and Archives. In the absence of copyright depository libraries, although an Act to this effect was promulgated in 1962, the work of the Unit was handicapped in the beginning. However, the Unit succeeded in bringing out the *Pakistan National Bibliography* for the year 1962 in 1966. In February 1967, enforcement of the Copyright Ordinance was announced. Subsequently, the National Library of Pakistan, Islamabad, the Central Library of Pakistan, Dacca, and Liaquat Memorial Library, Karachi, were designated as copyright deposit libraries under the provision of the Ordinance.

There are a number of organisations which have contributed towards bibliographical development. The National Book Centre of Pakistan, established in 1962 under the Unesco project on reading materials, has published a number of bibliographies in Urdu, English and Bengali. Similarly, PANSDOC has compiled more than 600 bibliographies on scientific and technical subjects. Other institutions and organisations which have contributed to bibliographical control include the Social Science Research Centre, University of the Panjab; Institute of Development of Economics, Dacca; Department of Library Science, University of Karachi; Institute of Business Administration, Karachi.

Library education

Training facilities for library workers were virtually non-existent when Pakistan came into being. This situation remained for years although a beginning was made by the University of the Panjab and various library associations by instituting courses of short duration leading to certificate level, to meet immediate needs. In 1956 a new force came into play with the institution of the Post-Graduate Diploma Course at the University of Panjab and Dacca in 1959, and the University of Peshawar in 1962. By 1959, the idea of a Degree Programme received a great deal of attention because of the need of more library facilities and the inadequacy of the one-year Diploma Course. Eventually, the universities of Dacca and Karachi raised their Diploma Programme to Master Level from 1962, and now the Diploma Course is considered the first year of the two-year Degree Programme.

In 1968, a Doctoral Programme was instituted at the University of Karachi. So far three students have been admitted to this programme.

The most important achievement in 1970 was the appointment of Dr. A. Moid and Dr. Anis Khurshid as Professor of Library Science and Associate Professor, respectively, at the University of Karachi. The Department of Library Science at the University of Karachi is now fully constituted with five full-time teachers. Other library schools are headed by university librarians with one or two full-time faculty members, but there is a trend towards fully constituted departments. A post of Professor has also been created at the University of the Panjab but the same has not yet been filled.

Research in librarianship
Along with development and expansion in library education, some research contributions have been made, particularly in the fields of cataloguing and classification. The rendering of Pakistani personal names, in the absence of a code, in library catalogues and bibliographies has always been a problem in Pakistan as well as outside the country. The need for a code was felt after the International Conference on Cataloguing Principles, held in October 1961, at Paris. The impact of this Conference was tremendous in the succeeding years. As a result of this, numerous efforts were made towards formulation of a set of rules for bringing uniformity in divergent existing practices. The most important of these was the *Cataloguing of Pakistan names* by Anis Khurshid. The rules suggested by Khurshid for rendering the names of person conform to the principles evolved by the Sub-committee of ICCP for Muslim names of the Indo-Pakistan Sub-continent and to the Statement of Principles adopted at the Conference.

The Dewey Decimal Classification, the most used scheme in Pakistan, was found inadequate for classification of material on oriental topics. A committee was, therefore, constituted in 1960 by the Department of Library Science, University of Karachi, with the late Muhammad Shafi as its Convenor, for the modification and expansion of the Dewey Scheme to suit local needs. The expansion was worked out for subjects such as Muslim Philosophy, Islam, Oriental Languages and Literature, and Muslim History, by the Convenor with the assistance of the Committee. The expansion is now widely used by small as well as large libraries in the country.

The following professional journals, brought out by various library associations, report regularly current developments in the subject:
Pakistan Library Review, Pakistan Library Association Journal, Eastern Librarian, Pakistan Library Bulletin.

In addition to these, monthly or casual newsletters are issued by some of the professional associations. The *PLA Newsletter* is the most popular and regular.

3 ASIA: FAR EAST

(a) Libraries and Librarianship in the Republic of Korea: I

KE HONG PARK

Librarian, Korea Institute of Science and Technology

Background

In September 1955, two years after the Korean War, only 70 libraries reported their operation with a total collection of 1,961,252 volumes, manned by 423 librarians and assistants, with the seating capacity of 6,504. There was only a small number of librarians who had proper modern library school training. However, 16 years later, these figures jumped to 3,121 libraries with 5,111 librarians, 16,087,285 volumes, and 302,903 seats.

This is by no means a miracle. Korea, throughout her history over centuries, flourished with many royal and private libraries. The first royal library with a substantial collection was founded in AD 918 and was expanded greatly by AD 982. About this time there came many libraries, i.e. the Central Royal Library, government libraries including government archives, the Royal College Library and nine private college libraries, and several Buddhist temple libraries.

A royal decree for the first modern national library was issued in 1906 and many collections, both royal and private, were gathered in a palace which used to be the living quarters of the Royal family. These collections were incorporated into the New Governor General's Investigation Bureau which was set up by the then occupying Japanese Governor General in 1911.

Privately endowed public libraries, in the modern sense, were established by several interested persons in Seoul in 1909, and in Pyong Yang in 1910. There were about 100 school libraries (college and school) in Seoul about 1910. Korea had her first modern special library in 1920 when the government railroad system opened a library.

At present Korea has 63 public libraries and 149 special libraries with a total collection of 596,548 volumes for public libraries and 1,577,388 volumes for special libraries.

Public libraries

Seoul, the capital of the country, had only two public libraries until the city opened a district library a few months ago. This is the first of the district public library systems which the city is going to establish. There will be eight more of this type of public library within the next five years in Seoul.

Chongro Public Library, one of the three public libraries in Seoul, just opened a book mobile service a few months ago. This is the first book mobile service in Korea. If the trial service brings more demand, the mobile fleet will be increased.

The Library Law, which was enacted in 1967, requires at least one public library for each county. This means that there will be 135 more county public libraries besides the city public libraries within the next 10 years.

A model county library system can be found at Kangjin County in Cholla Province. The main library is located in Kangjin, the county seat, and all micro-library programmes within the county were incorporated into a system which will, eventually, open town branches in the County.

Micro-libraries

Micro-library programme has been expanded greatly since its initiation in 1960. A micro-library, a small shelf with 300 to 400 volumes and a few magazines, is set up in each village if some person or the village will finance half the cost, the remaining half being contributed by the Micro-Library Association.

Most of these small collections usually comprise agricultural, horticultural or fishing handbooks with a few fiction. These books are often exchanged with nearby micro-libraries, and public libraries in the vicinity lend their collection to them. The contents of a micro-library varies depending on the nature of the village.

Special libraries

In 1966 the Korea Institute of Science and Technology was established with the financial support of the governments of the Republic of Korea and the United States. The Institute was officially dedicated in 1969 and now the KIST library holds over 1,300 academic journals with extensive back files and 25,000 volumes of books on science and technology.

The periodical collection at this library was computerised for management, location, and bibliographic purposes in 1970. This is the first electronic data processing system applied to the library service in Korea.

Two more science libraries are being organised with substantial stocks: one for the Korea Institute of Advanced Science, which is a graduate school; and the other for the Agency for Defence Development. A new research library in economic development and management is also being organised for the Korea Development Institute.

With a view to a joint library system or very close co-operation in the future, these four libraries are undertaking co-ordinated acquisition and unified processing of library materials. These four libraries, together with the Korea Scientific and Technological Information Centre (KORSTIC), will provide an enormous amount of scientific material to satisfy the information demands of the scientific community in Korea.

Co-operation

At present there are only a few technical libraries to meet the demand for scientific information in Korea. Notable ones are the National Institute for

73

Industrial Research Library, the Atomic Energy Institute Library, the Korea Institute of Science and Technology Library and a few libraries of the major universities.

These science and technology libraries do not have an official system for co-operation. However, with mutual understanding, they are closely co-operating in inter-library loans, photocopying services and co-ordinated acquisitions. KORSTIC publishes a union list of scientific and technological periodicals of key libraries.

There is an inter-library loan system among 16 libraries in Seoul since 1968. Member libraries are the National Assembly Library, the National Central Library, two special libraries, two public libraries and 10 university libraries.

The Medical Library Association, which was formed in 1968, publishes the *Union list of medical journals* of member libraries (28) and these medical libraries have an inter-library loan system among themselves. Other smaller libraries are waiting to join in these inter-library loan systems.

The National Central Library started compiling a *National union catalogue* in 1970. Each library was asked to send one copy of main entry cards of their recent acquisitions. Forty-seven libraries are co-operating in this project. The annual catalogue will be published in book form.

Library school

Yonsei University first opened a library science department in 1957. This is an undergraduate programme. There is a graduate programme in the Graduate School of Education. There are four undergraduate library science departments in four universities in Seoul. Ewha Women's University has both undergraduate and graduate programmes. Chung Ang University has only an undergraduate programme. Sung Kyun Kwan University has an undergraduate programme and this year inaugurated the Graduate School of Library and Information Science.

Apart from these formal educational programmes, there are a few other workshop programmes by which we train teacher-librarians or junior librarians. Except for these workshop programmes and undergraduate programmes, Korea lacks adequate staff and facilities for higher education in librarianship.

Future perspectives

When Yonsei University first opened its library science department in 1957, there were only a small number of trained librarians; most of the library staff were clerks or archivists.

The concept of library service was first introduced at this time, and a few librarians, including the author, experienced hardship in opening the reference collection to the library public.

Problems before Korean libraries and librarians today are manifold. The first and most basic problem is the lack of highly trained librarians and educational facilities as mentioned above. The flood of published or unpublished information will engulf us and throw us into an abyss unless we are ready, with trained staff, to process them for the best use.

We often hear that the problem is money. Of course we all have that problem, Korean libraries more so than other libraries. However, the author believes that man is more important than money because an able man can stretch a little money far further than others.

The second problem is the lack of enthusiasm and insight among librarians. This will be the cause of many discreditable situations such as indifference or refusal to co-operate in programmes in acquisition, processing, circulation and other field of services.

The third problem is lack of source information on library materials. The language barrier contributes considerably to this problem, and to the lack of international co-operation among librarians. However, if we have a fixed international channel through which we can exchange information, we could have better and more information in the future.

The fourth problem is the most common problem—money. The major portion of the budget for Korean libraries is spent on salaries, leaving only a small portion for library materials. However, the amount of the budget is increasing steadily, not as fast as we want to, but faster than the economic growth of the country.

Appendix I
Public and Special Libraries: Statistics

Year	Type of Lib.	No. of Lib.	Staff	Seats	Vols.	Budget (Won†)
1955	Public	12	113	1,784	476,844	
	Special	15	103	526	187,374	
1960	Public	18	143	3,422	576,260	
	Special	41	188	1,123	494,284	
1965	Public	49	412	8,909	694,515	9,106,936
	Special	71	472	2,721	623,850	20,683,918
1970	Public*	58	447	13,114	563,427	117,447,450
	Special**	134	543	3,343	1,548,550	375,637,343
	National Central	1	114	943	438,318	70,715,000
	National Assembly	1	185	68	125,820	143,718,900

† (370 Won=US$1.00).
* National Central Library is excluded from the public libraries.
** National Assembly Library is excluded from the special libraries.

SOURCES:
Korean Library Association. *Statistics of libraries in Korea.* Seoul, the Association, 1970.

Year	No. of libs.
1961	26
1965	4,240
1970	16,150
1971	20,310

SOURCE:
The Micro-Library Association, 1971.

(a) Libraries and Librarianship in the Republic of Korea: II

BYUNG MOCK RHEE
Instructor, Department of Library Science, Yonsei University, Seoul

1 College and university libraries

College and university libraries have been developing more actively and vigorously than any other types of libraries in Korea, though almost all of them have short histories of less than three decades. Among 129 college and university libraries reported in 1970, only 10 existed before 1945. In other words, nearly 90% of all college and university libraries have been established after the Liberation in 1945, and more than half of them appeared within the past 15 years.

Some of the determining factors why academic libraries had grown so rapidly during the 1950s and 1960s might be mentioned in two ways. First, in general, there was social recognition that universities should be regarded as major investments of human resources in the nation's interest. Secondly, in particular, the Regulations of the Standard of College and University Establishment influenced the development of college and university libraries.

The Regulation which prescribes the facilities of college and university education was promulgated by the Ministry of Education in August 1955 and later amended in September 1967. It provides for libraries of higher educational institutions, and the annual inspection of them according to the Regulation led the colleges and universities to expand their libraries.

It says in the Regulation that, among other things: 'A college and university library should have a reading room, stack room, and library office. The reading room should be furnished with a specified number of seats, more than 15% of total students enrolled. The library should be equipped with 30 or more books for each student, and 5,000 or more books together with five scholarly periodicals for each academic department.'

This Regulation brought about both favourable and unfavourable results in the course of academic library development; favourable for having more physical facilities and unfavourable for neglecting the quality of library collections due to the stress on the number of books.

Of the total of 5,158,702 volumes owned by academic libraries in 1970, 1,997,913 volumes were Western books, many of which had been accepted injudiciously as gifts, and consequently were of little value to the research and teaching programmes. Thus, naturally, there has been some discussion among academic librarians about raising the quality of the collections by either amending the Regulation or improving library acquisition practices.

The average size of the college and university library book collection reaches nearly 40,000 volumes and 33 volumes per student, but 40% of the total academic libraries house less than 10,000 volumes and only 12% of the total house more than 100,000 volumes. For periodicals, the average is 156 titles for each institution.

Total academic library budget for 1970 is 315,476,728 Won; only 7% of the libraries exceed one billion Won and 50% are under 1,000,000 Won. The average library budget is 2,445,630 Won, or 2,035 Won per student (US$1.00 is equivalent to 372 Won.)

It goes without saying that these figures are not only well under the standards of other developed countries, but also obviously inadequate to achieve fully the missions assigned to Korean colleges and universities.

All college and university libraries have organised their collections in one way or another according to certain established classification schemes and cataloguing rules; most of them have adopted either the Korean Decimal Classification System and Korean Cataloguing Rule or DDC and AACR with or without some modifications. Korean academic libraries usually maintain classified catalogues rather than dictionary catalogues.

Since printed cards are not introduced in Korean libraries as yet except in the National Assembly Library for its own use, college and university libraries have to do their own cataloguing. However, it is known that the Central National Library of Korea, serving as a centralised cataloguing agency in this connection, will take the initiative of producing printed cards for all Korean libraries in the near future. When the project is realised, then academic libraries certainly might benefit from it.

The need for trained librarians arises mainly from the rapid growth of new institutions of higher education and the expansion of the existing ones and has been fulfilled gradually by the regular production of library science graduates from the universities of Yonsei, Ewha Womans, Choong-ang, and Sungkyunkwan which have offered four-year undergraduate library science courses since 1957, 1959, 1962, and 1964 respectively.

According to the statistics, there were 331 professional librarians and 745 supporting staff, totalling 1,076 in 1970, while there were 207 academic librarians in 1955. The directorships of academic libraries are mostly occupied by senior professors except in two or three institutions. As highly qualified university librarians are of central importance to operate the libraries more effectively, the present situation should be changed when the younger, trained librarians are grown up ready to be selected or nominated as directors.

Academic status for professional library staff in Korean college and university libraries is still far off so long as the difference of educational background between the teaching staff and the professional librarians exists. At present, librarians can start their professional life with only a bachelor's degree whereas the teaching staff should start at least with a master's degree. As this is the prevailing obstacle to gain academic status as well as to promote professional librarianship, those who are concerned with library education are considering the elevation of the present education for librarianship from undergraduate to graduate level.

Meanwhile, it might be worthwhile to note that there is a tendency now to distinguish professional librarians from other administrative or clerical workers by giving the former a special stipend. Whether this can be called a part of academic status or not, it apparently is a creditable achievement to recognise professional librarianship as a somewhat 'special' occupation.

A recent academic library survey shows that 62 academic libraries, or 87.4% of a total of 71 college and university libraries, allowed circulation for home use. The survey reveals that the reason for not allowing home use was the lack of library collections and the anxiety of losing books. The loan period ranges from one day to more than one week. The number of books that can be borrowed at a time is usually limited to one or two items.

Reviewing the statistics above, it would appear that a great deal of co-ordination and co-operation among libraries is needed beyond the few cases of mutual co-operation that have been launched recently. Some of the academic libraries joined an interlibrary loan system which was initiated by the Central National Library of Korea in November 1968. Now nine academic libraries are participating in this system; Yonsei, Ewha Womans, and Sogang universities, all located side by side, have made an agreement to compile a union list of serials of their holdings in the early part of this year. This $2,500 project is to be completed by the end of this year. National college and university libraries have organised an association named 'Consultative Committee on National College and University Libraries' to deal with their specific problems. They have organised meetings at different national academic institutions in turn. This year they met in Taejon and discussed the manpower problems of national academic libraries. It is learned that the recommendations of that meeting have been submitted to the Economic Planning Board, a government bureau which is dealing with national budgets, to secure more funds for national academic library personnel.

Within the inner scene of academic library service, there was once severe criticism that the library collections had not been widely and fully utilised as they should be, mainly because book-oriented teaching is quite new to most older professors and, as a result, the students have no other way than to follow the lecture-memorisation way of studying. Thus, the trained librarians are trying to break this phenomena by having close contact with older professors for making library collections and class teaching interact, and by serving as teachers in introducing and guiding the students for their investigation and research. Another hope to solve this problem is Western-educated professors who do understand the library as a dynamic instrument of education, and the number of them is increasing year after year.

Table 1
Academic Library Development

Year	No. of Lib.	Size of Staff	No. of Seats	No. of Volumes	Size of Budgets (Won)
1955	44	207	4,194	1,297,034	
1960	68	405	14,610	2,285,335	
1965	109	838	28,231	3,951,379	51,276,147
1970	129	1,076	33,272	5,158,702	315,476,728

SOURCES:
Korean Library Association. *Statistics on libraries in Korea.*
Seoul, The Association, 1970.

Table 2
Some Statistics on Academic Libraries as of 1970

University and College Students: 155,763
Teaching Staff: 9,026 (excluding Nursing Schools)
Administrative Staff: 9,138 (excluding Nursing Schools)
Number of Librarians: 1,076
   Professional: 331
   Supportive: 745
   Professional vs. Supportive: 32.3%–67.7%
   Professional Librarian per Student: 1:470
Number of Libraries: 129
   Separate building: 43
   Attached: 86
Number of Seats: 33,272
   Seating Capacity: ¼ of total students enrolled
Size of Collections: 5,158,702
   Oriental: 3,160,807
   Occidental: 1,997,913
   Number of Books per Student: 33
Size of Budgets: 315,476,728 Won
   Size of Budgets per Student: 2,025 Won

SOURCES:
Korea, Ministry of Education. *Statistic Year Book of Education.*
Seoul, 1970.
Korean Library Association. *Statistics on libraries in Korea.*
Seoul, The Association, 1970.

2 Professional organisations

(i) *Korean Library Association*

The Association was originally founded on 30 August 1945, as the Chosun Library Association. The first and foremost aims of the Association were to organise libraries which had been under the hands of foreign occupants for our own system and to undertake programmes needed immediately for library development. Unfortunately its activities to achieve its goals could not continue due to the Korean War, which broke out in June 1950 and lasted until July 1953.

During the war, not only were many leaders in the library field either forced to flee or were even kidnapped and missing, but also a great deal of library facilities, both building and stock, were destroyed. When the war was over, all the librarians remaining gathered together and decided to reorganise the Association on 16 March 1955 with new officials and the new name of the Association. Thus the Korean Library Association came into being.

Later the establishment of the Association was legalised under article 13 of the Library Law and it now enjoys an annual appropriation of the governmental budget according to the Law as one of the corporate juridical bodies to which the financial support of government is given. Now the Association has a secretariat with seven staff members and is located at the Central National Library of Korea.

The Korean Library Association affirms its objectives as 'promoting and improving library services and facilities in Korea through mutual exchanges and co-operation among domestic and foreign libraries and librarians with the ultimate purpose of contributing to the cultural and economic development of the Republic of Korea'.

The general programmes of the Association to meet the defined objectives include: (1) Guiding the establishment and management of libraries; (2) Editing and publishing of library science materials; (3) Developing the social status of librarians; (4) Studying and analysing the current state of libraries; (5) Promoting and guiding reading campaigns; (6) Studying library construction and equipment; (7) Maintaining a reference material centre on library science; (8) Improving co-operation among libraries; (9) Maintaining co-operation with international library or related organisations, etc.

The major annual activities which the Association is carrying out now are: National Convention of Librarians started in 1962 for discussing, internally, the current problems that Korean libraries are confronted with and interpreting, externally, to government officials concerned as well as the general public better recognition of the importance of library services; National Library Week begun in 1964 for promoting library activities as a strong social movement; and National Book Week initiated in 1955 for developing reading habits of people.

The publishing programme of the Association attracts both practising and potential librarians since there is a lack of materials on library and library science as in other developing countries. KLA publishes its organ, the monthly

KLA Bulletin, and annual *Statistics on libraries in Korea.* In addition to those mentioned, a 20-volume project, 'Korean Library Science Series', and a 10-volume project, 'Library Science Korean Translation Series' are outstanding among its other publications.

The Association is organised with a president, a managing director, a board of directors (standing and general), a senate or membership board, a secretariat and seven professional committees, four divisions by type of libraries, and eight regional chapters. The Association is managed by three levels of governing bodies, namely the professional committee as the policy-formulating body, the board of directors as the decision-making one, and secretariat as the executive one.

The Association is financed by membership dues, income from self-supporting business, and government subventions. Although the Association today depends largely for its income on government subventions which amount to almost half of the KLA's budget, it is trying to make every effort to find ways and means to replace government subsidy with other income. The budget of the Association for 1971 indicates 3,148,000 Won from membership dues, 8,532,000 Won from self-supporting business, and 8,500,000 Won from government subventions.

There are four kinds of membership in the Association; individual, institutional, supporting and honorary. To secure an individual membership, he or she must have completed at least 18 units of librarianship at the educational institutes of library science. There are 353 individual members and 534 institutional members as of 31 December 1970.

There was a saying that KLA is an organisation represented by the older, senior professors—those who chair the KLA board of directorship only because they head university library directorships—but now the changing concept of the Association is permeating. For an example, a group of younger, professionally trained librarians acquired their positions within the various organisations of the Association at the last biannual conference in January 1971.

It is understood that there still remain many problems to solve even though the Korean Library Association has been endeavouring for the fulfilment of its objectives since its foundation. It will never cease its mission as the professional library organisation for the co-ordination and understanding among librarians with efforts to develop libraries and librarianship in Korea.

(ii) *Learned societies*
(a) Korean Library Science Society
The Society was founded as a learned body on 10 January 1970, in collaboration with the library science faculty members who had shown their keen interests in the formation of the Society. Up to that time some of the leading figures in librarianship, mostly those who are engaged in teaching library science, had felt the need for a research and scholarly organisation on a national basis in order to set up librarianship as a sound discipline and to present the

way to develop it, since we have the Library Law that affects library movement, library schools that produce professional librarians, and some reference materials and bibliographies that might be used as basic tools for daily library activities. That strong feeling led us to form the Korean Library Science Society.

The aims of the Society are 'to promote the study of librarianship, to further the co-operation among members of the Society, and to contribute to the development of librarianship through co-ordination with learned societies concerned within and outside the Republic of Korea'.

The programmes of the Korean Library Science Society are as follows: (1) Hold seminars and lectures; (2) Publish the organ of the Society and other research reports; (3) Maintain mutual relationships among foreign and domestic learned societies concerned; (4) Other programmes approved by the Board of Officers.

The officials of the Society comprise one president, four officers (administrative affairs, research, public relations, finance) and two auditors. Terms for each official run one year. As of 30 June 1971, the Society has 92 members.

The Society's first seminar/lecture programme was held on 7 November 1970, with the following lecturers and topics: (1) Problems of Descriptive Cataloguing on Korean Classics in the University Libraries in the United States, by Mr. Lin Paik of Seoul National University Library; (2) A Study of Author Notation for Korean Libraries, by Professor Jai Chul Lee of Yonsei University.

The first volume of the official organ of the Society, *Tosogwan Hak; Journal of the Korean Library Science Society,* was published in December 1970. It carries original articles on library and information science and is expected to appear annually.

(*b*) Library science student organisation and their publications.

Each library school has organisations of its students in a library science society and publishes its bulletin from time to time. Among those bulletins the following two examples are notable: (1) *Commemoration Papers of the 10th Anniversary of the Founding of the Department of Library Science of Yonsei University,* November 1968. This publication had been issued as volume 3 of the *Bulletin of the Library Science Society* published by its Society of Yonsei University; (2) *Commemoration Papers of the 10th Anniversary of the Founding of the Department of Library Science of Ewha Women's University,* November 1970.

(b)　A Survey of Library Development in Malaysia

PHILOMENA NG SOO CHING

Assistant Director, National Library of Malaysia

The library movement is a recent development on the Malaysian scene. Prior to 1945 there were few libraries in Malaysia. The concept of librarianship and the provision of public library services were unknown to the majority of people, while the benefits of having a well-developed nation-wide system of library services which catered for the needs of the various sectors of the population were not yet fully realised. There were no qualified librarians in the country and library training facilities for local librarians were non-existent. It is not surprising, therefore, that there was no planning or co-ordination of library development in the country. There were a few research libraries which served a small and restricted clientele, and there were also a few subscription libraries which were financed mainly through membership subscriptions with partial government support given in the form of grants. These subscription libraries were founded through the efforts of interested individuals, usually Europeans who were working in Malaysia. They had a limited membership as they catered in the main for those literate in English and they were located in urban areas.

It was after 1945 that most library development in the nation took place, the most significant developments occurring in the 1960s. There is now a growing consciousness among the people of the need for libraries, especially public libraries. A corps of qualified local librarians is gradually being built up and an increasing number of Malaysians are taking up librarianship as a career. A library association was formed, comprising librarians and those interested or engaged in library work in Malaysia. It is fully engaged in promoting the library movement in the country. There are now a few free public libraries and library services are no longer confined to the urban areas. The Government, too, began to take an active interest in library development. At national level, the Federal Government took steps to plan for the setting up of a national library which would eventually form the apex of a nation-wide library system. These measures finally culminated in the formal establishment of the National Library of Malaysia as a special unit within the National Archives and Library on 1 January 1971. At State level, State Governments are being encouraged by the Federal Government to operate state-wide public library services. It is hoped that the seventies will see the rapid development of public library services in the West Malaysian States, which at present are still lagging behind East Malaysia in the provision of state-wide public library services.

Professional association
The Persatuan Perpustakaan Malaysia (Library Association of Malaysia) is the only professional library association in Malaysia. It has won recognition as the only body representing the views of professional librarians in matters pertaining to libraries and library development. Its membership is open to all persons or institutions engaged in library work or interested in libraries in Malaysia. The present membership is approximately 400. It maintains very close ties with the Persatuan Perpustakaan Singapura (Library Association of Singapore), with whom it shares a common origin and pools together professional expertise for their mutual benefit.

The PPM originated from the Malayan Library Group, which was inaugurated in Singapore with 54 members from Malaya and Singapore on 25 March 1955. This was the first attempt made to unite librarians and it brought together those who were engaged or interested in the work of libraries in Malaysia. From 1955–8 the Group was very active. One of the most important projects undertaken by it during this period was the drawing up of a Memorandum on a public library service for the Federation of Malaya at the request of the Federation Adult Education Association. The Memorandum urged the introduction of legislation to set up a Library Board and the appointment of a suitably experienced director so as to provide a national bibliographical centre and a nation-wide system of public library services for Malaya. Unfortunately, no action could be taken on the Memorandum as the Government was then fully occupied with the Emergency and the issue of self-government. In November 1958 the Group was dissolved and replaced by the Library Association of Malaya and Singapore. This decision was taken mainly to show that the Group included both territories of Malaya and Singapore and also because it was felt that it had now become large enough to regard itself as an Association. However, through the vagaries of politics it was not possible for both countries to continue having one library association. Consequently in early January 1966, two separate library associations were formed: the Persatuan Perpustakaan Malaysia and the Persatuan Perpustakaan Singapura.

The objects of the PPM have not changed significantly from those of the Malayan Library Group however. They are:

(a) To unite all persons engaged in library work or interested in libraries in Malaysia.

(b) To promote the better administration of libraries.

(c) To encourage the establishment, development and use of libraries in Malaysia.

(d) To encourage professional education and training for librarianship.

(e) To publish such information as will be of service to members.

(f) To undertake such activities, including the holding of meetings and conferences, as are appropriate to the attainment of the above objects.

The PPM continues to co-operate with the PPS in joint projects whenever feasible. To maintain this close liaison with the PPS, a Joint Liaison Council composed of Council members from both Associations was set up. It meets twice a year, alternating between Singapore and Kuala Lumpur. Both Associations have held joint conferences, among the most recent of which were *Planning for the '70s; Joint Seminar of PPM and PPS* (1969) and the *Conference of South-east Asian Librarians* (August 1970). In 1971 a *Conference on Scientific and Technical Information Needs of Malaysia and Singapore* is scheduled to be held in September.

The two Associations formerly published a joint journal, the *Perpustakaan*. However, it was decided that, from 1971 onwards, each Association would publish a separate journal. The Malaysian journal is called *Majallah Perpustakaan Malaysia.* It will be published annually.

Apart from the Joint Liaison Council, there is a Joint Standing Committee on Library Co-operation and Bibliographical Services of the PPM and the PPS which was established in 1966. Its terms of reference are:

(a) To determine priorities in developing national bibliographical services.

(b) To provide and extend such services.

(c) To stimulate research and bibliographical services and to serve as a clearing house of information about research in progress and completed.

(d) To recommend policy and practice in the field of library co-operation with particular reference to:
   (i) Union Catalogue;
   (ii) Inter-library loans;
   (iii) Co-operative acquisition, storage and withdrawal.

(e) To act as a link with national and international bodies concerned with inter-library co-operation and bibliographical services.

The JSCLCBS has initiated a number of important bibliographical projects over the years. It initiated the *Union catalogue of scientific and technical serials* with the compilation of a list of library symbols. The union catalogue is housed at the National Library of Singapore. Twenty-five libraries from Malaysia and Singapore are participating in this project. Over 3,700 titles have been received and it is planned to publish this union catalogue in about two years' time.

The JSCLCBS was also instrumental in formulating the guidelines which were adopted by the National Library of Malaysia and the National Library of Singapore in the compilation of their respective national bibliographies. This project was undertaken so as to ensure uniformity in the information provided, the classification used and the cataloguing rules adopted. Other projects of the JSCLCBS include:

(i) Expansions to the Dewey Decimal Classification's geographical and period sub-divisions for Malaysia and Singapore.

(ii) Expansions for the languages and literatures of the Malay Archipelago and Oceania (Austronesian and non-Austronesian).

(iii) Cataloguing of Indonesian names.

(iv) Inter-library loan code and the inter-library loan request form.

(v) Standard lists of bibliographical terms in the Malay, Chinese and Tamil languages.

(vi) *Index to Current Malaysian, Singapore and Brunei Periodicals.* Two issues of this index for 1967 and 1968 have been published. Librarians from Malaysia and Singapore participated in this project which indexed local periodicals not covered by foreign indexing and abstracting journals. It has now been agreed that, from 1971 onwards, the National Library of Singapore will undertake to index Singapore periodicals and that the

85

PPM will index Malaysian journals until the National Library of Malaysia is able to take over this work.

The JSCLCBS has established two Standing Sub-committees:

(i) The Sub-committee on Microforms was set up on 19 May 1968 to look into the question of microfilm resources; to examine current microfilming programmes; and to make recommendations for co-ordinating these programmes at national levels. Its membership is institutional. At present its major concern is the rationalisation of the microfilming programmes of participating institutions. A schedule of priorities has been drawn up for the microfilming of newspapers and a start is being made towards a similar schedule for serials including government publications beginning with pre-war titles.

(ii) The Sub-committee on Cataloguing and Classification is a newly formed Sub-committee which was set up in March 1971. Its terms of reference are to consider problems, initiate or sponsor studies and recommend improvements in the field of cataloguing and classification, with special emphasis on Asian library materials and subject fields; to co-operate with national, regional and international organisations concerned with cataloguing and classification; and to keep informed as to research in progress in these fields.

The PPM's own programme of activities for the year include the following: it has so far organised a forum on *Training and Prospects for Future Librarians in Malaysia* which was held in July and hopes to hold once a month other library functions, such as training workshops, talks by prominent Malaysian authors, librarians and members of the book trade which would prove of benefit to the members, etc. In addition to the publication of the *Majallah Perpustakaan Malaysia,* it proposes to bring out this year a Directory of Libraries in Malaysia, a quarterly Newsletter and a Year book.

The PPM is carrying on its practice of providing short-term courses for those engaged in library work and who do not have any formal training in the profession. Details of these courses for the year 1971–2 are still being worked out. However, a long-term course consisting of 120 hours of lectures and practical work, to prepare candidates for the Part I examination of the Library Association, London, is scheduled to start in September.

The need to establish a library school has long been pursued by the PPM. Recently it has been felt desirable that a combined School of Librarianship and Archives should be set up which would cater primarily for training needs within Malaysia. This has led to the formation of a Working Party comprising librarians and archivists. The Working Party is working on a revision of the first draft of the memorandum on the library school with a view to establishing a School of Librarianship and Archives.

The PPM is also active in the field of school libraries. It resuscitated the School Libraries Committee in 1969. This Committee has since been engaged in helping to conduct short-term courses and in providing advice on the organising of school libraries. It is also assisting the Ministry of Education in the revision of the school library manual.

National Library of Malaysia

1971 is a historic year in the history of libraries in Malaysia. On 1 January this year, the Perpustakaan Negara Malaysia (National Library of Malaysia) was formally established as a special unit within the enlarged Department of Arkib dan Perpustakaan Negara (National Archives and Library). Prior to this, a Division called the National Library Service in the Arkib Negara Malaysia (National Archives of Malaysia) served as the nucleus since November 1966. The Director-General of the National Archives and Library is the overall head for both the National Library and the National Archives.

At present the National Library implements the policy decisions and directives of the National Library Committee which was appointed by the Cabinet in February 1966 with the following terms of reference:

(a) To advise and prepare the Government on the proposed establishment of a National Library.

(b) To report from time to time to Cabinet of its proceedings.

Members of the Committee include:

(a) Chief Secretary to the Government (Chairman)
(b) Representative of the Treasury
(c) Representative of the Ministry of External Affairs
(d) Representative of the Ministry of Education
(e) Representative of the Ministry of Works, Post and Telecommunications
(f) Representative of the Ministry of Information and Broadcasting
(g) Representative of the Public Services Department
(h) Representative of the Dewan Bahasa dan Pustaka;
(i) Librarian of the University of Malaya
(j) Director-General of the National Archives and Library (Secretary).

During its meetings the Committee studies matters related to the establishment of the National Library, such as functions, finance, staffing and the building. Well aware of the importance of the National Library project, it sought the aid of Unesco in providing the services of a library consultant who would advise on the organisation of the National Library and its legislation. The library consultant was attached to the National Library for three months from November 1970 to February 1971 and his report is being awaited. In the meantime the national library legislation is being drafted. A request has also been made for a second library consultant who will be advising on the national library building. The Committee has been instrumental in getting Cabinet approval for the formal establishment of the National Library and for the inclusion in the Second Malaysia Plan of provision for a national library building and for public library development. The National Library is taking measures to implement the latter two projects.

The Committee is aware, too, of the need to obtain funds in order to establish the National Library. Aid has been solicited from foreign countries, some of which have indicated interest in the provision of books, equipment, etc. At home a National Library Fund Raising Committee has been formed. It has met several times to discuss methods of raising funds. From the foregoing, it can be seen that the National Library needs the active support of the National Library Committee in order to enable it to carry out its plans for its future development and growth.

When the National Library was first set up, it was immediately involved in the operation of the Preservation of Books Act 1966. Under this Act, two copies of every publication published in Malaysia are required to be deposited at the National Library. It serves as the depository for these publications whereas formerly the deposited publications were redistributed to designated institutions. It maintains a catalogue of particulars of the books deposited and publishes this catalogue quarterly in the *Malaysian Government Gazette*. This activity has since been expanded to include the compilation of a current national bibliography. Two issues of the *Malaysian National Bibliography* for 1967 and 1968 have been published. It lists in classified subject order all books and periodicals published in the various languages which have been received and registered for the year, and includes an author, title and subject index. At the moment it is published annually. However, when difficulties in production are overcome and as there is an increase in the number of publications deposited, the issues will be published at more frequent intervals.

With the sanction of the National Library Committee, a start has been made towards the establishment of a union catalogue of the holdings of Government Department and Statutory Body Libraries. It was felt that the creation of this catalogue would lead towards a fuller programme of library co-operation and that it should be embarked on prior to other aspects of library co-operation. Initially this project is to be confined to about 20 libraries which have professionally qualified staff. The number of participating libraries will be increased only when the project is established on a sound basis.

There is one sphere where it is felt that the National Library must begin to play a more active role. This is the field of liaison with other libraries, especially public libraries. The National Library is expected to encourage and assist State Governments and local authorities to establish public library services for both urban and rural areas where such services are not available or are inadequate. Now that a provision for public library development has been included in the Second Malaysia Plan, it is imperative that the National Library take steps to ensure that the amount allocated is fully utilised. A first step in this direction is the creation of a new Division in the National Library—the Extension Services. This Division, which will be headed by an Assistant Director, will liaise with libraries and related institutions throughout Malaysia and especially with public libraries. It is hoped that staff for this Division will be recruited soon. It is intended that State Governments will be able to call on this Division for help in establishing public library services. It is also expected that, through this Division, the National Library will be kept informed of the latest library developments in the country and thus it will be in a position to co-ordinate the total library resources of the nation. It may be pertinent to mention here that a decision was reached recently to implement a uniform scheme of service for all library personnel in Federal Government Departments as a common user service. This would ensure maintenance of library standards in Government Departments and create career prospects for such personnel. The National Library will be responsible for the recruitment of all professional and clerical library personnel.

The National Library at present provides a limited reference service. It is faced with the task of building up a good reference collection so that it can provide a first-rate reference service. It also has to build up a comprehensive collection of literature pertaining to Malaysia. A start in this direction has been made with the acquisition of publications under legal deposit. It has received requests for advice and help from other libraries. There is a need, then, to build up a core of experienced and qualified librarians who could be sent out to help establish libraries and thus ensure that standards are maintained in the provision of library services. Such library personnel are also required to conduct in-service training courses for library staff within the National Library and in other libraries on request. It is necessary, too, to conduct surveys to gather data on the various fields of library activities and areas of library problems. Last but not least, the existing services of the National Library must be consolidated and their scope expanded. It is essential, therefore, that in view of the many problems facing the National Library, it requires provision in the next few years of an increased budget, book provision and staff if it is to carry out its various tasks properly. The National Library Service, when it was first set up in November 1966, had a complement of three staff which included one professional post of librarian. Today the staff strength has been increased to 41, with a provision for 10 professional posts, of which five have yet to be filled.

Public and subscription libraries
The Persatuan Perpustakaan Malaysia has played a major role in promoting public library development in Malaysia. In 1968 mainly through its efforts Mrs. Hedwig Anuar, Director of the National Library of Singapore, was requested to draw up a *Blueprint for Public Library Development in Malaysia*. The publication of this blueprint marks an important milestone in the history of public library development in the country. It was the first time that such a study in depth was carried out. From the data gathered, a clear picture emerged of the problems being faced by the existing public libraries.

It was found that, on the whole, the provision of public library services was very poor, with the result that these libraries were barely used. Among the most important services lacking were reference and information services and also services to children and the rural population. Public library provision in East Malaysia, however, which was on a state-wide basis, was better developed than in West Malaysia where three states, i.e. Pahang, Perlis and Trengganu, did not have any public library.

The book collections were of poor quality. There was an urgent need to build up collections of science and technology, children's books, as well as books in the national language and other local languages. Most libraries, too, had a very limited range of periodicals.

The lending of books was the chief service provided. Loans were generally restricted to members, and particularly to residents of the local authority area or state. Only two State Governments, Malacca and Selangor, attempted to provide a mobile library service to readers in the rural areas. However, both these services suffered from not having a central base of operations or full-time staff, apart from the drivers. They were also hampered by not being able to draw from a strong central bookstock.

Reference services were generally limited to provision of a reference collection of books and periodicals. A few libraries had other library services such as the provision of regular story-telling sessions for children, class visits from schools, and extension activities. Some also actively promoted knowledge of the public library and its services through press publicity, posters, annual reports, book weeks, etc. There were only three qualified librarians working in public libraries at that time: one in West Malaysia and two in East Malaysia. This staff shortage extended to the non-professional staff as well. Consequently there was a heavy reliance on volunteers.

Public and subscription libraries were financed from a variety of sources including federal, state and local governments. In 1966 West Malaysia spent 3.66 cents actual expenditure per head of population on public library service while in East Malaysia the figure was 12.13 cents. There was no public library legislation. Sabah and Sarawak already had state-wide public library services before joining Malaysia. To enable the West Malaysian States to do the same, the Incorporation (State Legislatures Competency) Act 1962 was amended to allow state governments to legislate for the setting up of state public library corporations.

Generally speaking, however, the picture of public library development is brightening. Perlis and Trengganu now have public libraries while Pahang has made provision to set up a public library in Kuantan, the state capital. Selangor is the first state to have enacted the Selangor Public Library Corporation Enactment 1968 which has enabled it to take over the Kuala Lumpur Book Club. Two more public libraries have been established in Penang: one at Ayer Hitam and the other at Butterworth. Penang Library and Sultan Ismail Public Library, Johore Bahru are now headed by qualified librarians. Sabah has started a mobile library service. Sarawak State Central Library and Kuching Municipal Library both have newly constructed library buildings.

There is a growing awareness, especially among government circles, of the important role which public libraries can play in nation building and that the provision of public library services is not a luxury but an economic necessity. This is borne out by the fact that public library development has been included in the Second Malaysia Plan. State governments, too, have been urged to include this item in their state development plans. The Director-General of the National Archives and Library has embarked on a tour of the states to explain to state governments what federal aid they can expect from the Second Malaysia Plan. It is intended that his visits should be followed up by the Assistant Director of the Extension Services, who is expected to work very closely with the state governments in planning for the development of public library services in the respective state.

University and college libraries
Taken as a whole, when compared to other types of libraries in the country, the university libraries are the best off. Their governing authorities as well as the Government realise the importance of having a first-rate library if it is to serve adequately the needs of the institution. Consequently the university libraries are in a better position to develop their collections and services as they are provided with a reasonably adequate library budget.

There are three universities in Malaysia. The University of Malaya, which was established in 1957, is the oldest of the three. From its inception until now, its library has grown to be the largest in the country. It has more than 330,000 volumes and, in addition to being one of the legal depositories for Malaysian publications, is a depository for UN, Unesco and FAO publications. Its seating capacity was increased to 1,500 when the third phase of its building programme was completed in 1969. The Medical Centre at the University of Malaya is one of the most modern and well-equipped hospitals in Asia. Its Library has been designed to provide for expansion over the next 20 years, thus making it the largest and most modern special library in Malaysia. It is developing to be the centre for medical information in this region.

The University of Penang was established in 1969. Its Library is being developed rapidly to meet the growing demands for research and education. Its collection now totals approximately 30,000 volumes. It is working towards achieving an intake of 20,000 volumes per annum. The Universiti Kebangsaan is the most recently established of the three universities and had its first student intake in May 1970. The medium of instruction of this university is Bahasa Malaysia. It is expected, therefore, that the Library will build up the most comprehensive collection of materials in Bahasa Malaysia and Bahasa Indonesia in addition to materials in English and other languages. Its book collection is about 20,000 volumes.

College libraries, on the other hand, suffer from insufficient funds, staff, book-stock and space. Very few of them are run by qualified librarians, the majority of teacher training college libraries being administered by teacher librarians or staff who have had some library experience. With few exceptions all these libraries experience a serious shortage of both professional and non-professional staff. A number of them are located in badly planned buildings. The library budget often falls far short of the standard set for college libraries, which is 5% of the total budget of the whole college.

School libraries
School libraries in Malaysia face four major problems. These are lack of funds, centralised physical facilities, trained library staff and inadequate book selection. However, the biggest hurdle they face is that of becoming integrated with the academic work of the school. There is no special division in the Ministry of Education responsible for looking after school libraries. The nearest approach to this is the Textbook Bureau of the Ministry which has begun to concern itself with school library matters.

Much improvement is needed in the area of staffing. Very often school libraries remain closed during school hours because of staffing difficulties. The majority of teacher librarians, who carry a normal teaching load, find it virtually impossible to carry out the task of making the library effective. Many open their libraries after school hours and some work during the school vacation to cope with arrears of work. As a result, there are frequent changes of personnel in the post of teacher librarian because the appointment is an onerous one. Some of these teacher librarians have attended library workshops and seminars. Although within the secondary school teacher training programmes there is provision for a basic course in school librarianship, this is an elective subject and will be held only if there are teacher trainees who elect to follow the course. The primary school teacher training programmes do not have such a course.

A large proportion of the book collection in school libraries is often unsuitable and either does not cater for the needs of the schools or is beyond the reading levels of the students. These books have usually been donated to the library. The book budget varies considerably between schools of comparable size. There is no grant from the Government for maintaining school libraries. They are regularly financed only by a library fee imposed on the students.

The Textbook Bureau of the Ministry recently conducted a school library survey in order to obtain an overall picture of the school library and the programmes now provided in the schools in West Malaysia. The survey covers both primary and secondary schools in all media. It is hoped that the results of this survey will give an adequate and comprehensive picture of the present position of school libraries and serve to direct their continuous development. The Textbook Bureau has also tried to assist schools in initiating library programmes and organising their book collections. It has revised and updated the basic library booklist for primary schools in Bahasa Malaysia and English to include all the latest titles published. The Ministry of Education will use this list as a basis to purchase books for school libraries in the rural areas.

Special libraries
There have been two surveys conducted on special libraries and scientific information facilities in Malaysia. The 1961 survey carried out by Mr. Wilfred J. Plumbe, former Librarian of the University of Malaya, covered 15 scientific libraries (which included the University of Malaya and the Technical College). It reported that most of these libraries were very small, only four of them

having more than 10,000 volumes. Between them, they had about 30,000 scientific books and approximately 1,000 serial titles available for research. However, only the longer-established institutions had long retrospective sets of many of these serials. Three institutions undertook translation work for their clientele and five of them maintained specialised indexes. At that time there were only three qualified librarians, all of whom were working at the University of Malaya Library, while the Librarian of the Rubber Research Institute of Malaya (RRIM) was then abroad studying librarianship. Most of the libraries provided reprographic facilities. Generally speaking, the condition of special libraries reflected the lack of funds, staff and bookstock which characterised the Malaysian library scene.

The situation of special libraries has improved much since that survey. The 1970, survey, conducted by Mr. J. S. Soosai, Librarian of the Rubber Research Institute of Malaysia, showed that the number of libraries which might be regarded as wholly or partly scientific and technical (including university and college libraries) had increased to about 30. These are mainly small libraries, as less than one-third of them had more than 10,000 volumes. It is estimated that probably not more than 150,000 scientific books and about 3,000 scientific serials were available for consultation. More than half this stock was held by the three leading libraries in this field, i.e. the Department of Agriculture, RRIM and the University of Malaya. As noted in the earlier survey, only the older institutions and the University of Malaya had long retrospective runs of many of these serials.

Some of the leading special libraries undertake to index papers published by Malaysian authors in their own field. The RRIM Library published *A Bibliography of contributions to natural rubber research from the Rubber Research Institute of Malaya 1927–67*. This bibliography lists all papers published by the RRIM staff up to 1967. The Medical Centre Library is compiling a comprehensive bibliography of papers on medical science published by Malaysians at home and abroad as well as papers published by foreigners on medical science in Malaysia. The Department of Agriculture Library has a comprehensive index of all its departmental publications. The Institute of Medical Research Library has also indexed all its published staff papers. Very few libraries index articles from the periodicals they receive, though exceptions are made for the indexing of articles which are of special interest to their staff. The RRIM Library has published a series entitled *R.R.I.M. Library Bibliographies* on subjects of topical interest to its staff.

The RRIM Library is the only library which provides formal translation services exclusively for its own staff. These translations now number about 800. However, the University of Malaya Library acts as a central clearing house. It maintains a panel of translators and puts the enquirer in touch with a prospective translator in the field. Document reproduction is playing an increasingly important role in the rapid dissemination of scientific information and almost all special libraries provide this service for their own use. The

G

University of Malaya Library and the RRIM Library also provide photo-copies of their holdings to enquirers who are not members of their staffs.

At present about 12 special libraries (excluding the university and college libraries) employ qualified librarians in their libraries. But so far the Rubber Research Institute of Malaysia Library is the only special library with two qualified librarians on its staff.

(c) Recent Developments in Librarianship in Singapore

HONG TOO LIM
Senior Assistant Librarian, University of Singapore

Singapore is a small island nation with an area of 224.6 square miles and a population of slightly over 2,000,000 people. Situated at the cross-roads between the East and the West, Singapore is also multi-racial and therefore multi-cultural. The population of Singapore consists of four main races, namely, the Chinese (76%), the Malays (15%), the Indians (7%) and the Eurasians who make up the majority of the rest. These divergent ethnic origins result naturally in a variety of tongues being spoken in Singapore, the main ones being Chinese, English, Malay and Tamil, all of which have been made official languages.

The history of libraries in Singapore dates back to 1823 when the first library was established, but modern librarianship as we know it today had not started until the 1950s. In 1955, the earliest professional library association, the Malayan Library Group, was organised with members from both Singapore and the then Malaya. There are now two independent national library asso-ciations: one in Malaysia, the Library Association of Malaysia, and the other in Singapore, the Library Association of Singapore. At the time of the incep-tion of the Malayan Library Group, there were only half-a-dozen qualified librarians in both Singapore and Malaya, but within the last 15 years or so the number of professional librarians increased sharply to over 80 in the beginning of 1971. With the availability of high-quality personnel, a number of significant developments took place. In this short paper, I shall attempt to describe briefly developments in the following areas: (1) bibliographical con-trol, (2) co-operation in microfilming programmes, (3) school library develop-ments, (4) regional organisation, (5) research libraries.

Bibliographical control
Significant progress was made in the attempt to achieve bibliographical con-trol recently. The most noteworthy is the publication of the *Singapore National Bibliography* and the *Index to Current Malaysian Singapore and Brunei Periodicals*. The *Singapore National Bibliography,* published by the National Library, is an annual, whose first issue came out in 1969 covering imprints of 1967. The publication of the *Index* was undertaken by the *Joint Standing*

Committee on Library Co-operation and Bibliographical Services (JSCLCBS), of the Library Associations of Malaysia and Singapore. The *Index* is also an annual, whose first issue was published in 1969 covering periodical articles appearing in 1967. Two issues of the *Index* have been published by the JSCLCBS. From the third issue onwards, the Singapore National Library will undertake the publication covering only Singapore periodicals, while the Library Association of Malaysia will do likewise for Malaysian periodicals.

It should be pointed out that the groundwork for the above publications was laid by the JSCLCBS, whose members are librarians from both Malaysia and Singapore. Most significant are the following bibliographical projects:

(1) *Revisions of Dewey Decimal Classification expansions for Malaysia and Singapore*

The expansions of the geographical and period sub-divisions for Malaysia and Singapore were undertaken by the Cataloguing Committee of the National Library and approved by the JSCLCBS. The expansions are now in general use, and are used for the compilation of the *Singapore National Bibliography* and the first issue of the *Index.*

(2) *Special Expansions for Languages and Literatures of the Malay Archipelago and Oceania (Austronesian and non-Austronesian Languages)*

These special expansions were prepared by Abdul Aziz bin Shaik Mydin for the JSCLCBS. They are used for the *Singapore National Bibliography,* and copies of them have been forwarded to the British DDC Sub-committee and also to the American DDC Editorial Committee.

(3) *Standard lists of bibliographical terms*

These lists, each for the Chinese, Malay and Tamil languages, were compiled by the various sub-committees of the JSCLCBS.

Another important bibliographical project is the compilation of the *Union Catalogue of Scientific and Technical Serials,* undertaken by the National Library. The *Union Catalogue* now has about 4,000 titles held in the various libraries in Singapore, and the work of compilation is still in progress. It is planned to include titles in social sciences. The *Union Catalogue* will be published eventually.

Co-operation in microfilming programmes
The JSCLCBS has a Sub-Committee on Microforms (SCOM). Originally set up for co-operation and co-ordination of microfilming in Malaysia and Singapore, SCOM is now extending its work to other international organisations, such as the South east Asia Microforms (SEAM), which is based in the Center for Research Libraries in Chicago. SCOM acts as an intermediary and clearing-house between SEAM and its own members. As part of its contribution to co-operation with SEAM, SCOM will compile:
(a) Lists of negatives already filmed.
(b) List of material on SCOM's list of priorities waiting filming.
(c) Wants lists of material required by members but not held in Malaysia and Singapore.

The Chairman of SCOM, Mrs. P. Lim Pui Huen, recently attended the first General Conference of SARBICA (South-east Asian Regional Branch of the International Council on Archives), held in Manila in May 1971, at which the question of international co-operation in microfilming programmes was discussed. Based on the existing relationship between SCOM and SEAM, the Conference adopted a set of principles known as the *Guide-lines for National and International Co-operation in Microfilming Projects,* a copy of which is appended (Appendix I).

School library developments

In 1969 the Library Association of Singapore set up a School Library Section in an attempt to promote library activities in the schools. Membership of the Section grew rapidly to over 200 in the beginning of 1971. In February 1970, the Section organised a Seminar on School Libraries, at which a number of recommendations were adopted. Acting in response to these recommendations, the Ministry of Education set up a Standing Committee on Libraries (Ministry and Schools) to advise on the establishment, development and management of libraries in schools and the Ministry of Education. The Standing Committee also works in conjunction with the School Library Section:

(1) To plan programmes of study and services for school libraries.
(2) To establish, evaluate and promote desirable standards in the quality of of school libraries.
(3) To organise activities and projects for the improvement and extension of services in school libraries.

One of the first tasks undertaken by the Standing Committee was to take steps to implement the recommendations of the Seminar on School Libraries. This resulted in:

(1) Regular meetings once a school term between principals, teachers and librarians.
(2) The setting up of a sub-committee to study standards for school libraries.
(3) The setting up of an *ad hoc* committee to review an instructions book on procedures relating to school libraries.
(4) The compilation of syllabi for library instruction in both secondary and primary schools.
(5) The planning of a pilot scheme for centralised purchasing and processing of library books in primary schools.

Regional organisation

The organisation of the Conference of South-east Asian Librarians (CONSAL) in 1970 was the first ever attempt in bringing about regional library co-operation within South-east Asia. The first CONSAL was held in Singapore, being jointly sponsored by the Library Associations of Malaysia and Singapore. At this first Conference an informal organisation, CONSAL, was set up with Cambodia, Indonesia, Malaysia, the Philippines, Singapore, Thailand and Vietnam as members. CONSAL will meet once every three years, and the

CONSAL Committee is charged with the responsibility of carrying out resolutions passed at the preceding Conference. A copy each of the CONSAL constitution and the resolutions adopted at the first CONSAL are appended. (Appendix II and III).

CONSAL is the first organisation in South-east Asia providing opportunities for South-east Asian librarians to come together to discuss matters of common professional interest. As all the national library associations in the regions are represented, it is evident that CONSAL will stimulate and expedite library co-operation and developments in these countries. CONSAL will act as a means of communication and clearing-house of information not only between its members, but also between the region and the rest of the world. With the establishment of CONSAL, it is possible for South-east Asian librarians to play a great part in the world-wide professional community. It is hoped that CONSAL will reach the happy relationship with IFLA that SARBICA enjoys with ICA. IFLA invites a CONSAL nominee to attend the 37th Annual Council and also this pre-session Seminar. It is possible that Unesco may be able to hold a regional meeting in Manila to coincide with the next CONSAL.

Research Libraries
Rapid progress in the economic and social fields has led to the setting up of a number of research institutions and agencies, both in the public as well as in the private sectors. Again, more significantly, taking advantage of the advantageous geographical position of Singapore, a number of teaching and research institutions of a regional character have been established. With the advent of these institutions and agencies, special libraries aiming to serve research needs have sprung up. These libraries require a greater degree of subject specialisation and adequate documentation and information services. A few prominent examples of these institutions are given below:

(1) The Institute of South-east Asian Studies.
(2) The South-east Asian Ministers of Education Organisation (SEAMEO) Regional English Language Centre—with Indonesia, Khmer Republic, Laos, Malaysia, the Philippines, Singapore, Thailand and Vietnam as members.
(3) SEAMO INNOTECH Centre (SEAMO Educational Innovation and Technology Centre.)
(4) Regional Institute of Higher Education and Development (RIHED).

REFERENCES
Conference of South-east Asian Librarians, Singapore, 1970. Proceedings. Singapore, 1971.
Lim, Hong Too. Library development in Singapore. The role of libraries in the process of modernisation: report of the Asia-Pacific Conference on Libraries and National Development, Seoul, May 1969. Seoul, Korean Library Association, [1970]. p. 85–92.
Lim, Pui Huen P. Co-operation in microfilming South-east Asian material. First General Conference of SARBICA, Manila, 1971.
Lim, Pui Huen P. South-east Asian librarianship: new prospects for co-operation. Twenty-eighth International Congress of Orientalists, Library Seminar, Canberra, 1971.
Library Association of Singapore. Annual report, 1969–70.

APPENDIX I

Guide-lines for National and International Co-operation in Microfilming Projects

Adopted at the First General Conference of SARBICA
Manila, 24–28 May 1971

1. National Microfilm Committees support the formation of international co-operative projects and in this context welcome the establishment of international non-profit organisations interested in microfilming South-east Asian materials. National Microfilm Committees extend their co-operation to such international organisations and will urge their members to do likewise within the framework of their programme and their members' individual needs.

2. National Microfilm Committees will act as intermediaries and clearing-houses between international organisations and their members channelling requests and requirements on both sides but negotiations will, however, be conducted directly by the particular institution concerned.

3. As part of their contribution to co-operation with international organisations, National Microfilm Committees will compile:
(a) Lists of negatives already filmed.
(b) Lists of material on their lists of priorities awaiting filming.
(c) Wants lists of material required by members but not held in their respective countries.

4. All parties should undertake not to reproduce from microfilms supplied but should refer prospective buyers back to the institution holding the negative and the copyright.

5. Microfilms will be supplied in accordance with the institution's normal charges.

6. Recommendations for Microfilm Units:
(a) Negatives should be retained by the institution owning the original material or by any other institution in the country it entrusts with the keeping of these negatives.
(b) Positives of negatives already made may be freely supplied at the discretion of the institution owning the original material.
(c) Material not yet filmed may be filmed at request of the international organisation if the item is on the National Microfilm Committee's lists of agreed priorities.
(d) Microfilms should be made in accordance with recognised technical standards.

APPENDIX II

Conference of South-east Asian Librarians Constitution

I
(a) The name of the organisation shall be the Conference of South-east Asian Librarians (CONSAL).
(b) South-east Asia shall be taken to consist of those countries in the region.

II *Objectives*
To hold conferences of South-east Asian librarians at least once every three years in order:
(a) To establish, maintain and strengthen relations among librarians, libraries, library schools, library associations and related organisations in the region.

(b) To promote co-operation in the fields of librarianship, bibliography, documentation and related activities in the region.

(c) To co-operate with other regional or international organisations and institutions in the fields of librarianship, bibliography, documentation and related activities.

III *Participation*

(a) Delegates shall be:
  (i) librarians working or resident in the region;
  (ii) representatives of libraries, library schools, library associations and related organisations in the region.

(b) Observers shall be those who do not qualify as delegates.

IV *CONSAL Committee*

The CONSAL Committee shall consist of:

(a) The Executive Board comprising the following office-bearers who shall be residents in the host country:
Chairman
Vice-Chairman
Hon. Secretary
Hon. Treasurer.

(b) Two members from each participating country in the region other than the host country.

V *Functions of CONSAL Committee*

The CONSAL Committee shall:

(a) Organise the next Conference, and publish its proceedings.

(b) Implement the resolutions adopted at the previous Conference.

(c) Appoint such sub-committees as are required.

(d) Seek appropriate financial and other assistance as required to carry out the aims of CONSAL.

(e) Publish a newsletter.

VI *Location of Conference*

The host country for the next Conference shall be decided by the Conference.

VII *Election*

(a) The Chairman shall be nominated by the delegate(s) of the succeeding host country and his nomination shall be endorsed by the Conference. In the event of there being more than one nominee, the Conference shall elect a Chairman from amongst those nominated.

(b) The other office-bearers shall be appointed by the Chairman in consultation with the library association(s) of the host country.

(c) The members from each participating country of the region shall be appointed by their respective national library association(s).

Ratified by the following official delegates:
(Signed) Thach Phiem
for Cambodia
(Signed) Winarti Partaningrat
for Indonesia
(Signed) J. S. Soosai
for Malaysia
(Signed) Estela M. Figueroa
for the Philippines
(Signed) Lim Hong Too
for Singapore
(Signed) Nitaya Chudhamataya
for Thailand
(Signed) Nguyen Ung Long
for Vietnam

Conference of South-east Asian Librarians
Resolutions

1. The Conference resolves that a directory of South-east Asian librarians be compiled and periodically brought up to date.
2. *Education.* In view of the varied needs of South-east Asian countries, this Conference resolves:
   (a) That basic training of librarians should be provided at national levels.
   (b) That in-service training be provided by libraries within the region.
   (c) That a programme of staff exchanges between South-east Asian libraries and library schools be initiated.
   (d) That library schools in the region be encouraged to make available advanced library education and training to librarians from South-east Asia.
   (e) That the project for a regional institution to provide advanced training for librarians in South-east Asia be further explored.
3. In view of the non-existence and/or relative ineffectiveness of legal deposit legislation in South-east Asian countries, the Conference resolves that measures be initiated at national level to formulate appropriate laws.
4. The Conference further resolves that national bibliographical committees be set up in each country and that effective liaison between these committees be maintained by the CONSAL Committee in such manner as it may deem fit.

(d) Some Aspects of the Recent Development of Librarianship in Taiwan

TZE-CHUNG LI
Director, National Central Library, Taiwan

Less than 100 miles off the coast of Fukien, looking much like a tobacco leaf floating on the China Sea, lies the island of Taiwan, also known as Formosa. Chinese settlement of the island began in the twelfth century and in 1886, Taiwan became a province of China. In 1895, at the conclusion of the Sino-Japanese War, Taiwan was ceded to Japan, remaining under the Japanese rule until 1945 when it was returned to China. Since the Communist occupation of mainland China in 1949, Taiwan has been the site of the Nationalist government.

In the first years after Taiwan was restored to China, the Nationalist government was faced with many problems of priority, such as stability of the island, resettlement, land reform, etc., having little time for the development and building of libraries. Librarianship in Taiwan remained stagnant until the mid-1950s when the National Central Library re-opened in Taiwan after a short recess and the creation of the Library Association of China. The library and the association have been the major forces in developing and promoting librarianship in Taiwan. This paper will present some aspects of recent developments of librarianship in Taiwan with particular reference to the work of the National Central Library and of the Library Association of China.

Bibliographical services

Most bibliographical services are provided by libraries. The National Central Library began its publication of union catalogues on certain subjects and periods in the 1950s. General union catalogues were not started until 1967, when the China Council of the Sino-American Co-operation in Humanities and Social Sciences directed funds to the National Central Library for the project. The union catalogue project includes four categories of items: Chinese rare books, Chinese documents, Chinese serial publications, and Chinese non-rare stitch-bound books. All, except the last one, have been completed.

General bibliographies are essentially library holding lists. Book-form holding lists were published by the National Central Library, National War College Library, Provincial Taichung Library, Tainan Municipal Library and many others. A monthly national bibliography has been published by the National Central Library since 1961. Though only an accession list of the library, it is the nearest approach to a national bibliography, since the library is the legal depository for all materials published in Taiwan.

Subject bibliographies are numerous with obvious emphasis on the humanities and the social sciences. Catalogues of publishers have been frequently published, but there is no general trade bibliography equivalent to the American publication of *Publishers Trade List Annual* or *Books-in-Print*.

Indexing services have fairly good coverage, though lack of recency. General indexes have been published by the National Taiwan University Library, National Chengchi University Social Sciences Materials Centre, the National War College Library, and the National Central Library. The National Central Library's publication of a monthly periodical index since 1970 has an extensive coverage of 480 periodicals. Since 1969, the Scientific Documentation and Instrumentation Centre of the National Science Council has provided indexing services in pure and applied sciences.

In general, bibliographical services are reasonably adequate, though not without flaws. Their main weaknesses lie in the lack of co-ordination, lack of recency, and lack of cumulation. There are at least four libraries engaged in indexing services. Their efforts overlap to a great extent. Most indexes are retrospective in nature. Even the monthly index of the National Central Library lags a few months behind its publication, thus enlarging the gap between the publication of articles and that of the index. Current trade bibliography is lacking. No bibliography has attempted to include non-book materials. There is no national bibliography in the strictest sense. In general, cumulation is rare.

On the other side of the ledger, the bibliographical control of Chinese rare books, documents, and serial publications is much better. Though far from prompt, indexing services are extensive. A surprisingly large number of union catalogues and book-form library catalogues has been published.

Centralised process of cataloguing

There are three major classification schemes presently employed for classification of Chinese materials, but the cataloguing rules are more or less the system developed by the National Central Library. The library's *Cataloguing Rules,* published in 1946 and revised in 1959, has been used by almost all libraries in Taiwan. This is an obvious advantage for the National Central Library to start the centralised cataloguing process.

Beginning in February this year, the National Central Library began issuing printed Chinese catalogue cards. Any title deposited in the Library will be catalogued and the catalogue card printed and distributed to libraries needing them. Each card records title, author, imprint, collations, series note, tracings, card number, price, etc. In addition, romanisation of title and author is also supplied.

A new service was initiated by the National Central Library in June this year, that is, publishers are invited to register their books with the library. Any book registered will be assigned a printed card number and, after it is received, will be catalogued in printed form and listed in the monthly *Chinese National Bibliography.*

Along with the printed card project, as of 1 May, the National Central Library has been working on the creation of a National Union Catalogue. Participating libraries include the National Central Library, National Taiwan University Library, National Normal University Library, Fu Ssu Nien Library of the Academia Sinica, Provincial Taipei Library, Taipei Municipal Library, Tung Hai University Library, Taiwan Provincial Cheng Kung Unversity Library, Kao Hsiung Municipal Library, Fujen University Library, Soochow University Library, and Tamkang College Library.

Each library, when making the set of catalogue cards for a new book, is required to make an extra card and send it to the National Central Library. The library is responsible for maintaining the national union card catalogue and will eventually publish it in book form.

Microproduction and reprints
Microproduction was introduced to Taiwan rather late. In the late 1960s, both the National Central Library and the Social Science Materials Centre of the National Chengchi University started their programmes of microproduction. The centre has primary interest in producing newspapers and periodicals on microfilm. A list of microfilm journals in the social sciences was published by the centre in 1970.

The National Central Library began production of Chinese rare books on microfilm in 1967. A total number of 449 titles of Chinese rare books has been made on microfilm, including 11 titles of Sung imprints, 10 titles of Yuan imprints, 375 titles of Ming imprints and 53 titles of Ching imprints. All microfilm-positive are available for sale or exchange.

The recent financial aid of the China Foundation equipped the library with new microproduction facilities. The library plans to reproduce all its collection of Sung, Yuan and Ming imprints on 16 mm microfilm within the next two years. In addition, all Chinese newspapers in the collection of the library will be put on microfilm.

In recent years, reprinting of Chinese old imprints has become popular. Reprinting of the strong collection of rare books at the National Central Library has also attracted the interest of many publishers. As of 1970, 315 titles of Chinese old imprints, mostly rare books, in the collection of the National Central Library were reprinted by 35 publishers. 63% were published by four publishers: Student Book Company (98 titles), Cheng Chung Book Company (44 titles), Kwang Wen Book Company (34 titles) and Han Hwa (23 titles). In 1971, six publishers contracted with the library to reprint 53 titles of Chinese rare books in its collection.

Reference services
Reference services are virtually lacking in public libraries. A recent survey indicates that among the 14 public libraries which supplied information, eight libraries answered an average of 15 inquiries per month and six libraries answered no inquiries at all. The situation in college and university libraries appears to be better. Twelve college and university libraries replied that they answered from 5 to 312 inquiries per month, with an average of 133 inquiries per library. No library, however, has created a department or section especially for reference services.

The main reason for the lack of development of reference services is two-fold. There is a shortage of trained personnel who have good knowledge of reference tools. Secondly, most library budgets are too meagre to enable them to build strong collections of reference works.

Reference services are provided by the National Central Library though not effectively since its resumption of duties in 1954. The financial aid of the Asia Foundation and the China Foundation in recent years has enabled the library to build a collection of reference works gradually both in Chinese and Western languages. This collection is by far the best in Taiwan. In June of this year, a reference section was created with two trained librarians in charge of reference services. During the first month of operation, the library answered about 170 inquiries from patrons both domestic and foreign.

Library education
Formal library education in Taiwan began in 1955 with the establishment of a library science section in the Social Education Department of the National Taiwan Normal University in Taipei. With the assistance of the American Library Association, the Department of Library Science of National Taiwan University was established in 1961. By the end of 1969, a total number of 345 students were graduated from the two schools.

The World Junior College of Journalism in Taipei has been offering library science programmes since 1964. The college, originally a vocational school established in 1954, offers two library science programmes: a three-year pro-gramme for senior high school graduates, and a five-year programme for junior high school graduates. No degree is conferred. Since 1956, the Library Association of China has sponsored the Summer Library Workshop every year except 1962. From 1956 to 1970, 14 sessions were conducted with a total enrolment of 862.

In spite of the large number of library science students produced during the past decade, there is a serious shortage of trained library personnel, particularly in public libraries. Seventeen university and research libraries employed a total of 479 librarians in 1971. Of these, 76 or 15.8% have college degrees in library science and 119 or 24.8% received some library science training. The National Chengchi University, a public institution, employs 44 librarians of which there are none with library science degrees. Only 12 of the 116 librarians employed at the National Taiwan University have library science degrees.

Eighteen public libraries employ a total of 207 librarians. Of these, only one has a library science degree, constituting 0.4% of the total. The number of librarians with library science training is also meagre: 62 out of 207, constituting 29% of the total number.

The shortage of trained librarians may be attributed to three factors. Firstly, many locally trained librarians have left for North America. It is estimated that over 90% of the library science graduates from the National Taiwan University have gone abroad. Secondly, libraries in general, and public libraries in particular, have been slow in their development. Very few libraries offer reference services. Library holdings are meagre in most libraries and library funds are far from adequate. Thirdly, the importance of the library as a social institution has not been fully recognised. The low status and, as a result, the low salary scale, are the major factors barring some qualified librarians from working in the field of their interest.

It is anticipated, however, that the shortage of manpower in libraries will be eased by 1973, and by the middle of 1970s many libraries will be adequately staffed with qualified librarians. Fujen, the Catholic University of China, started its library science programme in 1969, and graduates of library science are expected in 1973. Tamkang College plans to begin its library science programme in 1972, as does the College of Chinese Culture. The National Taiwan University has recently decided to begin its graduate programme in library science and will begin, hopefully, this fall. The National Taiwan Normal University will follow suit by beginning its graduate programme next year. In addition, this year's Summer Library Workshop conducted at the National Central Library has a 50% increase in enrolment, totalling 138. By the mid-1970s, the number of trained librarians will be doubled. This should substantially solve the problem of shortage of library manpower in Taiwan.

In summing up, one could say the current status of library science in Taiwan looks very promising. In every area of library science, new programmes have been initiated, to bring Taiwan's library service up to modern-day standards. Current emphasis on library education will soon supply libraries with an adequate number of qualified personnel who can carry out those programmes, bringing modern, convenient service to library patrons throughout Taiwan.

(e) Library Development in Thailand: An Appraisal and a Forward Look

SUTHILAK AMBHANWONG

Librarian, Central Library, Chulalongkorn University, Bangkok

Libraries in Thailand have been in existence since the past century, but their development is painfully slow. Some outstanding progress probably began 20 years ago, and may be noticeable in the areas of academic and research libraries, documentation and bibliographical service, library education, the Thai Library Association and library co-operation. This paper will cover these aspects with a look into their impact on future developments.

Academic libraries
A significant event in the field of academic libraries is the appointment of a Committee on the Improvement and Co-ordination of University Libraries by the National Education Council in 1968. Members of the Committee, comprising chief librarians of the 10 universities and an official of the Council, serving as secretary, work together to improve their libraries. Major works advocated by the Committee are the Book Programme, the Union Catalogue Project and the recommendations for the Development of University Libraries.

Made possible by a substantial fund jointly allocated by the Thai and the United States Governments to the 10 academic libraries for the purpose of helping strengthen book collections in the fields of science, technology and social sciences, the Book Programme has resulted in a considerable increase in the quality and quantity of library resources in the universities.

A union catalogue for university libraries is being developed, whereas a union list of serials in the 10 universities and some government libraries is in preparation. The completion of the union catalogue will certainly help augment the inter-library loan service among libraries.

Recently, recommendations for the Development of University Libraries were adopted by the Committee. The main recommendations, comprising the development of a centralised library system, the improvement of status for trained librarians and the increase of book funds commensurate with the student enrolments, have been accepted and implemented in different stages by each university.

It is evident that the future plan of co-operation among academic libraries will be in the form of co-operative acquisitions, the development of a Farmington Plan-type programme with well-defined subject and area responsibilities for each academic library, the exchange of duplicate materials, and the inter-library loan service.

Research libraries

Considerable development has taken place in the field of research libraries. The new building dedicated in 1963 has made it possible for the National Library to extend more services to its clientele, who can avail themselves of the reading room facilities and the various adult education programmes and exhibitions in the library auditorium. Several subject and author bibliographies have been made available. Two research libraries, recently opened, namely Phya Anuman Rajadhon Memorial Library and the Library of King Rama VI, form a most welcome addition to the National Library.

Some other outstanding research libraries include the library of the Department of Science, Ministry of Industry, Siriraj Medical Library, the National Institute of Development Administration (NIDA) Library, the Bank of Thailand Library, Education Materials Centre Library, the Siam Society Library, and the Asian Institute of Technology (AIT) Library. Most of them have extensive reference, bibliographical and indexing services in their specialised fields for researchers.

The Asian Institute of Technology (AIT) Library, noted for its collection on engineering and technology, is the pioneer in introducing two computerised systems to library work. The Computer-aided Journal Listing and Control System is designed to provide a machine-readable data base for both the current and non-current journals in the collection, including information on title, library holding, subscription and history of the journals. The Computer-aided Acquisitions and Accounting System intends to print out the multiple order form, a book-on-order list, a monthly New Titles List, and list of orders to be claimed; to keep a detailed and up-to-date account of encumbrances and expenditures; and to keep statistics of the library accessions. The accomplishment of the computerisation at the AIT Library sets a pace in this field for other academic and research libraries.

The future plan of the AIT Library is to serve as a regional information centre for science and technology in South-east Asia. Soon a study will be begun on the possibility of obtaining MARC (Machine-Readable Cataloguing) magnetic tapes of the Library of Congress for use in book selection, cataloguing, SDI (Selective Dissemination of Information) service, etc., and of other machine-readable data bases such as *Chemical Abstracts Condensates, Engineering Index Compendex*, the Highway Research Information Service data file and the MEDLARS (Medical Literature Analysis and Retrieval System) when a larger computer system is installed. If the plan can be implemented, the computer application will be made available to other libraries in Thailand and to national documentation centres of South-east Asian countries on a cost-sharing basis. Thus it will help expand the scope of bibliographical service in this region.

Documentation and bibliographical service

The centre for documentation service is the Thai National Documentation Centre (TNDC), established in Bangkok in 1961, with the assistance of

106

Unesco. Services beginning from December 1964, which include indexing, abstracting, translating, compiling bibliography, reproduction and reference services, have been extended to researchers in other countries as well.

Bibliographical activities began to flourish in Thailand in 1960. Bibliographies, compiled and published, include bibliography of government publications, current bibliographies, author bibliographies, subject bibliographies, bibliographies of theses and research reports, list and union lists of serials, indexes to Thai periodical literature and newspaper indexes.

It is anticipated that the computerised method will be used to some extent in the near future to print out Thai bibliographies, periodical indexes and other lists; more co-operation among libraries will be strengthened to ensure the compilation and production of comprehensive subject bibliographies and indexes so as to meet the needs of researchers in the various fields.

Library education
There are five library schools in Thailand, of which the library school at Chulalongkorn University is the oldest. Founded in 1955, it now operates three programmes, namely, the graduate programme leading to a Master's degree of Arts in Library Science, the graduate diploma and the undergraduate programmes. The College of Education, Prasarnmit, offers a graduate programme towards a Master's degree in education, with a major in library science, and a specialist programme. The library schcools at Thamasat and Chiengmai Universities have only the undergraduate programme, and so has Ramkamhang University, which inaugurated its programme this year.

Basic courses in the library schools include the following: Libraries and Society, Classification and Cataloguing of Books, Book Selection, Library Organisation and Administration Reference Service, Bibliography in several fields and English for Librarians. In addition, a course in Classification and Cataloguing of Thai books is offered, whereas knowledge on the various aspects of Thai librarianship and Thai materials form an integral part of most courses. Advanced courses are in the fields of technical services, cataloguing and classification, subject bibliographies and administration of each type of library, audio-visual materials and services, government publications, research in librarianship, and comparative librarianship.

This year, changes have been made in the three library science programmes of Chulalongkorn University. Two more electives are added in the curricula of the graduate and the graduate diploma programmes, namely Teaching Method in Librarianship, designed for students interested in a teaching career in the field of librarianship, and Mechanisation of Library Information Sciences, which intends to give an introduction to mechanised systems of the storage and retrieval of recorded information. Students interested in computerisation may take one more course entitled Computer Programming and Digital Computer, offered in the Department of Computer Science.

More electives for the undergraduate programme include School Curriculum Materials, Administration of Archival Materials, Rare Books and Manuscripts,

Area Studies in Librarianship, Bibliography of South-east Asia and Bibliography of Special Subjects.

It is evident that library science courses offered are extensive in scope and built on a sound basis to meet the need of present demands of the country, and also to broaden the outlook of students in international librarianship. Professional literature used to supplement the courses is composed of American and British books and periodicals since there are only a few books published in the vernacular.

Research in librarianship has been encouraged and produced in the form of theses as required in the Master's degree programme at Chulalongkorn University. In addition, a monograph series of Library Science Papers has been issued since 1965, with a coverage of students' research papers and the faculty's writings on some aspects of Thai librarianship.

Teachers in the library schools consist of full-time and part-time persons. Part-time teachers are drawn from practising librarians in several libraries. In some years, American teachers, sponsored by American Foundations or Peace Corps volunteers help teach the courses. A majority of Thai teachers graduated with Masters' degrees in library science from different American library schools. There is a great need for them to take refresher courses or observation tours of libraries abroad so as to keep abreast of professional knowledge and new techniques in this field.

Graduates of all library schools at present number around 600; they hold important positions in the various libraries. One hundred is an average number of graduates from all library schools each year. This small number fails to meet the increasing demand for trained librarians to work in all types of libraries, but, the expansion of library education is not feasible at present due to the inadequacy of teachers, professional books and periodicals. It can be said that the accelerated growth of library education in Thailand is partly engendered by more recognition being given to the library profession, and partly by the contribution of the library school graduates to the library career. There is evidently a great need for the expansion of library education in all library schools to meet the acute shortage of trained librarians.

Thai Library Association (TLA)

Recognition is also given to the Thai Library Association for its role in training librarians without qualifications for admission to a library school. There are five types of workshops performed by the TLA, namely school, public, special and regional libraries, and one for teacher librarians which is organised in co-operation with the Teacher Training Department, Ministry of Education. The attendance of the five series of workshops from 1956 to December 1970 totals 8,088. The duration of each workshop varies from 10 days to two months. Basic courses in library science are offered together with some practical work. It is evident that the workshops help solve problems in the shortage of trained librarians in Thailand.

Apart from the workshop programme, the TLA has extensive activities in promoting library service. It holds an annual conference for librarians, conducts radio and television programmes to promote reading interests, organises a library for its members, publishes several professional books and periodicals, supervises school libraries upon request, and specifically helps to encourage public acceptance of libraries as an integral part of education.

Library co-operation
Co-operation among libraries or librarians is noticeable through the TLA activities and the library committees, and results in the free flow of information and effective library service. Foreign relations are carried on by academic and research libraries through the exchange of publications. The TLA also extends its service in the acquisition of Thai government publications to libraries abroad.

Last August, Thai librarians participated in the first Conference of Southeast Asian Librarians (CONSAL) held at the University of Singapore. Some recommendations of particular interest include the exchange of staff between South-east Asian libraries and library schools, and a project for a regional institution to provide advanced training for librarians in South-east Asia. Thai librarians are looking forward to the implementation of these recommendations.

A look at the future
A review of the library activities in the past 20 years presents an encouraging picture of library development in Thailand. The only serious handicap lies in the lack of good public library service due to the absence of library legislation, which should be enacted in the near future. Furthermore, the administration of public libraries is the responsibility of the Ministry of Education, whose main task is to develop schools for children and young people. Thus public libraries are not much developed; they suffer badly from the lack of financial support and positions for trained librarians.

In the recent years, school libraries received more attention from the authorities of the Ministry of Education. Several projects for the development of schools include the improvement of their libraries. Emphasis has been placed on developing schools in the provincial towns. Nevertheless, only a few school libraries meet the standard set up by the Ministry.

It should be noted here that the first attempt of Thai librarians to set up a national plan for library development was made in 1968. Standards for each type of library and a detailed plan for development were drafted in the hope that they would be accepted as part of the Five-Year National Plan for Economic Development. Unfortunately, the plan was turned down.

However, it is hoped that a national plan for public library development could be made possible through the assistance of an international organisation. If so, a model public library should be established in Bangkok to set a good example of public library service and perhaps public and school libraries

H

should be consolidated in the organisation and building, as practised in some Scandinavian countries for economical purposes and for the extension of reading facilities to more people.

REFERENCES

Conference of South-east Asian Librarians 14–16 August 1970. *Resolutions.* Singapore, 1970.

Lee, Hwa-Wei. *Library mechanisation at the Asian Institute of Technology.* Bangkok, AIT, 1971. (Xeroxed.)

Spain, Frances Lander. *Some notes on Library development in Thailand, 1951–65.* Library Science Papers No. 2. Bangkok, Department of Library Science, Faculty of Arts. Chulalongkorn University, 1965.

Suthilak Ambhanwong. *Libraries and librarianship in Thailand.* Library Science Papers, No. 5: Bangkok, Department of Library Science, Faculty of Arts, Chulalongkorn University, 1967.

Thailand. National Research Council. *Thai National Documentation Centre; an account of the planning, establishing functions and services of the Centre.* Bangkok, TNDC, 1966.

4 CARIBBEAN AND CYPRUS

(a) Recent Developments in Librarianship in Barbados

MICHAEL E. GILL

Librarian, University of the West Indies, Cave Hill, Barbados

There have been three recent developments which are expected to influence the field of librarianship in Barbados. All are evidences of a spirit of co-operation and all have grown out of the need to provide solutions to problems which the profession faces.

The Library Association of Barbados, now in its fourth year, became a possibility when, in the 1960s, a number of new libraries were established (at the Cave Hill campus of the University of the West Indies, at the Centre for Multi-Racial Studies, at the Department of Archives and at the Caribbean Meteorological Institute) to join the long-existing Public Library system. This Association has turned its attention to the training of the clerical and sub-professional staff in an attempt to improve their status, performance and remuneration, and to arrest the rather rapid rate of turnover of staff at that level.

The Association is also studying the provision for professional staffing in its member libraries which include, in addition to the ones already listed, school libraries and libraries in several government departments, because there exists some indication that such provision is not uniformly adequate. Recommendations should soon be ready for transmission to the appropriate authorities.

Another recently formed association is ACURIL (The Association of Caribbean University and Research Libraries—originally . . . Research Institute Libraries, hence the acronym, but broadened to include Public Libraries which in the West Indies are frequently the only source of much research material—particularly in Local History). ACURIL is in its second year of operation and has produced a questionnaire to determine the state of the art in the area and to provide a framework within which its own standing committees may plan. The constitution provides for membership by libraries in all the Caribbean territories and the countries and states in South, Central and North America which border on the Caribbean sea or the Gulf of Mexico.

And the third development is the establishment in October of this year of the School of Librarianship at the University of the West Indies at Mona in Jamaica. This school will provide initially undergraduate courses and hopes to add postgraduate courses in three years. It is being set up with assistance from Unesco and is certain to relieve the manpower shortage the profession has faced in Barbados and the rest of the West Indies.

In spite of these advances, certain problems still exist, e.g. the absence of a

National Library—something perhaps not feasible as a separate entity in a country the size of ours. The Public Library, of course, fills several of the functions of a National Library but lacks the staff to do a complete job. Also, the collection of the nation's and its nationals' publishing output is complicated by the fact that the literature is mostly published abroad and that the production at home is dominated by Government publication which is notoriously difficult to control bibliographically.

However, the outlook is encouraging since the new developments tend to suggest that, through co-operation, significant advances will be made.

For a more detailed treatment of the historical development of Librarianship in Barbados readers are referred to Ifill, E.L.V. *The public library movement in Barbados and Jamaica from the middle of the nineteenth century to the present day.* 1968. (A thesis accepted for Fellowship of the Library Association obtainable on microfilm from University Microfilms Ltd., St. John's Road, Tylers Green, Penn, Bucks.)

(b)   Possible Impact of Recent Developments in Library Education on Librarianship in Jamaica

S. W. FERGUSON
Chief Librarian, College of Arts, Science and Technology, Kingston

Historical, Geographical and Socio-Economic Background
Jamaica, a former British colony has been independent since 1962. The island with an area of 4,411 square miles has a population of 1.9 million.

The economy, which was formerly based on agriculture, is increasingly being diversified; consequently, light manufacturing, bauxite mining, manufacturing of alumina and a thriving tourist trade now contribute substantial amounts to the GNP of the island annually.

The island is characterised by rugged hills which form a backbone in the interior along its longitudinal axis. These hills rise to a height of over 7,000 feet at the eastern end of the island contributing much to the scenic beauty for which the country is noted. The hilly terrain of the interior is surrounded by a narrow coastal plain on which most of the large towns are located.

Social services are being developed apace with the economic progress taking place to adequately serve the growing population, 45% of which is under 14 years of age.

Libraries
Libraries are among the services being developed. The island is adequately served by a Public Library Service operated by the Jamaica Library Board, a statutory body, under the auspices of the Ministry of Education. The Jamaica Library Service offers a reference and lending service through 269 service points consisting of 13 main libraries in the capital towns of the parishes or local government administrative areas, 69 branch libraries in the smaller towns

and 120 book centres in the small villages. This is supplemented by a book mobile service at 67 points and a postal reader's service. In addition, the Institute of Jamaica, located in Kingston the capital city, is the home of a comprehensive West Indian Reference Library and also serves as a legal deposit library for Jamaican publications.

Government libraries
Government departments are served by libraries of varying levels, ranging from small collections operated by clerks to well-established libraries operated by professionally qualified librarians. There are 30 such libraries at present.

Educational libraries
A comprehensive library service to 813 primary schools is operated by the Jamaica Library Service on behalf of the Ministry of Education. This schools' library service is based on a once per term visit to each school by the book mobile which is staffed by a trained librarian who carries out book exchanges and gives professional guidance to staff and students of the schools.

In the 42 junior secondary schools, separate accommodation is provided for libraries, and again with the help of the Jamaica Library Service, libraries have been established. Libraries have also been established in the 53 high schools and although the standards vary widely, efforts are being made to ensure that adequate library facilities and trained staff are available in these institutions.

Institutions of higher education include the six Teacher Training Colleges and the College of Arts Science and Technology with libraries of varying standards, also the University Library which serves over 3,000 students and staff.

Special libraries
Special libraries are of relatively recent origin in Jamaica, but development is being accelerated in this field since many commercial and manufacturing firms as well as specialised government institutions realise that well-organised libraries are vital to the success of their organisations.

Some recent developments in librarianship in Jamaica
There have been many important and far-reaching developments in the field of librarianship in Jamaica recently. Among these are the following:
(a) The emphasis being placed by Government on establishing school libraries at Primary and Junior Secondary School levels.
(b) The introduction of a course for Teacher Librarians in Teacher Training Colleges.
(c) The establishment of a library school at the University of the West Indies in October 1971. This is being done with the assistance of Unesco.

Of these developments, the most far-reaching are the developments in library education as listed in (b) and (c) above. Up to the present, most librarians in Jamaica received their training on the job and qualified as librarians under the British system either by private studies or by attending library school in England through a limited number of scholarships granted by the Jamaica Library Board. A small number of librarians have been trained under the North American system of post graduate study at universities in the USA or in Canada. Except for the Eastern Caribbean Regional Library School which operated in Trinidad during the 1950s and early 1960s, there has never been any facility for library education in the English-speaking Caribbean. As a result, the percentage of unfilled posts, especially in the early years, has been high.

In Jamaica at present, there are approximately 100 established posts for qualified librarians, of which approximately two-thirds are filled. Predictions are that in the next five years there will be an additional 50 established posts for librarians in addition to those for Teacher Librarians. Under the present costly system of training abroad, there would be no hope of filling this need for qualified librarians or teacher librarians in the country. It can therefore be seen how important it is that provision is now being made for the training of Librarians and Teacher Librarians in the island.

Some details of the library education proposals for Teacher Librarians are as follows:

The aim should be to provide as soon as possible enough Teacher Librarians to work in Junior Secondary, Comprehensive, Technical, Vocational and Primary Schools.

The training programme should recognise the fact that a Teacher Librarian is a specialist in two fields—education and librarianship, thus recruitment should be conducted through either of the professions.

The training programme in the Teacher Training Colleges should be suitably co-ordinated with the programme at the University's School of Librarianship to ensure the continuing education of Teacher Librarians.

The syllabus will include courses on the following:

(a) The introduction, origin, scope and function of the school library.

(b) Children's literature and reading habits.

(c) Teacher library skills.

(d) Reference materials and their uses.

(e) Administration and organisation of the school library.

(f) Principles and practice of classifying and cataloguing.

(g) Other facilities outside the school.

The syllabus of the School of Librarianship, UWI, is still under consideration, but proposals are that it will contain compulsory and elective courses to be taken over a three-year period along with other academic courses leading to the professional qualification to be granted by the University. A decision is yet to be taken on the name of the degree to be awarded.

The well-needed development in education for librarianship will have an immense impact on the profession not only in Jamaica but in the entire English-speaking Caribbean.

(a) The returns of numbers trained in terms of cost will be greatly increased. Formerly it cost £1,600 approximately per annum to send one student to library school in England. Now this amount can train approximately five persons per year at the local school of librarianship at the University of the West Indies.

(b) The increased number of graduates will help fill the many vacancies which now exist in a much shorter time than could have been achieved under the old scheme of training abroad. It is envisaged that the school will turn out 30 graduates per annum, of which approximately one-third should be Jamaicans. Compared with the two or three which have so far been trained annually, this will be a vast improvement.

(c) The establishment of a library school at the University will enable the profession to compete on more equal grounds with other professions in the recruitment of staff. Hitherto, the poor facilities for local training, and the long wait before a young recruit could expect to gain a scholarship to library school abroad discouraged many suitable qualified persons from entering the profession. They preferred instead to join other professions with better facilities for training or to go directly to university after leaving school.

(d) Such a school can only result in improved status and improved salaries for librarians since the layman and the employer will more readily accept university qualifications as a symbol of professional status and efficiency.

(e) The course offered by the local university will, of necessity, be more relevant to a developing country with its attendant social and economic problems and its tropical climate and weather conditions. Studies in the planning and design of library buildings will now emphasise conditions in a tropical rather than a temperate country.

(f) To date the profession in Jamaica is dominated by women. As part of the general studies Department of the University, there is a possibility that men will be attracted to the profession.

(g) There should be an improvement in the quality of the service offered at all levels as trained librarians fill the vacant posts now being staffed by clerks. This improvement in the quality of service offered should result in increased recognition of the value of librarians and improved professional status.

(h) When the postgraduate course gets under way, it is expected that original research undertaken will result in contributions to the literature of librarianship, particularly for developing countries.

(c) Libraries in Cyprus

COSTAS D. STEPHANOU
Chief Librarian, Paedagogical Academy, Nicosia

Although it is a small island, with a population of only 600,000 people, Cyprus nevertheless has a considerable number of libraries—public, special, college and school—situated in all the towns and in many of the villages.

Libraries in Cyprus may be traced back to ancient times, the earliest ones being those attached to the temples in which archives were kept; these included such famous temples as that of Aphrodite at Paphos, the temple of Apollo at Curium and of Cybele at Aepia.

The earliest known public library in Cyprus was in the City-State of Soli where, according to a source from Laphitos and Chytri, 'there was a public library (Bibliophilakion) and a special man, Apollonions, in charge of the library, and he was also a priest of Cybele, here called Pammateira'.

During the early Christian period, along with the development of Christian literature, libraries became part of the ecclesiastical organisation and it was the general rule to attach a library to every church. Cyprus being among the first places to be converted to Christianity, we can thus assume that there were libraries in the churches there, although for the early period no evidence of this has been found. Later, many codices and manuscripts of Christian authors, particularly the lives of Saints, were kept in the churches of Cyprus and today these are to be found in various great libraries in Europe (at the Vatican, in Venice, etc.).

In the Frankish period 1191–1571, there were libraries in the court of the Lusignan kings and the Latin churches, monasteries and abbeys. Etienne de Lusignan, in his Description of the Island of Cyprus, Paris, 1580, states that he used the library of the abbey of St. Dominic, at Nicosia, where he found many books of classical Greek writers such as Strabo, Plutarch, Plato, Pliny, and George Bustron, a Cypriot nobleman.

During the Turkish period 1571–1878) there were no libraries other than the very small ones kept by monasteries and churches. After 1821, a small library was formed at the Archbishopric, Nicosia. All books saved from ancient collections in the various monasteries and bishoprics were collected in this library. The library of the Archbishopric, which has originated from those earlier collections, has now about 5,000 volumes as well as many codices and manuscripts.

In 1840, Archimandrite Hilarion donated his library to the Hellenic School of Nicosia, which was founded in 1812. This school is known today as the Pancyprian Gymnasium and it is the oldest secondary school of Cyprus. Its library, which originated from this donation, today contains about 34,000.

At the beginning of the nineteenth century, a small Turkish library of Turkish, Persian and Arabic works, known as the Sultan Mahmut II Library, was established by the Ottoman Government of Cyprus. Originally the library was housed in the medieval building behind the cathedral of St. Sophia. It now has its quarters in the Evcaf premises and numbers about 4,000 volumes.

After the secession of Cyprus to England, for administrative purposes, in 1878, there was an increase in the number of books imported, mainly from Greece and England, and the situation improved. In 1887, the British Government of Cyprus passed a law providing for the preservation of copies of books printed in Cyprus, and a depository of copies of printed books was set up in the office of the Chief Secretary. Two copies of each book were sent to the Keeper of the Department of Printed Books at the British Museum. The law has recently been amended and the depository has been transferred to the Ministry of the Interior.

However, little was done for the establishment of new libraries or the improvement of the existing ones, and until 1927, apart from those mentioned above, there were only a few small libraries in government offices and some private libraries. During the period 1927–59 some new libraries were established by school committees and the Church of Cyprus. The public library of Nicosia, established in 1927, was transferred in 1936 to the municipality of Nicosia and it now contains about 6,500 volumes.

The Phaneromeni Library was founded at Nicosia by the Church Committee in 1933 and it has now 28,000 volumes including a special collection of works on Cyprus and Byzantine history. It is a reference library only.

The library of the Antiquities Department was founded in 1943 and housed at the Cyprus Museum, Nicosia. It has 8,000 volumes of books and magazines, most of them donated in 1941 by Zenon Pierides and Rupert Gunnis. The library possesses a fine collection of books on Cyprus, especially on the archaeology of Cyprus; it is also a reference library.

The public library of Limassol was founded in 1945 by the Municipality. It has 16,000 volumes, mainly Greek, English and Turkish, and an interesting collection of paintings.

The public library of Paphos was founded by the Municipality in 1946 and is housed in an attractive building of classical style, erected specially for the purpose. It has 8,000 volumes.

The Leontios Library in Paphos—named after Bishop of Paphos Leontios, and later Archbishop of Cyprus (1897–1947), who donated the complete collection of books—has now 6,000 volumes, mainly on religion, and is a reference library only.

The public library of Famagusta was founded by the Municipality in 1953. It has 16,000 volumes. An art gallery is also attached to it.

A number of new libraries have been founded since Independence (16 August 1960):

The library of the Paedagogical Academy with 18,000 volumes.

The library of the Higher Technical Institute with 6,000 volumes.

The library of the Ministry of Education amalgamating the libraries of the Greek Office of Education and the Greek Communal Chamber, which were founded in 1960 and 1961 respectively, was set up in May 1966 in Nicosia, the

117

capital of Cyprus. It serves as the central public library for Cyprus, at the disposal of all citizens, and has established a mailing system for readers who are not residents of Nicosia. In 1967, by decision at the Council of Ministers, the Nicosia Municipal Library passed to the Ministry of Education. By decision of the Minister of Education, the Municipal Library was incorporated in the Library of the Ministry of Education and now it is housed in the premises of the Library of the Ministry of Education. The Library of the Ministry of Education has now 35,000 volumes and serves as a lending and reference library. It also has sub-offices with small collections in the district education offices.

Since 1960 the Cultural Department of the Ministry of Education has founded 72 rural public libraries, which are now serving about 120,000 people in rural areas. There is also a mobile unit and a second one is going to start functioning. Thus a population of about 40,000 more people will be served by the two mobile library units. One of the units was donated by Unesco.

The high schools of Cyprus have their own libraries with a total of 300,000 volumes.

The following libraries are run by foreign missions and embassies in Nicosia and they are very helpful: British Council, Bibliothèque du Centre Cultural Français, the United States Information Services and the Goethe Institute.

Government departments and ministries have their own specialised libraries. These are the libraries of the House of Representatives, the Ministry of Agriculture, the Presidential Palace and the Cyprus Broadcasting Corporation.

The Government of Cyprus decided to create a state library with a state gallery, giving for the purpose the sum of £162,000.

The problem with the libraries in Cyprus is one of personnel. We have no trained librarians. The reason is that the job is not well paid.

The Greek Library Association of Cyprus is doing everything to improve libraries and librarianship.

REFERENCES

Hill, George. History of Cyprus. Cambridge, 1948, vol. 1, pp. 66 and 110.
Bible: Acts of Apostles 23: 4–14.
Inscriptiones Graecae ad Res Romanas pertinentes. Paris, 1906, vol. III, p. 933.
Papaioannoi, Charilaos. Catalogue of manuscripts of the Archbishopric of Cyprus. Athens, 1906.
Tornaritas Criton. The Statute Law of Cyprus. Cap. 79, III.

PART II

*Surveys of Recent Developments in
Advanced Librarianship*

5 PUBLIC LIBRARIES

(a) Recent Developments in Advanced Librarianship Affecting Public Libraries

H. C. CAMPBELL

Chief Librarian, Toronto Public Libraries, Toronto, Canada
President, International Association of Metropolitan City Libraries
(INTAMEL)

The basic function of the public library today is still to bring books to people, and people to books. This activity has been carried out in Europe and North America by the public library for over 100 years, and the audience now reached by metropolitan area public libraries alone can be estimated at more than 70,000,000 adults each year, as well as millions of children. A growing number of persons are also being served in Asia, Africa and Latin America. Since the days of its foundation, the function of the public library has never altered. Its duty is to further the literary, ideological and practical interaction of people with the themes and artifacts of their cultural heritage. In doing so, the public library makes use of print and those newer developments of print and the graphic arts that the past few decades have introduced into our lives.

The responsibility which faces those who have to direct and guide public library service is to determine how best to achieve these goals. In this seminar we will be concerned with the present-day developments which are bringing about changes in all countries and forcing our services to adapt to meet the needs of our citizens. For this reason, it might be well to try to agree on a definition of what we mean when we speak of 'advanced librarianship'. The main feature which I believe is characteristic of 'advanced librarianship' is its *international* component. While there has always been a certain amount of borrowing of methods and techniques in public librarianship from one country to another, it is clear that today the advances in librarianship being made throughout the world are coming from all countries. It is therefore necessary for every country to be prepared to adopt practices and discoveries which it can find abroad. No country that wishes to put into action forms of advanced library service can do so without looking abroad for help and assistance. This applies equally to the 'advanced' or 'developed' countries as to any other.

In the public library in which I have been for the past 15 years, since leaving the staff of Unesco, I have been concerned in applying ideas and concepts of librarianship from all parts of the world and from all areas of library service. I have borrowed and used ideas that come from university, national or technical school libraries, from bibliography, documentation, reprography and management. It is not easy to know which foreign practices are the ones which should be adapted to one's own conditions. I have found as the best guide in making a choice the methods of comparative analysis, in which I and members of my staff attempt to look across our national and cultural boundaries and, without bias, consider objectively those ideas and practices from other libraries which seem to be pertinent to our needs.

The use of the comparative method on an international basis is to me the essential ingredient in making advances in public library services. I think it is, therefore, very appropriate that a seminar sponsored by IFLA should concentrate on the study of what is needed in order to bring about advanced librarianship. On the basis of the above definition, it follows that no one country has the unique claim to be alone in providing advances in librarianship. It will be part of our task to find out from each other what the recent advances are in all fields which can be used in public librarianship and how these may be applied.

I would first like to make clear that the public library system, particularly in Western Europe and North America, is today in a state of change. While it is not possible to discuss here all of the reasons for this state of change, I would like to suggest several causes which I feel are responsible for bringing this about. These are, first, the impact of the new world-wide information technology on public library systems; second, the shifting role of the public library in relation to other municipal and national education and information services; and third, the developments and practices in the staffing and administration of our library services which make it necessary to have people with a wide range of specialised abilities, not only those who know and love books.

As well as the changes in library methods, there are social changes taking place around us, and the public library has had to respond to these changes. The continuing movements of citizens to secure more participation in their own government is one of the basic facts that is bringing change to the public library system. The public library has to adapt itself to new forms of government and to the increasing demand for fuller participation of citizens in the planning of their own lives. Where revolutions have brought dramatic changes to nations, it is interesting to observe the role of the public library before, during and after the revolutions.

Because of the growing numbers of people who need to express their ideas in their own languages, who need to create their own journals and books and develop the applied and social sciences to meet their own national needs, there has been a phenomenal increase in printing and publishing in all countries of the world. The public library, in company with other libraries, has to face the challenge of providing bibliographical control and access to this new output. For this reason librarians today are adopting new tools and machines from other areas of industry and business and applying them to their daily work. This to me is the meaning of the phrase 'new information technology'. We see growing up around us a vast number of machines and tools which have been adapted by librarians in order to make the handling of information more effective and reliable. I need not give examples; they will occur to all of us. Probably the most glamorous of these tools is the computer. Public libraries have as yet made only slight use of the computer in order to meet the requirements for books of our citizens. Some of us have adapted the computer to serve some of our administration needs. Some of us have done it to handle stocking of our library shelves. It is my view that much more will need to be done by public libraries to adapt the processing power of the computer if we are to meet the demands being made on us by our citizens.

Let me remind you that the computer that we know and use today is only a pale reflection of the computer that we will have tomorrow. According to Edward David, Science Advisor to the President of the United States, we are on the threshold of entirely new computer capabilities. These new capabilities will enable us to solve problems by techniques now considered infeasible, or even beyond our conception. We are now within reach of computers at least two orders of magnitude faster than those available today, and this is not the end of the development road. For example, if we have a problem for which a clearly defined criteria for a successful solution exists, and if 100 instruction steps are sufficient to test each solution, then we can examine 107 solutions per second with the new 1,000 MIP (millions of instructions per second) computers that are coming along. Our planning for the future must take into account the changes in information technology which lie ahead of us.

We will be required in the future to develop methods of selective dissemination of knowledge to our users in the large- and medium-sized public libraries, if we are not doing this now. Our users will not be content simply to be provided with a wide range of books. They will ask us for more guidance and assistance in securing non-book and current technical and scientific information.

For these reasons I see in all countries, both those in the developed and the so-called underdeveloped parts of the world, a growing need to utilise methods of communication between and within library systems and to develop library communication networks capable of sending and receiving messages between the various libraries. To my way of thinking, the most important new technology for information handling which we in public libraries should study are the methods of operating communication network systems between our individual libraries. These need not be sophisticated electronically, but they must get the message across speedily, accurately and reliably.

Just as the production of printed and graphic material is rising, so also is the national and international production of radio, television and motion picture materials. The impact of these on our culture poses serious problems for the public library. It has been essential in many of the developed countries for the public library to clarify to its users to what extent it is prepared to offer assistance in securing film, radio and TV materials. In some countries the public library has opened its doors to the free circulation of film and sound recordings just as it has to books and periodicals. In other countries access to film and sound recording material is handled by other agencies. There is no particular barrier to the public library becoming a vehicle in the field of film, TV and sound recordings. It is my view that public library services will need to enter this field more and more.

A further area in which the public library in many countries is now playing a substantial role is in handling information secured from commercial sources. The public library in recent years is becoming more and more a source that purchases commercial information services, both national and international, and makes these available to its citizens. The value of the public library doing this is evident. It provides to the widest possible range of persons in the community those very specialised commercial information services to which use would be restricted otherwise only to those who had the ability to pay.

A further area where the public library has had to make advances is in the area of post-secondary and informal education for adults. In countries where a larger and larger percentage of the population are completing primary and secondary schooling, the question of their continuing education is a matter which has concerned the public library. In countries where formal education is not keeping up with the growth in population, then the challenge is even more serious. This is a challenge which is of special concern to the developing countries and for which some assistance from developed countries should be provided.

A final area which I would like to touch on briefly deals with changing practices in staffing and administrating our public library systems. Just as the public libraries in their beginnings were very much a voluntary activity, so it is clear that we should retain much of the strength of voluntary assistance if we are to reach the widest number of our citizens. If we are to open up new areas of services, we must count on using para-professional and non-library-school-trained staff members. We will require persons with widely different outlooks and talents. I mentioned the action of many libraries in making available audio-visual materials and special information services. It is my view that we will require technologists and specialists in these fields to work alongside traditionally trained library staff members. Where public libraries are concerned with their role of community leadership, then it will also be necessary to employ staff who have the confidence of their community and understand its needs. Finally, in our vast urban metropolitan centres it is clear that the forms of municipal government are changing in keeping with the growth and complexity of our cities. The public library has an important role to play in providing information needed by all those, both citizens and officials, who are concerned with the replanning and organisation of our metropolitan urban way of life.

I would like to mention briefly several basic works, listed as an annex to my outline, which may be of some value in our study of these problems. These works are not offered as the only ones which deal with developments in advanced librarianship, but I would recommend them as being relatively unbiased and technically sound.

Since this is the opening session of our seminar, I have had to speak in very general terms about some of the recent advances which I see affecting public libraries. My purpose was not to pronounce which advances are the best, but to try to show how I feel we can approach the study of adapting such advances to our own needs in a practical manner. I trust that I have been able to provide some points that we can discuss, not just now, but all through the seminar, and also take on to other seminars and conferences which IFLA may be in a position to organise in years ahead.

REFERENCES

Hicks, W. B., and Tillin, A. *Developing multi-media libraries.* NY/London, Bowker, 1970. 199 p.
Heilinger, E. M. and Henderson, Paul B. *Library automation: experience, methodology, and technology of the library as an information system.* NY, McGraw-Hill, 1971. (A volume of the McGraw-Hill series in Library Education. Extensive bibliography (1,029 entries)—not annotated.)
Penna, C. V. *The planning of library and documentation services.* Second ed. Unesco, Paris, 1970. 158 p. (A selective bibliography of recent general works is to be found on pages 83-7. Further references to Central and South America, the UK, the USA and the USSR are contained in the chapters on these areas.)
Morgan, Roger P. *The new communications technology and its social implications:* a symposium at Ditchley Park, Oxfordshire, 2–7 November 1970. Rome, International Broadcast Institute, 1971. 74 p.
Jackson, M. M. Jr. *Comparative and international librarianship:* essays on themes and problems. Westport, Conn., USA, Greenwood Publishing Co., 1970. 307 p.

(b) Commentary and Record of Discussion

T. K. LWANGA
University Librarian, Makerere University, Kampala, Uganda

General Comment on the theme of the Seminar was that 'it was bad'. The participants would have preferred to discuss common problems and examine, wherever possible, solutions suggested by colleagues from advanced library systems. This approach would have led to comparative analysis and study, and a critical examination of the applicability to developing countries of solutions to library problems of developed countries. It was generally recommended that Unesco should note this point when organising future seminars of this kind.
[Discussion was led by: Mr. Pala (Kenya); Mr. Lwanga (Uganda)]

Library Technology. There was general disagreement with Mr. Campbell's definition of library technology. The participants saw library technology, or new information technology, as nothing more than the application of technology to established library techniques to meet the complicated demands of library users. The technical methods used, by themselves, are not part of librarianship.

Library technology has little relevance, yet, to public library services in developing countries, where the demands of the readers are far less complicated to require the use of sophisticated technological gadgetry. It was agreed,

125

I

however, that library technology could be profitably applied to university and special library services in the developing countries. A number of examples were given of the computerisation of serials records, indicating perhaps that this was the priority field for library technology in most developing countries.

[Discussion was led by: Mr. Kalia (India); Mrs. Ogunsheye (Nigeria)]

Changing Practices in Staffing and Administration of Public Libraries. There were two distinct points of view regarding the use of para-professional and non-library-trained specialists in such fields as: Community leadership, Audio-visual technology and information, Urban planning and reorganisation, etc. One view was that these services should not be performed by librarians, but by specialists recruited specifically to help the librarian in planning library services. The other was that, because of the acute shortage of highly trained manpower in developing countries, the librarian has to be a person of many trades. There is, therefore, a need to include in our curriculum specialist topics for services related to the fields mentioned above.

[Discussion was led by: Mr. Tawete (Tanzania); Mrs. Ogunsheye (Nigeria); Mr. Park (Korea)]

Planning of Public Library Services. There was unanimous support for the view that developing countries should avoid the rigidity of function of the various types of libraries. The aim in planning should be to develop multi-functional libraries. Planning public libraries should, therefore, be part of a national co-ordinated development programme, which would ensure the economic use of resources available. Developing countries should avoid the mistakes of developed countries and plan for a national library system. In such a system you could plan for, say, a research library at an experimental station in a rural area to serve as a public library. The same additional function could be allotted school, college and university libraries.

[Discussion was led by: Mr. Lwanga (Uganda); Mrs. Pankhurst (Ethiopia)]

The Future. The future of public library services in developing countries was seen as essentially depending on good planning and ample financial support for purchase of books, erection of buildings and training of staff. The participants did not agree with Mr. Campbell's view that technological changes will radically lead to the disappearance of the public library as one knows it today. It was pointed out that the 'book' will continue to be the basis of the public library service in developing countries for many years to come.

[Discussion was led by Mr. Pyadasa (Ceylon]

Conclusion. The session was, on the whole, disappointing mainly because, after Mr. Campbell's introductory remarks, there was very little time left for discussion; also the participants got bogged down with definitions. It was also felt that, for fruitful discussion. Mr. Campbell's paper should have taken into account the problems of developing countries in establishing public library services.

126

(c)   Impact of Recent Developments on the
Organisation of the Library Profession—Public Libraries

F. K. TAWETE

The IFLA section on public libraries had eight items to discuss on the agenda. The most important items were: the Working Party on revision of standards for public libraries, revision of Unesco Manifesto, library services to young adults, election of secretary, audio-visual aids sub-section and International Book Year. Added to these items was a paper, 'The organisation of our profession', by Dr. P. Van Swigchem, Chairman of the Dutch Association of Librarians.

The organisation of our profession
In this paper Dr. Van Swigchem raised two questions:
(1) Whether public librarians should have their own library association outside a general professional library association, and
(2) Whether the Public Librarians' Association should include members other than the professional librarians.

His argument for question one was that public librarians have their own needs which they need to discuss outside other members of the profession. Secondly, he argued that since IFLA has a separate section for public libraries, it seems there is need for such an organisation.

His argument for point two was that, since the public librarians were serving the public, he thought that it would only be fair if the latter were allowed to join the association so that they would know what is discussed for their services.

Both arguments are true but my comments are that to have a separate organisation for public librarians in a country is a duplication of effort. The principles of librarianship are the same and they can be discussed by all professional librarians. What differs is the application of these principles. But the application cannot warrant the formation of a separate organisation for public librarians. Even IFLA does not allow the formation of subject specialised organisations. What IFLA has allowed is the formation of subject committees which then report their discussions to the general council. This move was in an effort to make the functions and activities of IFLA efficient.

From the developing countries' point of view, the move which Dr. Van Swigchem advocates would mean decentralisation of the strength of the profession. Librarianship in developing countries is still very young and therefore cannot begin to think of such a move. What would happen is that some librarians would not belong to any association if such a move were taken.

In developing countries where national library service boards exist, the general public's interests are discussed by the national board. In my opinion, members of the public are included in such associations not because we want to discuss their interests but because they themselves are interested in the promotion of libraries and the profession in the country. In that case it is not necessary that they should be in the public librarians' association only.

Draft standards for public libraries
My general comment on these standards is that it would have been proper if IFLA invited views from developing countries on the setting up of these standards. Several items have been overlooked due to this factor. For example:

Principles on which a public library must be based
Items 3 and 4: In some developing countries the local authorities are not strong enough to finance a library service. There should be legislation which should name a governmental ministry (preferably the Ministry of Education) which should be responsible for providing public library service.

Item 14: Here the draft has omitted the inclusion of microfilms and microfiche.

The size of the library unit
Item 5: Public library service: It is not indicated in this item whether the 3,000 people mentioned here should all be literates. In some developing countries, only a quarter of this number may be literate. Thus it will not be wise to start a library service at such a place.

Cost of the public library service
In this item the percentage of salaries is too high compared to the percentage of materials. In countries where they depend very much on materials from overseas, the percentage on materials should have been higher and that on salaries lower. This would take into consideration transport charges for the materials.

On the whole the standards are quite fitting for the majority of the developed countries.

6   UNIVERSITY LIBRARIES

(a)   Recent Developments in University Librarianship

K. W. HUMPHREYS
Librarian, University of Birmingham

Problems have been created for university librarians by the rapid growth of student numbers (and consequently of academic staff numbers), the increase in the number and range of new publications, the demand for more personal service to research workers, the development of new techniques in teaching, the use of management methods for library administration and perhaps, above all, the application of the computer to library routines and to information services. At the same time, in this period of an unprecedented rate of expansion, demands for new buildings have forced the librarian to take up a position in relation to some of the older types of problem like centralisation versus decentralisation or open versus closed access.

In such circumstances one may echo Wordsworth's words 'Bliss was it in that dawn to be alive, But to be young was very heaven'; if you are not so young or enthusiastic, you might prefer to remember that Wordsworth was speaking of the French Revolution. Still, as one not so young, I must immediately say that I regard this as one of the most exciting periods in the history of librarianship. It could also be one of the most disastrous, if techniques are substituted for books and technology for culture. We must be clear that most of the advances of which I shall speak are intended to improve our ability to offer the reader more economically and/or efficiently the material he requires, whether it is a photograph (or even the original) of a Tibetan manuscript or the completed print-out answer to an obscure medical question. In other words, we must preserve a sense of proportion and, despite the words of Professor Robbins in his Report on Higher Education that computers are more important than libraries to the running of a university, *we* must assume that the intention is more important than the method.

Perhaps I should firstly discuss recent attitudes to old problems since we must not assume that all countries or all librarians take the same view of the solutions which generally seem to be acceptable. The arguments about centralisation and decentralisation, for example, continue to be important on the Continent since so many universities are organised in a decentralised pattern so that university librarians still live with seminar, departmental or institute libraries which are not in any way under their control. As a result they have been looking for ways to improve relationships and to obtain some form of co-operation. At the same time it is significant that not all new German universities have accepted the idea of one centrally administered library service.

At Konstanz, in fact, the library was originally set up as a series of decentralised units. Libraries in seminars and institutes have still been the common situation in many of the new universities in Europe. In general, the new British universities have been established with one central library, although the battle for departmental collections has not always been won by the librarian.

In France the Libraries Division of the Ministry of Education has laid down a pattern of development for universities in relation to new buildings. This necessitates a division of the library into several sections, of which the most common are humanities, science and medicine. Very few examples of the division into undergraduate and research libraries exist in Europe, although the arrangement in some central libraries allows the research worker to be separated from the undergraduate. One or two British libraries are now considering the possibility of separate undergraduate library buildings as, for example, at Leeds.

Another library problem which is still important in Europe is that of the amount of material which should be available on open shelves. In European libraries it is still very unusual for the majority of the stock to be immediately available to the readers. Only reference works can usually be found on open shelves in all countries, although recent buildings in France have greatly increased the number of open shelves. Only a few new buildings in Germany, of which Frankfurt was the first, reflect a new attitude to the old idea of a single large reading room with closed stacks. In Britain open access is generally acceptable, although there have been a few critics. Dr. Radcliff and Mr. Ceadel, for example, have expressed some doubts, but these are largely based on the difficulties which result for the library administration rather than on readers' wishes. Certainly in evidence to the Dainton Committee on the National Library, it was clear that readers accustomed to using open access libraries were almost entirely in favour of this system.

There may well be other aspects of library organisation which you wish to discuss, but I should now devote my time to the developments which may be seen to be of a more contemporary nature.

The first significant change in university librarianship over the past few years has been the result of a new attitude to library use. Whereas it was common for a library (and not only a university library) to provide materials for the students and staff, but little service, the tendency now is to offer very developed and even sophisticated services. It is likely that the East European countries would be convinced that their attitude has always been to consider the needs of their readers and that their bibliographical and methodological departments, which are an important part of their libraries, are devoted entirely to the demands of readers. In the West, however, the purpose of the library is different and a do-it-yourself type of method was thought to be preferable. It is, however, clear now that students and academic staff are in need of assistance in the use of the library and that it is important for them to receive instruction, not only in library use, but in the bibliographic resources of their subject, whether it is in the humanities, social sciences or sciences.

The effect of this interpretation of the library's role is to bring it more closely into the general teaching pattern of the university. Library buildings tend to become centres for instruction as well as for individual studies. Further, they are organised on a subject division basis, so that library staff, expert in the subject concerned, are immediately available for consultation. The whole question of the utilisation of subject specialists for reader services I have treated elsewhere, so that I shall not spend any time in elaborating it here. There is a difference of opinion about their use as it is still believed on the Continent and in the USA that they should apply specialisation to selection of books. In a number of British university libraries, however—as well, of course, as in the United States—staff have increasingly been orientated towards reader service.

As I have said, the library may now undertake considerable programmes of instruction. All students are shown the library and how it works, usually by conducted tours by library staff and the issue of guides to the library. Film and video tapes are also becoming popular for this kind of instruction.

The education of students and even of staff must include some knowledge of the literature of the subject with an understanding of reference tools. Sometimes this has been the responsibility of the department but it is gradually being assumed by the library, so that classes, seminars and courses are available in the library on scientific and technical literature, abstracts, reports, conference papers, etc., or on the social sciences and government or non-governmental publications or on the bibliography, say, of medieval Egypt. Again, these may be supported by films or by video tapes and slide tapes. Several university libraries in Britain have co-operated in providing slide tapes, for example, for a number of subjects, including MEDLARS, Chemical Abstracts, etc.

Another experiment in the United Kingdom, financed by the Office for Scientific and Technical Information, is the establishment of a number of scientific information officers whose job is to offer instruction on scientific literature and an information service. It is hoped that they will be able to make use of the various machine-readable systems on behalf of the staff and to evaluate them in the university context. So far this promises to be a valuable experiment and it is likely that universities will wish to continue to employ these information officers after the funds from OSTI have run out.

A word here, too, about an aspect of university organisation at least in the United Kingdom which has some bearing on the efficacy of the library's relations with the readers. In some universities the proposal of the Parry Committee on University Libraries that a library liaison representative should be appointed in each department of the university has been accepted. This ensures that a department is fully consulted on any changes in library administration, on suggested courses for research students and on other similar questions.

These library representatives are particularly important in determining the material which should be on restricted access for student use. The provision of multiple copies of textbooks and of periodical articles in the reserve collection of an American university was familiar to all university librarians, and it is perhaps worth noting that a similar pattern is to be found in many British libraries and that even on the Continent the central university library may have a textbook collection. The recommendations of the Deutsche Forschungsgemeinschaft, in fact, included the provision of finance for textbook acquisition. In Britain, where students' grants contain a notional element for books, the reserve collections attempt to provide the background reading materials rather than textbooks.

Mention has already been made of the role of the library as part of the teaching function of the university. In recent years there has been a considerable development in teaching methods and attempts have been made to offer the individual student a greater part in his education. This can include more time available for reading in the library and opportunities for studying through the use of the so-called new media—i.e. language laboratories, television, learning machines, video tapes, slide tape courses, etc. Libraries have had to decide how far the library should be concerned in these media and I think that most would now feel that a logical position has been established.

A reasonable formula seems to be that the library would not normally produce films, tapes, slides, etc., except possibly in relation to teaching aids for students on the use of the library itself. On the other hand, it may provide equipment for using the media, store it and generally make it available. It may also provide an information service on the availability within the university and perhaps outside the various types of new media especially those which are published. We have a session in the general IFLA Conference later on this subject, so I shall not pursue it further here.

It has been necessary to include facilities for using these media in recent library buildings and the form and content of many have included other features which reflect the influence of a number of different trends. It has been generally accepted in the United States and the United Kingdom that new buildings, in order to be as flexible as possible, should be constructed on a modular basis and that ceiling heights should be adequate for reading, stack and staff areas. All services (plumbing, lighting, heating and ventilating) should be contained in the structural frame of the building so that floor areas are open and can be used for almost any purpose. Reading and stack areas are often mixed and divided according to broad or even specific subject fields. Open access is the rule rather than the exception. In these multipurpose buildings, full air-conditioning is essential, with adequate air changes for readers in all usable parts of the building even though it may normally be used for stacks. Plans are usually made so that further building phases can be foreseen and expansion space provided for as long a period as possible. This supposes an almost limitless size of the library and no proposals have yet been made to suggest that the library should cease to grow beyond a certain point, although the problem has been tackled from two directions—the establishment of criteria for effective withdrawals of stock and the rationalisation of collecting by means of co-operative planning.

A great deal of progress has been made over the past few years in the field of national and international co-operation. The work of ARL in the United States and of SCONUL in the United Kingdom has been so impressive that attempts have also been made to apply this pattern on a regional or international scale. As a result, we have the SCAUL and its regional offspring SCAULEA. During the past year, too, an organisation (LIBER) has been established to foster greater co-operation between research libraries in Western Europe. This meeting today, and the many other ventures of IFLA, indicate the increasing value of this international body.

Some of the results of co-operation will be well known to you in the Farmington Plan and PL 480 in the United States, the Scandia Plan for the Scandinavian countries and the Sondergebiet scheme for Western Germany. In some other countries, for example the United Kingdom, similar schemes have been evolved to cover a more limited range of material or a more restricted area of the world so that we have committees concerned with co-operation in African, Russian and East European, Oriental and South American materials. Libraries, too, have often agreed locally or regionally to limit their collections in fields of overlapping interests. University libraries have thus been required to make their collections available to readers outside their walls. This is often a considerable burden since outside users may include the staff and students of neighbouring smaller universities, colleges of education, polytechnics and similar institutions as well as associations of doctors, lawyers and scientists and the staffs of hospitals. In many cases no additional financial assistance is given either by the bodies themselves or by the University Grants Committee.

The latest example of co-operation is in the field of automation. It would not be appropriate here to record the progress made internationally in the field of shared cataloguing or in aspects of machine compatibility. It is, however, of some importance to note the work which has been undertaken by universities, especially in the United States and Canada, but also in Germany, France and the United Kingdom. Co-operation has been often on two levels—international and local. Whilst in the United States and Canada some libraries have been able to develop their own systems, in other countries libraries have instituted their research by sharing the work and the costs. I am concerned, for example, with a project involving two universities and a public library and, for some aspects of the system, two other universities. This has resulted in a close relationship between different types of library which has had a very important influence on all aspects of co-operation. As you will know, the MARC format has been very satisfactorily applied to the British National Bibliography and the project MONOCLE at Grenoble has shown its use for French publications. It is further hoped that the West German National Bibliography will be produced in this form next year. Many university libraries have utilised the MARC tapes for their catalogues and for selective dissemination of information on new publications for book selection purposes. In view of the fact that the tapes are not yet sufficiently up-to-date, it is suggested that

Whitaker's should issue tapes of forthcoming books and this could be matched by Bowkers and possibly even by similar organisations in France and Germany to provide acquisition information rapidly.

Other aspects of automation applied to library processes include listing of periodicals, financial control and, perhaps above all, circulation records control. Attempts have also been made to provide automated periodicals registration.

I should not here try to describe all the various projects, both successful and unsuccessful, but rather to indicate in general terms that progress has been made on many fronts in computer application to library methods. Problems, however, arise from two questions at least: one is the fact that in many cases automation has increasingly taken over the manual methods without sufficient consideration being given to their appropriateness in a modern library, and the other is the high cost of development and even of running an automated system—especially if the university computer centre does not provide the expertise and computer time. In any case, even if the university does provide systems analysts and programmers, it is my belief that library staff must be free to study all aspects of the processes to be developed.

The need to examine library processes and services, and also to be able to cost them accurately, has given rise to a new attitude to librarianship. A surprising amount of research has been undertaken in recent years by specially formed units, by the staffs of individual libraries and even by professional consultants on library systems. Studies have been made of the user's approach to the literature of his subject, to catalogues, classification schemes, library staff, etc., to try to assess the efficiency of collections and their availability. Management studies have been applied to the organisation and control of library staffs and library processes have been subjected to the scrutiny of economists. Units have been set up in the United Kingdom at Lancaster University and at Cambridge to investigate methods, to study particular problems and to create models. The ARL has commissioned a firm to examine the relevance of management studies to libraries. Finally, attempts have been made by a number of libraries to define and cost the various aspects of library work. The problems, too, of determining efficiency not only by cost but by other quantitative and qualitative methods have also been studied.

In general terms, therefore, the image of librarianship which still survives, of a quiet absorption with trivia or of a gentle retiring scholar locked away from the readers in an ivy-grown ivory tower, living on the scent of decaying leather bindings, is no longer a true one. He has scholarly interests certainly, but he must be a manager, an organiser and an administrator with an adequate knowledge of building problems, computers, statistics, trading methods (for binderies and photographic departments), the book market, modern educational techniques, personnel management, and possibly even of a particular curricular subject as well. In listing these qualifications it will be appreciated that I have not included many others, like tact and diplomacy, courage or a strong constitution. I am sure that all of you have these qualities and will face the future with enthusiasm for

'There is a tide in the affairs of men,
Which, taken at the flood, leads on to fortune;
Omitted, all the voyage of their life
Is bound in shallows and in miseries.
On such a full sea are we now afloat,
And we must take the current when it serves,
Or lose our ventures.'—Shakespeare, *Julius Caesar,* Act iv Sc. iii.

(b) Report on the Session on Recent Developments in University Librarianship

I. D. MAMOUN
Librarian, Shambat Library, University of Khartoum

Mamoun: Sudan

To have the general administration of the branch librarian under the charge of the professor or the dean of the faculty and the technical side under the university librarian, e.g. classification and cataloguing, certainly diminishes the efficiency of the library and the prestige of the university librarian. The university librarian is certainly more familiar with library problems than the professor or the dean, technically or administratively.

I feel that there is no need for the university library to be computerised technically, as there are computer centres for information storage and retrieval regionally, e.g. MEDLARS for medical and veterinary literature in Western Europe. But it might be quite advisable that each university library should exploit the computer administratively, e.g. registration of journals, as that might facilitate and diminish the huge volume of routine work done by the library staff. This could be done in developing and developed countries alike. For example, the computer in Khartoum University used for accounts and other matters could be used as well for the purpose of library routine.

Almost all librarians are suffering from the inadequacy of buildings for their libraries. In most developing countries we only convert old buildings for the purpose of libraries, and therefore we cannot get what we want.

Chairman: As mentioned earlier, library problems differ in developed and developing countries.

T. K. Lwanga, Uganda

The role of the university library in our part of the world, East Africa (Kenya, Uganda and Tanzania), is different. Our university library serves all students in Uganda. We open it to the whole public as well as on a national basis. Our university library has the same role as a national library, including library training.

Co-operation with the subject specialised staff of the university is an ideal procedure for any library. In Makerere, co-operation of the teaching staff is ensured. Each department has a member of the staff working with the library staff. There is not enough money, but there is precise co-ordination.

Demands for readers' services forced us to use the computer for the processing of periodicals, which number 4,500 in our university library.

M. N. Nagaraj, India

The main problems facing us in India are of language. Many languages are spoken in India. English is a second language. Books are written in different local languages according to each area. To translate a book to any of the local Indian languages, one should translate it first into English and then to the required Indian language. Co-operation among Indian libraries is rather difficult, as there is no one union catalogue. Grants are utilised for development within each library. In some universities the computer is still primitive.

K. H. Park, Korea

asked about the co-operation of ARL (Association of Research Libraries) with other international organisations.

Miss Rita Pankhurst, Ethiopia

Most African countries have only one university each. Communication is not adequate. In 1964 a meeting was convened for the exchange of information. The first Regional Library Association met in February 1971, for the purpose of arranging international exchange of publications.

M. E. Gill, Barbados

There are several developments of library services in the West Indies. The Spanish areas are going on a separate way. The association of public, university and research libraries, which started two years ago, is fostering co-operation.

F. O. Pala, Kenya

Mr. Pala thought that it would not be adequate to have a university library serving as a national library. It proved to be a hard job in Uganda, Kenya and Tanzania, where each country has only one university and one university library. Mr. Pala consequently thought that where the university enrolment of students is large, the university library would find it difficult to cope with research needs. He concluded that a university library acting as a national library would not be accepted in future.

Kalu Chima Okorie, Nigeria

The situation in Nigeria is different. Nigeria has five university libraries in addition to the national library, and other research libraries. The demands of students are on a higher level. Co-operation of libraries is partly hampered by the inadequate communication and postal problems. Each individual university has its own programme. Although, on the other hand, university libraries have excellent collections, students do not use the libraries as they should. They use them for passing examinations. Libraries should organise orientation courses for new students and should introduce new techniques. Academic staff do not appreciate the role of the library.

D. R. Kalia, India
Problems in India are peculiar. There are 110 universities, 3,500 colleges and affiliated universities and 3,000,000 student population. The University Grants Commission gives financial assistance to universities and colleges alike. There is modern air conditioning and computer utilisation. Universities are in towns. Affiliated ones are in remote places, usually with a population of 5,000–10,000. Such affiliated universities and colleges look very poor and neglected, whereas universities in towns are well looked after. Students are not interested in reading except for examinations, and likewise most of the teaching staff. More and more specialists are coming on to the scene. Certain libraries are allocated particular subjects for special readers. Religious and social sciences literature is seriously required.

Translation is very complicated, as literature should be translated from a local language to English and then to the other local language. Standards of students are going downwards, as they are not fully occupied.

T. G. Piyadasa, Ceylon
Ceylon has peculiar problems. Since 1943 compulsory education has been implemented for all. Since 1959 the number of universities has increased to four. The professors and the heads of departments like to locate more funds for their own subjects of specialisation. Inter-library loan is operating. The official language is the national one, English is the second. Not many books are produced locally.

(c)   IFLA Sub-section on Social Sciences

FRANCIS OTIENO PALA
Chief Librarian, Kenya National Library Service

The Sub-section held its meeting on 31 August 1971, under the chairmanship of Mr. D. A. Clarke, Librarian of the British Library of Political Science and Economics.

Two papers were read during the meeting: one by Mr. D. A. Clarke entitled 'Notes on some economic and statistical libraries in Great Britain' and another, by Dr. Gyorgy Rosza on the 'Role of the social science librarian in a changing world, or The Problem of two cultures'.

Mr. Clarke's paper was a fairly directory type of work and gave salient descriptive data about a number of British libraries which would be of interest

137

to social science librarians. Dr. Rosza's paper, on the other hand, although a short one, was a fairly precise exposition on social sciences in the midst of advancing science and technology. The paper also attempted to define the role of the social science librarian in the above context, emphasising that while science and technology were important, development in any culture must necessarily be directed by, and be consistent with, the humanistic considerations in a given culture. It was important that a successful marriage should be attempted between science and technology on the one hand, and social and humanistic education on the other, if society were to function as a sound organic unit.

Little discussion ensued from the two papers, but it seemed clear that the participants were in agreement with the gist of both.

1972 meeting at Budapest
It had been agreed during a meeting of the Sub-section held in Brussels in December 1970, that a directory of Economics libraries should be attempted and a draft of the European part should be ready for discussion and approval at Budapest next year. Madame Philips of Belgium undertook to prepare a draft questionnaire which was presented to the current meeting for approval. It is not possible to comment in detail on the questionnaire as it was not available in the English language. However, it was generally felt that it was an extremely detailed questionnaire. It was, therefore, decided that an earlier questionnaire, which was designed in 1965 by Unesco for a survey on libraries, archives and library schools in Africa, be adopted and adapted. It was further agreed that the Directory of Economic Libraries should eventually cover the whole world but that by next year, at Budapest, a draft for Europe should be ready. It was also hoped that the following papers would be read at Budapest:
  (i) Libraries of Economics in Hungary.
 (ii) Libraries of Economics in the European Community.
(iii) An outline of Social Science libraries in Germany.

There was some strong disagreement as to whether a further paper should be prepared on the economic collections in the libraries of the UNO family although some members felt that this was desirable.

Further papers would be welcomed, provided that they were made available early enough to enable participants to study them prior to coming to the Conference.

Assistance to delegates who wished to attend the conference
It was not possible to reach any resolution on this subject but it was the view of the majority of the participants that the matter should be raised with the IFLA Secretariat particularly with regard to the developing countries.

Comments
Although the Sub-section had an international façade, it seemed to the writer to be primarily concerned with European problems. It was not understood, for

138

instance, why the first questionnaire should not be circulated on a global scale right from the start. If this were done, it would be possible for the total size of the problem to be assessed early enough for a realistic budget and plan to be prepared. It also seemed to the writer that, even if it were conceded that the problems of Europe were immediate and pressing in this respect, to attempt to solve the problem on a global scale at the outset would not be an obstacle to the immediate preparation of a European directory which could be treated merely as a first instalment towards a final global directory.

The writer is prepared to state further that, on the whole, IFLA still seems to lack a true global character even though this is the chief moral purpose of its existence. The writer wishes to have it noted that the true virtue of any international federation is the achievement of sharing among dissimilar members and that until IFLA makes a deliberate and continuing effort to achieve this objective, it will be failing in one of its most fundamental moral duties.

7 ADVANCES IN LIBRARY EDUCATION

Education for Librarianship

Dean, School of Library Science, Kent State University, Ohio, USA

An 'advance' is more than a 'change'—the word is linked with the concept of progress. To speak of advances in education for librarianship is, therefore, to point out progressive developments. But 'progress' implies movement along a path, or up a scale, toward some goal; and if the goal is unclear, progress is difficult to evaluate. We shall begin, therefore, with some thoughts on the goals of library education.

It is axiomatic that the goals of any professional training must grow from the goals of the profession itself. One who educates future librarians is preparing them for service in the library profession; if we know what the profession is trying to accomplish, we can devise educational programmes which are pertinent to those efforts. Indeed, it might be more useful to identify the ideal goals of the profession, as opposed to the practical transient goals which are observed in actual situations.

Clearly, we are addressing the venerable question of a 'philosophy of librarianship'. It presents us with an intriguing arena for reflection and discussion—but on this occasion we shall resist the temptation to debate this fascinating topic. Instead let us take our philosophy from a blend of theories, leaving for another time the problem of fitting the elements into a balanced combination. I suggest, for our point of departure, that the ideal goal of librarianship is to provide for the educational and information needs of every individual. To the extent that other agencies of society may provide for these needs, librarianship can assume a supplementary, supportive role.

The knowledge base of the library profession must have a number of components if such a lofty objective is to be pursued in a meaningful manner. Those components point to corresponding elements in training programmes for librarians. Let me point to some of these relationships between the knowledge needed by librarians and the kinds of things they need to be taught. Some of the connections are obvious: it is, for example, clear that the librarian needs to know how to organise the books and other materials of his library—and every library training programme has accordingly included instruction in the art of cataloguing and classification. It is also plain that a knowledge of reference books and bibliographical structure is essential; and library education has recognised this need with courses covering that field. Of a less obvious character is the connection between knowledge of the information needs of individuals, or of society, and the kind of formal instruction appropriate to it. Indeed studies of this kind are not often found in the curricula of library schools, outside the industrialised nations—yet their value would seem as great for the emerging nations. Another aspect of the librarian's knowledge spectrum is awareness of subjects themselves: the contents of the books in his library. With the proliferation of published materials throughout the world, it becomes increasingly difficult for a librarian to maintain a rapport with the topics, issues and authors represented in his collection—but unless he can do this, his ability to give advisory and reference service to his patrons can only be superficial. In the library science curriculum it is not practical to give direct instruction in literature, science, art history, and social problems—hence there is the growing perception among library educators in all countries that formal library training must stand upon a foundation of university studies in general subjects. There is not universal agreement upon the manner of putting together the general subjects and the library science subjects which, in combination, provide the knowledge base for modern librarianship. In the Soviet Union, for instance, these two categories of subjects are presented simultaneously in a co-ordinated programme of study. In North America the general studies—up to the point of a university degree—will come before professional library training, which takes place at post-graduate level. The important thing is to have both elements in the total educational programme.

A further implication of this desideratum—that of rapport with the topics of the collection—is specialisation by subject, and specialisation by type of library patron to be served. This development grows from the vastness of subject literatures and from the particular needs of readers in popular libraries as opposed to readers in academic or scientific libraries. In the context of library training, it is therefore advisable to give instruction in the special kinds of organisation and services found in libraries which are concerned with specialised readers—among which we should include such reader groups as children, artists, executives in business corporations, etc. The kind of deep knowledge of narrow subjects which is required for librarians giving intensive service to specialised readers cannot be directly imparted in the library training programme itself; it must come from the non-library element of the student's total education. Yet the library school can endeavour to give a focus to certain aspects of specialised topics through surveys of their literatures and bibliographic structures; and it can endeavour to advise the student regarding courses in other university departments which will assist him in mastering his chosen specialisation.

In this introductory analysis we derive the goals of library education and the kinds of courses or other activities which implement those goals. In that framework we may pursue the question of 'advances' or 'progress' in the field of training for librarianship. Let us concentrate on developments of the past three to five years.

In view of the very substantial knowledge base which is required by the librarian, it is plain that his course of study cannot be limited to a few months; even the traditional one-year programme of many library schools cannot be

K

justified unless it follows a much longer period of pre-professional studies in general subjects. It appears that one sign of true progress in the world of library education is the movement toward increasing the amount of time involved in the professional programme, and in placing the professional programme later in the total academic period of the student. Advances of this kind have occurred recently in several countries. Let us identify some of them.

In North America, postgraduate level instruction, terminating with the master's degree, has been accepted as the basic professional qualification. Among new postgraduate programmes, commencing in 1968–71 and giving the master's degree, are the University of Alabama, University of South Carolina, University of Puerto Rico, University of Alberta, and Dalhousie University in Nova Scotia. Altogether there are now more than 120 postgraduate library science programmes in the United States, and eight in Canada; of these, 55 have received accreditation by the American Library Association. Nineteen of those accreditations have been awarded since 1965.

In Senegal, a School for Librarians was established in 1967, at Dakar University. The Ghana Library School, which opened in 1965, offered a postgraduate diploma beginning in 1967. The University of Teheran initiated its programme in 1966, offering both university level undergraduate and postgraduate training. Three new institutions are reported in Australia: Queensland Institute of Technology, to open in 1972, giving postgraduate training; Canberra College of Advanced Education (1970), also postgraduate; and the Tasmanian College of Advanced Education, planned to open in 1972 and to commence postgraduate instruction within three years.

A new undergraduate level programme at the University of the West Indies—beginning in 1971—is expected to develop within three years into a postgraduate curriculum. In Taiwan, innovations are the postgraduate programme at National Central Library—beginning 1971—and at National Taiwan University, beginning 1972. Two other postgraduate programmes have begun in Seoul, Korea, in 1971. The University of Ibadan, Nigeria, commenced postgraduate instruction in 1969.

In Ceylon, Vidyalankara University has offered, since 1969, postgraduate level instruction for teacher librarians, within the Faculty of Education.

The Philippine Normal College began to give the master's degree in 1968, joining three other postgraduate schools in the Philippines. The first class of master's degree recipients at Chulalongkorn University, Thailand, graduated in 1966. In India there are many recently established postgraduate programmes: Aligarh, Jammu and Kashmir, Bhagalpur, Burdwan, Gauhati, Ujjain, Gwalior, Bombay, and Banares Hindu Universities; also at INSDOC and the Documentation Research and Training Centre.

In Great Britain, we find that Sheffield University introduced, in 1968, both an MA in Librarianship and a Master of Science in Information Studies; it was the second—after London—to offer these degrees in relation to specific curricula—though both master's and doctoral degrees had been available in other British schools earlier for persons who had written acceptable theses.

I should stress that attention is drawn to these particular institutions because I believe they represent one aspect of true progress in library education: placement of library science training at the postgraduate level. On this basis, recognition must also be given to the further extension of library science into curricular for the doctor's degree. Of the 18 United States universities which give the doctorate in librarianship, 10 have begun this programme in the past five or six years: University of Maryland, University of Pittsburgh, Syracuse University, Florida State University, Indiana University, University of Minnesota, University of Wisconsin, North Texas State University, University of Texas, Texas Women's University and University of Southern California. In Canada the doctorate is being initiated at the University of Toronto, which will be the only school in the country to offer the degree.

There is a new doctoral curriculum at the University of Karachi, the first in Pakistan, which began its programme in 1967.

In this brief survey of recently inaugurated postgraduate programmes, we have seen examples of progress of one important type. There is growing acceptance, around the world, of the principle that library training—if it is to be professional, rather than clerical in nature—needs to occur at a high educational level. A second, related trend may be discerned from the short inventory just given: there is an increasing tendency to extend the total period of training which takes place at the postgraduate level. This is clearest in the United States, where the ambitious student who has earned a master of library science degree no longer considers his formal education to be complete; he will very probably give thought to a doctor's degree as an ultimate goal. Even if he does not reach the doctoral level, he finds that another level has recently become available. This is the so-called Post-Master's programme, which is given in 19 universities. Most of these Post-Master's programmes are of very recent birth. They provide an additional year of formal study for the person who does not wish to enter a Ph.D. programme.

Still another new development supports the concept of the extended period of postgraduate study for the master's degree. In 1970 most of the Canadian library schools lengthened the time required for a master of library science degree from one year to two years. In the United States, the University of California at Los Angeles has introduced a two-year master's programme, which is an optional alternative to the one-year programme. Educators in the United States and elsewhere are very interested in observing the outcome of these changes.

Another aspect of curricular progress is the movement toward more specialisation, so that training can be intensively concentrated on the needs of specific types of libraries. Significant efforts in this kind of differentiation can be observed in several countries. The Soviet Union is strongly committed to specialised training; indeed Professor Gastfer has written that 'the outstanding feature in the development of the system of training for skilled librarians has been the increase in the degree of differentiation'. The principal thrust of this movement in the Soviet Union is toward the demands of scientific and industrial libraries; consequently the training programmes will give much attention to courses in the actual subjects under consideration—such as physics, chemistry or geology—and to the bibliography of those fields. There will also be greater concern for the area of information retrieval, documentation, and mechanisation.

Recently the American Library Association issued an official policy statement about library education. One element which is stressed is the need for 'intensive specialisations' at the postgraduate level which are seen as 'a logical development in professional library education'. In Britain, the Schur & Saunders report of 1968, entitled *Education and training for scientific and technological library and information work* offers recommendations for specialised coursework in technological information as well as information retrieval.

New courses and programmes of this nature are found in considerable numbers; only a few examples can be identified in this paper. The Documentation Research and Training Centre, Bangalore, India, has offered a 14-month advanced course. In Delhi a 12-month course at postgraduate level was introduced at the Indian National Scientific Documentation Centre in 1964. In the same year, the Indian Association of Special Libraries and Information Centres, Calcutta, initiated a six-month postgraduate course leading to a diploma in special librarianship. North American library schools, as might be expected, are very active in bringing forward new courses dealing with special library problems, particularly in connection with mechanised and computerised techniques for information control. During one recent year, 38 such courses were initiated in the schools of the United States and Canada. Warsaw now gives courses in information retrieval. In Berlin, Humboldt University and the Berlin School of Librarians give instruction for documentalists. In Britain there is the recent development of the centre of special librarianship and information science at Loughborough. There are also new courses at Sheffield, Newcastle, Aberystwyth, Belfast, and elsewhere.

To give a closer view of content in such programmes, permit me to offer the descriptions of two courses given in my own institution, Kent State University. I believe they are rather typical of what is found in North American library schools. The first, 'Data Processing in the Library', considers:

Computer and other machine application to library cataloguing, acquisitions work, serials control, circulation routines, inventory control and reference work; administrative uses, including personnel and budget work. Systems analysis.

The more advanced course, entitled 'Information Retrieval in the Library', considers:

Types of information systems; co-ordinate indexing; automatic indexing and abstracting; current awareness services; retrospective search services; hardware and software.

Students in these courses become very familiar with the computer's value to library and bibliographic work, not only in theory but through practice in

144

handling equipment and through observation of actual systems. For example, they can see how the MARC system is utilised in the pioneering Ohio College Library Centre located in Columbus, Ohio. At that Centre the computer can quickly determine which library in Ohio has any book that has been processed through the MARC tapes; the inquiry can be made by remote access from any library in the State which is a co-operating member of the Centre.

In addition to these examples of recent efforts in training persons for scientific libraries and for work in mechanisation, there are many other kinds of specialisation which may be identified. In America, it is now possible for students to enrol in courses which offer intensive preparation in such diverse fields of librarianship as law, medicine, music, art, archives, maps, and rare books. Special courses for primary and secondary school librarians are multiplying. Similar trends appear in Britain. A unique new programme at the University of Maryland prepares black librarians to serve the 'informationally deprived' residents of large cities.

Another point of interest in a discussion of advances in library education is that of progress in teaching methods. Again we will avoid commenting on mere innovations and experiments, but will instead take notice only of those new techniques which appear to further the goals of library training. In this section, specific examples of practice are drawn from American schools. We may begin by citing the distinguished book by Josefa E. Sabor, published by Unesco under the title *Methods of teaching librarianship*. In that volume, Professor Sabor elaborates on several of the topics I am treating in this presentation. One statement by Professor Sabor may well serve to introduce a subject which is of fundamental concern: commenting on the controversy between those who prefer formal class lectures and those who prefer less structured discussions by the students, she says:

'The idea that, with only a series of reading assignments—often mutually contradictory—and comments on them in class, young people will be able, on their own, to subject these texts to the required analysis and criticism and draw valid conclusions is in most cases a delusion.'

This is the traditional position among library educators, and it is by far the most common attitude throughout Europe, Asia, Africa, and South America today. In North America much of classroom instruction has moved away from the formal lecture to devices which involve greater student participation. Let me say why I consider this movement to be progressive, within the context of the North American situation.

We must bear in mind first of all that professional training in North America is concentrated at the postgraduate level; therefore the students have considerable maturity. We must also recall that North American university libraries are well supplied with reading material, in book and journal form, on every subject of the library science curricula. Fortunately for that region, it enjoys the services of full-time professors who have—for the most part—long experience as well as high academic qualification. With such a combination of factors, the hazards suggested by Professor Sabor are minimised.

Students read carefully in advance of the class period several journal articles and parts of books relating to the topic of the day. In the classroom, the professor raises a provocative issue and calls for response from the group. He encourages expression of differing views, even if he personally does not find them convincing or interesting. His objective is more centred on promoting methods of inquiry and criticism than it is with announcing established truths. When this approach is successful, it furthers the goal of preparing librarians who are able to think effectively about changing circumstances, about new kinds of problems, and without reliance on the beliefs of authority figures.

A legitimate question may be asked about the application of this discussion method in countries where reading materials are not abundant. I think it can still succeed as a method, but with an additional burden on the professor— who must then elicit ideas from a small group of source materials, and must draw more extensively on his own background knowledge to fill in numerous details that the discussion may require.

For certain subjects, however, it is clear that a free discussion will have less validity: for example, instruction in cataloguing cannot benefit a great deal from such a technique, since it consists essentially of stating accepted principles or rules and of supervising practice exercises. Discussion appears to be most valuable in topics which have strong subjective elements, such as the place and role of libraries in society, the selection of library materials, and the problems of internal organisation and administration in large libraries. Professor Sabor is entirely justified in her critical comments regarding techniques of teaching book selection along unrealistic lines which have been all too common. A modern approach to this subject is suggested by the outline and reading list in her book. It must be said, however, that even her outline bears traces of the archaic, from the viewpoint of contemporary North American instruction. In selection for popular libraries, we give scarcely any thought to the traditional 'criteria' of judgment about individual books, those criteria which call for evaluation of the author's qualifications or style, nor do we give attention to the physical structure of books under consideration. Just as the library's goal is to meet every informational and educational need of its patrons, the library school's goal is to introduce all the types of materials to suit those needs, and the means of locating comparative evaluations when similar materials are available. For popular libraries, the concept of true value or worth of a book— for example, a novel or book about politics—is not primary. Public interest in a book or topic or a type of material is sufficient value; yet the librarian's judgement is still operative as he tries to identify the works that will best implement the public interest. Another consideration in the contemporary North American book selection course is that of censorship, or intellectual freedom. This is a controversial topic, which lends itself well to class discussion, and also to certain other techniques to which we may now turn.

In dealing with a subjective issue, such as censorship of books or films on the basis of their alleged obscenity, the book selection class may use the technique of case study. This approach, which was introduced to library education by Kenneth Shaffer of Simmons College in Boston, requires detailed study by the class of actual (or imaginary) events relating to the topic. Generally, these events are given to the students without their termination; in other words the students see only the problems imbedded in the occurrence, but not the solution. In some cases there is no solution, since the event is unfinished. Through analysis and discussion, the class attempts to determine what should have happened, or what ought to happen as a conclusion for the case. Case studies are popular in North American schools, particularly in the courses dealing with administration and selection.

A newer instructional device is called simulation. The students take roles or parts and act out situations which might well occur in a library. In book selection, they may act out the roles of a library committee or library board members, when they are meeting to determine whether a popular library should subscribe to the more spectacular 'men's magazines'. Each actor makes the best possible presentation of a certain viewpoint which would exemplify that of a typical member. At the end of the simulation, the rest of the class may offer judgment regarding the most effective and persuasive performances. Simulation is also suitable for practice in talking with patrons who desire reference assistance, in handling problems of personnel, and in other courses. In a more sophisticated form, the simulated drama is recorded on magnetic tape or even on video tape, so that the actors may observe their own presentations.

I would like to emphasise that such activity is worth pursuing only if substantial preparation accompanies it. Students learn to improvise and respond within the context of the simulation performance—and this is valuable as a prologue to life experience—but they will learn very little unless they come to the class with full knowledge of the issues and of the literature regarding those issues. Discussion, case-study, and simulation may all be viewed as means of bringing into sharp focus what the student has already studied.

Certain teaching techniques have come into use because they are seen as time savers. The trend toward expansion of the postgraduate study period has brought with it attempts to reduce the amount of time which is spent by students (and professors) on the mastery of each subject. In particular this is true of the most basic subjects. One approach has been through self-study. For example, at Kent State University elementary instruction in cataloguing, reference, selection and library organisation is available in regular classes or, as an option, through guided self-study which leads to proficiency examinations. The industrious student can thereby cover the content of one or two full terms by study at home during vacation periods and in whatever spare time he can devote to the project. At the University of Wisconsin, similar self-study courses are presented through the device of 'programmed learning'. In one sense, these American innovations are simply affirmations of older world-wide practice, in which university students work independently in preparation for examinations; the novelty—the advance—is through the systematic guidance now being given to the self-learner.

It is now common in the United States to find university courses offered via home television. We have not made much use of this medium for teaching library science, however; although the University of Illinois has developed a television course in children's literature. Television is used at the University of Pittsburgh for instruction within the library school building. This is known as 'closed-circuit' telecasting. Its purpose is to make possible the accommodation of very large classes (several hundred students, in some cases) without losing visual proximity to the professor and the materials he is showing. I would view as progressive the potentiality of television for bringing home instruction to persons who would otherwise not have access to library studies; and I would view as progressive that aspect of closed-circuit telecasting which facilitates demonstration and illustration through close views—but I am not sure that dealing with very large masses of students is itself an 'advance' in library training.

So-called visual aids are in regular use among professors in North American schools. Most schools maintain collections of colour slides, transparencies, films, filmstrips and other pictorial materials; these are in some manner projected on to screens in the classroom to illustrate facets of numerous courses. Among the many films which are available on loan for library schools, special interest has been shown in those which illustrate the operation of computers and which describe mechanised information retrieval. Another popular group of films relates to the functioning of primary school libraries, or 'media centres' as they are now called in the United States. The range of available films touches upon virtually every topic of the library training curriculum.

Although newer methods of teaching, such as discussion and visual presentations, have tended to reduce dependence on textbooks, such books continue to be published and to be used. Indeed, it is a sign of progress that so many modern textbooks are available, in English if not in many other languages. Fine new series of texts are coming from the presses of McGraw-Hill and Libraries Unlimited, in the United States; from Hafner, London House, Pergamon, Lockwood, and Bingley in Britain. In both countries, the library associations are also active in producing textbooks. A serious problem for the emerging countries is the lack of library science textbook material in local languages, but even certain European languages do not provide sufficient scope for the purposes of instruction in librarianship.

Turning to a new topic, it is interesting to observe the emphasis now being given to research within schools of librarianship. Again I draw my examples from the United States. Several library schools have established, in recent years, organised centres for research in library problems. Such centres are concerned with two functions: collecting of specialised, unusual materials and publishing the results of original research. Among the first of these research centres were those in the University of Illinois and in Case Western Reserve University (Cleveland); in the late 1960s research centres were created in the

University of California (Berkeley), University of Pittsburgh, Kent State University, and Indiana University. Some library schools have initiated research centres that deal intensively with certain well-defined areas of librarianship: for example, we have the Urban Library Research Centre of the University of Pittsburgh, and the new Centre for the Study of Ethnic Publications (non-English writing in America) at Kent State. All these research centres are valuable because of the investigations they carry out, and also because of the opportunity which they present to the students for involvement in actual scientific investigation of library questions.

While British schools have not yet created such research centres, at least two schools—Sheffield and The Polytechnic of North London—have emphasised staff research and have been successful in gaining outside funds for many projects.

Let me mention just one other country in this connection. The Unesco Delhi Conference of 1960 urged that library schools 'actively take up research on library problems'. The concept is certainly going to spread to library schools in every nation, because of its obvious relevance and usefulness.

Faced with the complexity of librarianship today, no one would suppose that a librarian has completed his professional studies upon receipt of his diploma or degree from a library school. There is world-wide progress in provision of additional training for practising librarians, so that they may benefit from new developments and thinking in librarianship. I shall mention only a few examples.

The South African Library Association and the University of South Africa are expanding their long-standing series of summer courses for librarians to include advanced topics. In Thailand, a very impressive series of seminars—or 'workshops'—which began in 1956 is increasing in scope; those workshops offer from 10 days to two months of advanced study for librarians in service. A select group of librarians in Indonesia were invited to advanced seminars held in 1969 (two months in duration) and 1970 (three months); it is planned to hold these seminars each year. A Unesco Seminar on electron data processing in libraries was conducted in the Federal Republic of Germany, at the University of Regensburg, from 13–18 April 1970. Fifty participants represented 17 countries. Ibadan University has also conducted information science seminars.

The Inter-American Library School in Medellin, Colombia, has been active in arranging seminars for Latin American librarians. Six special courses for medical librarians have been presented, the most recent being in 1970, from July through November. In June of this year an elaborate seminar was conducted in Medellin on the subject of automation in libraries, under sponsorship of the Organisation of American States. Another seminar on library service in primary and secondary schools was held earlier this year. Elsewhere in South America, the University of Guyana held a three-day seminar for experienced head librarians in May of 1970. It was the first such event in that new nation.

Important programmes in continuing education have been presented at the

Royal School of Librarianship in Copenhagen. Unesco sponsored a course held in Copenhagen from May through October 1966, which was attended by 18 participants from Asia, Africa, and Latin America. The purpose was to give basic training to promising persons already engaged in library work who had not had the advantage of formal study in librarianship.

Another notable seminar was conducted in Copenhagen during 1968: it was specifically for individuals who teach library courses themselves. Fifteen persons from Africa, Asia, and Latin America were brought to Denmark, with results generally thought to be very satisfactory.

Another seminar for teachers of librarianship was presented at the University of Delhi, in 1966.

A great variety of short courses and seminars for librarians are available each year in Great Britain, sponsored by the Library Association, the Association of Special Libraries and Research Bureaux, and individual universities. Some of the topics covered in 1970 were subject cataloguing, British government publications, mechanisation, microfilm, management, bookselling, social science literature and chemical literature.

In the United States, a massive stimulus to continuing education came with the Higher Education Act, passed by the Congress in 1965. A provision of this legislative act made possible the financing by the government of hundreds of seminars. These have been generally called 'institutes'. While funds are diminishing from this source, there are still 28 institutes scheduled for 1971–2, ranging from two days to one full year in duration.

While viable activity in continuing education is not yet as universal as we would wish, there are encouraging plans being formulated in certain nations which have not yet been able to sponsor such events. For instance, an article published in 1970 sets forth a systematic scheme of further education for librarians in Czechoslovakia.

Now let us give brief notice to three final aspects of progress in training for librarianship: student involvement in governance, co-operation among library schools, and the development of international perspectives.

In most countries, the concept of university students taking part in the governance of their university would seem very curious. In the United States, however, there has been considerable effort in the past five or six years to give students a voice in the policy decisions of their institutions. In American library schools it is not unusual for students to have a place on the governing council—in partnership with professors and administrators—and the result appears to be most beneficial. When professors and students share the responsibility for making changes in curriculum and policy, a better rapport develops in the school 'community' and there is less student dissatisfaction. I would hope that this practice, which simply acknowledges that students are also citizens in the school, will become widespread; but I do not have evidence of such a trend in other nations.

Co-operation among library schools appears to be rudimentary. I am not aware of systematic efforts by two or more schools to share resources or programmes. However, there are associations of library schools in Canada, United States, and Latin America which provide a means of communication among library educators, a forum in which common opinion can be expressed, and a potential base for setting of standards in the profession. The full potential of such associations—as of co-operation in general—is far from realisation.

Our final topic is international concerns of library schools and library educators. Essentially we are speaking now of any activity within the scope of library training which extends beyond the borders of a single country. The oldest manifestation of such international concerns seems to be 'study abroad': students going from their native country to another country which is better equipped to give the kind of library training desired. Another aspect is 'comparative librarianship', the study of libraries and library problems among several countries; this subject is becoming most visible in library school curricula of North America and Great Britain. An interest in comparative librarianship is often supported by the acquisition of source materials about libraries from countries which are of particular interest to each school. Two noteworthy examples of such international collections of library source material are at the University of Pittsburgh and Pratt Institute in Brooklyn, New York. Systematic exchange of publications often accompanies the development of such international collections. For instance my University sends copies of American library annual reports to the College of Librarianship in Wales and to the Bibliothèque National, Paris, in return for copies of British and French library reports. We also exchange materials with Chulalongkorn University, with the University of the Philippines, and with the University of Malta.

An ultimate stage in the international concept is found in the creation of regional study and research centres whose governance and finance is shared by several nations. Through Unesco, IFLA, and other international organisations, some encouraging steps have been taken in this direction. The Inter-American Library School in Colombia is now in its second decade, endeavouring to help meet the library training needs of all Latin-America. In 1967 the School for Librarians, Archivists and Documentalists was formed in Senegal, at Dakar University, with the financial assistance of Unesco. This school has the task of training librarians from all French-speaking Africa. Currently under discussion among librarians in South-East Asia is the possibility of a regional school to serve seven countries. An idea of even larger scope, which would develop a chain of regional schools under central direction by Unesco, has been debated in IFLA for two years.

So we come to the end of our survey. All the advances which we have examined contribute toward the fulfilment of major professional goals. Through expansion of postgraduate training facilities, and through extension of time which the postgraduate student may spend in his studies, we have moved towards establishing a proper place and scope for the professional curriculum. Through an increase in kinds of specialised training we have provided more opportunity for educating librarians who will work with particular types of

151

readers. By utilising new teaching methods and devices, we are improving the quality of education and saving the time of both student and professor. By systematic research into library problems, schools of librarianship are adding to the knowledge base of the profession and giving students the opportunity to participate in actual research. Through multiplication of seminars, workshops, and institutes, library schools are helping to bring awareness of current developments to practising members of the profession. In co-operative efforts, library schools are beginning to establish means for communicating among themselves, for making policy and standards, and for sharing resources. Through various approaches which focus on international concerns, library educators are removing boundaries from their curricula and from the thinking of their students. And in the development of regional training schools there is the splendid hope of a world-wide community for library education, in which every nation will be equally privileged to participate in the progress of the library profession.

8   NATIONAL LIBRARIES

(a)   Report on National Libraries Papers

H. LIEBAERS and D. ANDERSON

M. N. NAGARAJ, *India*

Dr. Liebaers said that the objectives of a national library can be best achieved when it has drawn up a list of functions which a national library system should perform. From among the list of functions priorities should be identified. It should not be forgotten that we are all conditioned by the situations existing in our libraries. Unesco, in 1958, convened a Seminar on European National Libraries. This was the first critical view of the roles of national libraries within the general framework of the projection of their objectives. The outcome of the Seminar held at Vienna has been very well reviewed by Kurt Wormann. After a period of inertia, national libraries had become conscious of their roles. Kenneth Humphreys, in his paper published in *Libri,* outlined the functions of the modern national library.

Dorothy Anderson then said that a national library system as such had not up till then existed in Britain. The various functions of the national library had been covered by many organisations, leading to duplication of effort. A government command paper provided for the British Museum Library, the National Reference Library for Science and Invention, the National Central Library, the National Lending Library for Science and Technology and the British National Bibliography to come under one umbrella to be known as the British Library. The Reference section was to be in Bloomsbury; the Lending section at Boston Spa. An organisational committee had been set up and planning officers had been appointed.

Discussion

Uganda: The problem in our country is to make the resources available to develop library services. Is it necessary to have an apex for the various objectives?

DA: A national library system is essential, but not necessarily a national library.

Liebaers: Basically there is no difference between developed and undeveloped countries.

Iran: How about HMSO Publications?

DA: The British Museum is receiving all HMSO Publications; the BNB is including only a few.

Gill: In the West Indies we have a special problem where books written by West Indians and on West Indies are published in Britain.

Liebaers: In our countries 30% of books relating to our interests are published abroad.

Nigeria: Co-ordination is very necessary for the proper functioning of any of the plans.

DA: Fourteen planning officers are working on the master plan for the British Library.

Kenya: The bookseller should, if he is selling books about the country, be made to send a copy to the library.

DA: The possibilities of gift should be explored.

Snape: BNB has been a commercial undertaking and it has had to pay its way.

Urquhart: We have in national libraries a bogey of legal deposit; all the materials received are not useful.

Nagaraj: The problem in India differs. The area of the country and the languages spoken pose a problem. Identifying the publications and getting them to the national library under the Act is a formidable task. We have no penal clauses in the Act.

Liebaers: The penal clauses do not help; we must educate the publishers about the advantages of a legal deposit and publicise their material by way of national bibliographies, documentation lists, etc.

DA: The publishers sometimes send as many as 40 free copies to various libraries, review journals, etc.; it is odd that they should quibble at one for legal deposit.

Liebaers: During the International Book Year we should explore the possibilities of a fruitful dialogue between the librarians on one hand and the printers, publishers and readers on the other.

(b)   IFLA Section on National and University Libraries: Report

Mrs. RITA PANKHURST

Both meetings of this section were held in the Local History Library on Tuesday morning, 31 August. They consisted of papers, most of which had been previously circulated, followed, at the first session, by discussion.

The first meeting, held jointly with the Committee on Rare and Precious Books, opened with an introduction by Dr. C. Reedijk, Chief Librarian, Royal Library, The Hague, followed by a summary of his paper, 'Inquiry into the present state of historical research in bibliology and librarianship: Final Report.'

The results of the inquiry were based on a questionnaire mailed to 114 national libraries or library associations in 58 countries of which 43 from 36 countries replied.

Dr. Reedijk outlined the substance of the questionnaire and noted that response did not warrant drawing extensive general conclusions. Nevertheless the following points could be made:

(1) Useful information had been collected on 155 agencies active in the field covered by the enquiry and, by coincidence, the same number of periodicals had been reported as dealing with it.
(2) Good progress had been made in cataloguing manuscripts, incunabula and early printed books.
(3) Historical research in bibliology and librarianship was not being carried out extensively; these 'historical' disciplines were somewhat neglected at library schools and so was the training of codicologists and incunabulists.
(4) Librarians were dissatisfied with the present state of affairs and many offered useful suggestions to be followed up.

Dr. Reedijk ended optimistically with the view that: 'the complex of disciplines regarded as the historical and cultural conscience of the profession is by no means extinct'.

In the course of the discussion the following comments were made:

(1) The Florence flood disaster had revealed a scarcity of experts in the field under discussion. IFLA should develop exchanges of experts, encourage trainees and develop international standards in these fields of librarianship.
(2) The term 'incunabula' should be flexibly interpreted with reference to early printed books of countries where printing began several centuries later than in Europe.

This paper was of particular interest to me in the light of Ethiopia's heritage of manuscripts and the urgent need to preserve and register them. International standards would offer welcome guide lines; expert assistance and training facilities for prospective Ethiopian codicologists and incunabulists. Incidentally a catalogue of books printed in Ethiopia between the beginning of printing there in the 1880s and 1936 was entitled *Ethiopian incunabula* (compiled by Stephen Wright).

The second paper, by Mr. Kenneth Garside, Librarian of King's College, London, was on 'the professional organisation of academic libraries'.

This paper, too, was based on a questionnaire. It was distributed to academic librarians in 29 countries from 22 of which there were responses.

Mr. Garside surveyed the position of academic libraries in national library associations; standing conferences of academic libraries, national and regional; and governmental and quasi-governmental bodies.

He concluded that:

(1) Academic librarians in countries with well-developed library systems required a forum either through a separate association or in a separate section of the national association.
(2) In addition, in such countries, there was a need for a voluntary or government-sponsored policy making body consisting either exclusively or partly of head librarians. In his view government-sponsored bodies were preferable as they tended to attract better government support.

155

(3) In developing countries standing conferences could bring great benefits in co-operation and exchanges of experience.

The discussion period was taken up by further information about such organisations in different countries.

The paper was a useful summary of the state of academic library organisation in many parts of the world. It seemed to me that point (3) applied equally to all countries, as much as points (1) and (2).

Miss W. E. S. Coops, Chief, Library Section, Unesco Library and Documentation Services, then reported on a third questionnaire requesting statistical data on national libraries to which 34 out of 110 national libraries responded.

Her conclusions were:

(1) A statistical survey based on data received would be of limited use given the disparity between the national libraries and the poor response to the questionnaire.

(2) Information from the questionnaire could, however, be used selectively to detect trends and make use of data in support of budget requests, etc., for libraries operating in comparable circumstances.

(3) The alternative next steps could be:
    (a) Publication; or
    (b) Storage in a clearing house—possibly the Royal Library, The Hague, which had offered to store and service it.

The discussion centred on the options presented under item (3) with opinion evenly divided.

In either event it was most useful that such a survey, however incomplete, had already taken place and to know that the information would become available in one or other form. The clearing house would seem the better option because:

(1) Information would become available very soon.

(2) It could be subjected to regular and incidental revision without too much expense.

(3) It would encourage librarians to be less inhibited in the information they supplied and in their comments.

The second session of the section was devoted to planning, programming and budgeting in national and university libraries.

Mr. Thomas R. Buckman, University Librarian and President of the Association of Research Libraries, summarised a paper, unfortunately not available, on the 'Programme, planning and budgeting system, or PPBS'.

He outlined the characteristics of the system, whose distinctive features were:

(1) Fixing attention on primary objectives, i.e. units of service in a library.

(2) Categorising and sub-categorising these.

(3) Programming for their implementation.

(4) Devising control and reporting methods for measuring achievement.

Mr. Buckman cautioned the audience that PPBS was not a panacea and could not replace judgement; he noted that it could be applied on a limited scale, that it needed time and indicated that, to a limited extent, it was being put into operation on an experimental basis by several library systems in the United States. He listed conferences where the programme approach had been discussed and gave additional references.

Mr. Etienne Dennery, General Administrator of the National Library, Paris, described the 'Application of PPBS in French libraries' in connection with the preparation for the sixth five-year plan. Despite problems, such as those arising over the choice of indicators and the fact that there had not yet been time for evaluation and control, Mr. Dennery came out strongly in favour of PPBS. He thought it brought clarity and coherence into library planning and budgeting.

Mr. B. P. Kanevski, Head of International Book Exchange, Moscow, described planning and budgeting procedures in the USSR. He noted that state planning and definition of objectives had existed in the Soviet Union since the 1930s; he stressed the democratic nature of decision-making about these objectives and pointed out that evaluation and control were regular features of library as well as other planning.

Long-term planning in the USSR was regularly practised and the Lenin Library had forecast its likely development to 1990.

The final paper, by Mr. F. de Vrieze, Curator of the Royal Library, Brussels, described 'PPBS in operation in the Royal Library'. It was introduced by government decree in 1970 after a consultative group had studied the system and had offered to collaborate. He described the various steps taken and was positive about the benefits despite qualifications, especially on categorisation.

Mr. de Vrieze believed PPBS would lead to more complete and meaningful library statistics, especially about readership and that it would stimulate research into evaluation of previously sacrosanct aspects of certain programmes (e.g. the catalogue).

There was no time for discussion.

It is clear that the programme approach to planning and budgeting advocated in the course of this session is more rational and scientific than the traditional approach.

It is also clear that the new system is still in its experimental stages and will require further refinement.

Once the exploratory stage has been passed, this system promises to gain wide acceptance and I should be glad to attempt to apply it at the Haile Selassie I University Library, although the University would require plans and estimates presented in the traditional form.

The advantages seem to be that:

(1) It is a clearer and more pragmatic instrument of internal organisation and administration.

(2) It identifies problems more specifically.

(3) It offers a more intelligible justification for greater funds.

L

General suggestions

(1) More time should be allowed for discussion.

(2) Two-page summaries of all papers should be available in advance.

(3) Without wishing to denigrate the valiant work done by the librarians-turned-translators, it might be worth the expense to obtain professional translators for languages such as Russian from which a large majority of the audience appear to require translations.

The pre-conference seminar

The limited number of participants sharing a hall of residence was conducive to stimulating discussion during sessions and outside them.

The dichotomy between the concerns of the participants and those of the lecturers became immediately apparent.

Nevertheless, personally, I was grateful to have the opportunity to hear directly from experts engaged in the fields they discussed of recent developments in advanced librarianship. It is important that *all* librarians, even those working in the least developed of countries, should have some inkling of recent advances on the various library fronts. If they cannot apply them today, they may wish to plan for them tomorrow.

It was also a great privilege to be able to meet and talk to, at Dale Hall and during the seminar and conference, so many distinguished librarians whose names had been familiar only in print.

No less useful was the opportunity of meeting colleagues with problems so very similar to one's own, differing often only in degree. It helped to see one's own problems in proportion, and strengthened a belief in the need for exchanges of views and co-operation between the developing countries themselves.

The exhibition

This contributed considerably to an understanding of the themes of both conferences, especially as so much useful literature was available free to digest properly at a later date.

Upon further reflection, I agree with Mr. Soosai's suggestion that IFLA should consider establishing a section, or, perhaps something less formal and permanent, along the lines suggested by Mr. Ofori, on librarianship in developing countries.

Much could be learned from the techniques used in developing countries, and for underprivileged minorities. Although there are special *additional* problems in developing countries, almost all aspects of librarianship normally discussed at IFLA meetings are, of course, also relevant.

9 NATIONAL TECHNICAL LIBRARIES

(a) Recent Developments

D. J. URQUHART

Director, National Lending Library for Science and Technology,
Boston Spa, Yorks

The first libraries began over 2,000 years ago. At that time and for a long time afterwards it took a great deal of human effort to make a copy of a book. Moreover, the transport system for centuries was slow and uncertain and the rate of social change was not appreciable. It is not, therefore, surprising that at first major libraries were reference libraries more concerned with preserving documents for posterity than anything else. This outlook did not clash to any great extent with the needs of the library users who were mainly scholars reading for their own intellectual satisfaction. These scholars were, as a rule, prepared to travel to remote libraries and pursue their studies in a leisurely fashion when they arrived.

But in the last five centuries the interweave of social and technological changes has altered the library requirements. Possibly the key to these changes was the development of printing in the western world. The power to multiply the copies of reports on observations and theories about natural phenomena made it more possible for these to bear fruit in other minds. So a chain reaction began which is now called the scientific revolution. In this chain reaction on average each idea gave birth to another idea approximately every 15 years so that, in this sort of period, the output of scientific literature doubled and then doubled again in the next 15 years or so.

At first the library problem of scientific literature was quite small. In 1665 there were two scientific periodicals and they began only in that year. Newton could have, and probably did, read all that was written about science in his time. But as the scientific explosion continued, this became more and more impossible. New ways of handling scientific literature developed. To a great extent periodicals replaced books and special guides to the contents of periodicals appeared. The social changes which flowed from scientific developments changed the nature of scientific activity itself. Scientists ceased to be only learned men studying for their own intellectual satisfaction and became more and more servants of a society which employed them and wanted the produce of their labours. These changes altered the relationship between learned men and their libraries which had gone on almost unchanged for some 2,000 years.

The individual changes seemed small in themselves and often they were primarily a change of emphasis. Periodicals became more important than books. It was more economic to move the documents to the reader than the reader to the documents. It was more important to make today's information available today than to preserve yesterday's information for posterity.

The national libraries which had grown in importance in the nineteenth century found great difficulties in adjusting themselves to these changes of emphasis. Those libraries which had become depositories for ancient documents had also become the depositories for library traditions and these they could not easily shed. So to meet their needs, the scientists and technologists created their own libraries based on their societies and institutions. When the continuous expansion of the output of scientific literature made this difficult, the scientists sought a national solution and, in many of the more developed countries, national technical libraries developed separately from the national libraries.

Such has been the path of national library development in the United Kingdom. In the middle of the last century, Panizzi at the British Museum Library was hoping to index all scientific periodicals. At the same time the Royal Society was preparing a catalogue of scientific periodicals. It used the British Museum collection to supplement the Royal Society's own holdings. At the beginning of the twentieth century, the major scientific libraries were undoubtedly those of the learned societies and professional institutions and the Patent Office Library. By 1948 when the Royal Society Scientific Information Conference was held, most of the learned societies and professional institutions were finding it increasingly difficult to keep pace with the scientific output. That conference passed a resolution recommending the Government to give increased support to the main national scientific libraries, in particular the Science Museum Library and the Patent Office Library.

In the United Kingdom the wheel has now nearly gone full circle. Under the proposals which are now being discussed, the library which was the National Lending Library for Science and Technology, which developed from the Science Museum Library and the Patent Office Library, is to become linked with the British Museum Library in a new organisation which is to be called the British Library.

The important point is that it is not necessary to have separate national technical libraries provided that the library techniques adopted permit material to be made available almost as soon as it is published, and providing that the majority of items can be made available where scientists work.

These requirements make it necessary to consider an entirely new approach to library records. It is not sufficient for us to say 'Let us use computers', any more than it was sufficient some time ago to say 'Let us use typewriters'. If you ask what difference the industrial revolution made to library technology, the answer appears to be that before the industrial revolution library records were written out by hand, and now they are written out by hand and then typed.

What is necessary is an entirely new approach to library records. It seems strange when you think about it that many academic libraries spend so much human effort describing the books they hold when the periodicals they hold are somewhat vaguely described as 'volume 1 and onwards'. For the contents of periodicals most scientists and technologists are prepared to use the published guides. Why should they not also do this when they require something in the nature of a book? If this attitude were generally adopted, then the records of the holdings of most libraries would have no special importance from a bibliographical point of view, and the research worker would be able to ask the essential question: what exists on the topic in which he is interested, rather than the question: what does a particular library hold on this topic? Of course it is important that there should be comprehensive bibliographies of the output of particular regions but all that most libraries appear to need is some simple system of knowing where the items they hold have been shelved.

This approach visualises that there will be some simple arrangements for supplying readers with publications which are not immediately available in the libraries they use, and clearly the development of a suitable system to achieve this is important. Such a system must recognise that no library can ever be self-sufficient and it is becoming more and more difficult even for the complex of libraries in any country to be self-sufficient in the publications of the world. Thus, we must seek to establish an efficient system which would enable the major libraries in one country to obtain publications rapidly from the major libraries in other countries. The development of such a system has been pioneered by IFLA, but it appears to me that the existing arrangements need a complete overhaul to provide a more rapid service. The United Kingdom is prepared to contribute to such a system, for it has established in the National Lending Library a system for dealing with most requests the day they are received.

This speed of service depends mainly upon two factors. First, the procedures used within the NLL permit most items to be found without consulting any record. Secondly, the issue system used eliminates accounting and clerical operations within the library when a request is received. For instance, if a charge is to be made for postage or photocopying, this has already been paid when the form is dispatched from the requesting library. A fuller description of the issue procedure used is given in one of the papers for the IFLA conference. A visual demonstration of the use of prepaid forms was seen at the NLL stand in the conference exhibition.

(b) Comments on Dr. Urquhart's Paper: National Technical Libraries

Dr. Urquhart, in his paper, emphasised that the requirements of scientific activity necessitated that publications should become available as soon as they were published both within the library and throughout the country. If the national library could achieve this, there was no need for a separate national technical library. However, should the national library be unable to do so, then a national technical library appeared to be essential.

The following points were made in the ensuing discussion:

(1) It is essential that the total resources within a country should be made available for use to the fullest extent. This gives economy.

(2) As long as the most recent scientific and technical literature can be made available rapidly by an institution within a country (developing or developed), there is no need to establish a separate national technical library. Any institution which can perform these functions should be allowed to do so. This also applies to the establishment of national scientific documentation centres.

(3) It is hoped that the Bill to establish the British Library will be passed in 1972. This Bill will nationalise the existing British national libraries including the British National Bibliography Office. In the meantime an Organising Committee, including librarians and the heads of the institutions to be nationalised, has been set up to discuss problems, find methods of simplifying the work to be undertaken by the British Library, to re-organise the set-up where necessary, etc.

(4) Elaborate records of books do not prevent books being lost. However, records are made to show what is available within a library. Although the aim is to make materials available as rapidly as possible, this should not be done at the expense of creating proper bibliographic records.

(5) There is no complete collection of British scientific and technical literature.

(6) Do not duplicate existing services, e.g. abstracting, indexing, etc. Check first before undertaking such a service. However, contribute to existing services by feeding them with information about local publications so that those indexing know what is available in their subject field. It is the responsibility of each country to give abstracts and indexes of publications in its national language, in an international language, and also to provide translation services.

(7) National libraries should fill gaps in the book resources within its country. The other libraries should then fit into this collecting pattern. Special libraries should question the need of buying certain publications. It might be preferable for them to borrow these publications on inter-library loan. National libraries should lend such materials to other libraries. This would cut down on unnecessary duplicate purchase of materials. Both national and local libraries should be used, as this would provide an improved library service.

(8) Inter-library loans would not cut down sales of a publication appreciably because people in the publishing country wish to see the publication for themselves.

10 INTERNATIONAL CO-OPERATION

(a) Recent Developments in Unesco Library and Documentation Activities

Miss W. E. S. COOPS

Chief, Library Section, Unesco Library and Documentation Services

Library and documentation work is of necessity international in scope. We cannot work on our own, but rely on inter-library co-operation, and have become gradually internationalists in practice. It is fitting that the library profession be recognised as of basic importance for the intellectual, artistic and technological development of mankind.

According to the Constitution of Unesco the aims of the Organisation are 'to contribute to peace and security by promoting collaboration among the nations through education, science and culture'. To attain these objectives Unesco is—amongst other ways and means—called upon to:

—collaborate in the work of advancing the mutual knowledge and understanding of people through all means of mass communication;

—maintain, increase and diffuse knowledge by assuring the conservation and protection of the world's inheritance of books, by encouraging co-operation amongst the nations in all branches of intellectual activity, including the exchange of publications and other materials of information and by initiating methods of international co-operation calculated to give the people of all countries access to the printed and published materials produced by any of them.

The Department of Documentation, Libraries and Archives grew out of the Libraries Division in the Department of Cultural Activities. It is symbolic for the great importance which Unesco through the years has come to attach to the role of library and documentation work that a separate Department, a part of the Communication Sector of the Unesco Secretariat, was established in 1967.

The International Advisory Committee on Documentation, Libraries and Archives (IACODLA) advises the Director General on questions of documentation, libraries and archives in general, and in particular those related to subject fields of interest to Unesco.

The promotion and co-ordination of research and international co-operation is undertaken by providing information and issuing publications relating to the improvement of documentation, library and archives services as well as of exchange of publications; by co-operating with, and consulting the international non-governmental organisations and other international and national institutions active in the field of documentation, libraries and archives, by fostering the co-ordination of their activities, and by granting them subventions.

In the Exhibition of Library Technology you will find copies of recent Unesco publications and periodicals, such as the second edition of C. V. Penna's *Planning of library and documentation services*. Due to appear shortly there are *A draft model law on archives*, F. M. Gardner's *Public Library legislation: a comparative study, Bibliographical services throughout the world, 1965–1969*.

I should also like to draw your attention to a document prepared by F. N. Withers: *Standards for library service* (COM/WS/151, October 1970) which may be requested from the Department.

Studies and research projects presently undertaken include the planning of documentation and library services, professional education of library personnel and of teachers of library science, the development of special teaching techniques, and the initiation of library users; the application of new methods, including the automation of information processing and the standardisation of library and documentation techniques and terminology.

Encouragement is given to the establishment of regional and national research and training centres, and a bibliography will be prepared on the training of technicians.

A consultation with a group of experts on the promotion of research and development in documentation and librarianship took place in June 1971. Advice was sought on a project for a computer-based system for the collection, storage and dissemination of information on research originating from member states of Unesco, and from international organisations. The discussions were guided by the FID report *Project ISORID; international information system on research in documentation* and by Unesco's programme on the state-of-the-art surveys in documentation. The consultants recommended that Unesco should develop, in close co-operation with the relevant international and national organisations (both governmental and non-governmental), a system for collecting, processing and disseminating information on research and development (R+D) in documentation which could also be regarded as an important element of Unesco's UNISIST programme; the co-operation of Unesco member states should be sought in the creation and development of the proposed system and in providing the input for it in the form of information on research and development projects completed, in progress or planned in their countries and on research and development reports; and also co-operation of member states in providing copies of research reports free of charge for setting up a special collection of reports in the Unesco Library; these reports should be processed by the Unesco Computerised Documentation Service. All information thus received by Unesco should be communicated to FID which would provide a referral service in this field; FID should provide the Unesco Computerised Documentation Service, which will process the R+D reports, with all the necessary supplementary information; Unesco should provide, on request, information on R+D projects and reports in the form of current printed indexes and searches; it should not, as a general rule, distribute copies of reports, but should encourage its member states to establish national centres to discharge this function.

The group also recommended that Unesco should commission state-of-the-art surveys in priority fields making use of the collection of R+D reports. Subjects to be covered might include: decision models for acquisition of materials, vocabularly control, relevance and user evaluation, information networks, and cost effectiveness of documentation activities.

The Unesco Archives are a section of the Unesco Library and Documentation Services where a complete collection of Unesco documents as well as publications can be consulted. The Archives indexes them all, and also publications sponsored or subsidised by Unesco. Indexing is at present limited in depth, with the exception of Executive Board Decisions and general Conference resolutions. The former are listed in the systematic indexes to the ARC/Lists issued annually, the latter are covered by a separate index.

The *List of Unesco documents and publications* is produced six times a year in four sections: (1) Unesco documents issued in Paris headquarters. (2) Unesco publications published in Paris. (3) Documents and publications issued by Unesco regional centres or offices. (4) Materials published by other publishers.

Microfiches of all experts' reports on the field missions undertaken by them are held in the Archives, and also in the regional documentation offices in Bangkok, Santiago de Chile and Dakar.

The Computerised Documentation Service of Unesco is still in its preparatory stage but we are confident that it will become operative before the end of 1971. The CDS uses an ICL 1902-A, a third-generation computer which can be compared to the IBM 360.

The decision to establish the CDS was taken when the importance of such a service in Unesco was realised. Valuable services could be rendered to member states if Unesco would devise a system that would serve as a model for comparable situations to demonstrate the advantages of using modern techniques and as a medium for training.

In January 1970 preliminary work began on systems analysis, charting the flow of work through the projected service, systems design, and computer programming. An amended MARC II format was selected, compatible with existing automated documentation systems (ILO, Library of Congress, BNB). A Unesco list of descriptors was drawn up, partly based on the Aligned list used by ILO, FAO, OECD, and several national organisations.

It is estimated that in 1971–2 the CDS will process some 30,000 Unesco documents and publications, covering all currently produced documents and publications, plus a selection of about 6,000 items from the retrospective collection in the Unesco Archives.

Indexers' worksheets are typed out on a Friden 7102 Communication Terminal which creates a hard copy for proof-reading and a punched paper tape for input in the computer.

Master records (main entry, title, date of publication in ascending and descending sequence, language, country of publication, subject entry or descriptor, series entry, etc.) can be provided in a variety of formats. Listings can take the form of a simple answer to a query, a bibliographic list or a complete print-out of the files. They are produced daily on the computer line pointer at 1,350 lines a minute (upper case, without diacritical signs). Documents such as the *List of Unesco documents and publications* will be produced through computer-driven photocomposition, allowing for various type fonts, diacritical and special characters.

Processed documents are microfiched by the photographic laboratory of the Centre National de la Recherche Scientifique in Paris. UN microfiche standards are used.

The CDS will thus be able to produce current and retrospective indexes, bibliographic listings on request, retrieve information, provide selective dissemination of information (SDI), and microfiche or hard copy of processed documents, not only for headquarters and field staff, but also for member states, UN organisations and other intergovernmental organisations as well as non-governmental organisations and national institutions.

In co-operation with the regional Unesco offices, the Unesco Library and Documentation Services will explore the possibility of organising workshops for the staff of depository libraries and other interested institutions, with a view to helping them to make greater use of, and ensure wider dissemination of, Unesco documents and publications in member states.

The Unesco programme for 1971–2, as approved by the 16th Session of the General Conference last year, contains various activities in the library field.

The *Education Sector* provides educational information and documentation services through the International Bureau of Education (IBE) in Geneva, since 1969 incorporated in Unesco. In the IBE Library particular attention will be given to the acquisition of reference works, national reports on education and comparative studies. Abstracts of educational policy documents will also be obtained from a large number of member states, and consultants will be invited to advise on the development of the IBE Information Service.

In recognition of the essential need of creating national library systems as support for economic and social development, the International Institute of Education Planning (also integrated in Unesco) has included the planning of these systems in its regular courses.

The feasibility study conducted by the *Science Sector* of Unesco and the International Council of Scientific Unions (ICSU) for the establishment of a world science information system (UNISIST) was recently completed and the final study report and a synopsis of it were issued in English, French, Russian and Spanish editions. (UNISIST is a made-up word; the initials do not have any particular significance.)

IFLA, FID and ISO were represented at the meetings held by the Central Committee of the Unesco/ICSU joint project on the communication of scientific information.

A UNISIST Working Group on bibliographic descriptions met six times in

1969–70. Final agreement was reached on the international list of periodical title word abbreviations, rules for citing authors' names, rules for supplementary elements, and character sets.

The establishment of UNISIST is intended to ensure easy access by the world community to the collective store of scientific and technical information through integration and co-operation at all stages of information transfer, and also to reduce unnecessary and costly duplication of information processing. The UNISIST system will be multi-national, multi-disciplinary and multi-functional. As an organisation, UNISIST will require some kind of inter-governmental machinery to co-ordinate and catalise the efforts made towards the harmonisation of information transfer methods. Particular attention will have to be paid to the participation of developing countries in the system, and to their access to it, as well as to the training of information specialists.

It should be stressed that, while UNISIST aims at a world-wide network in scientific and technological information, the elements forming this network consist of national infrastructures, which are the particular concern of the Department of DBA.

The *Sector of Social Sciences, Human Sciences and Culture* contributes to the development of social science information systems based on modern data collection, storage and retrieval techniques. Efforts will be made to link these activities with UNISIST.

The *Communication Sector* is responsible for the programme to promote the free flow of books. One of its main features is the organisation of the International Book Year (IBY) in 1972. Both IFLA and FID have, from the beginning, been closely associated with this project, and they have, and especially IFLA, actively taken part in the preparation of detailed suggestions concerning the IBY and activities related to it. Representatives of IFLA and FID attended the preliminary meetings held in Unesco House, and at the first session of the IBY Planning Committee in April 1971, the IFLA president was elected chairman.

In a description of Unesco's library activities, its own Library and Documentation Services (which include the Unesco Archives) should also be briefly mentioned. It is essentially a reference service for the staff of the Unesco Secretariat. A *Guide* provides concise information on the activities of this Division of the Department of DBA.

Colleagues visiting the Unesco Secretariat are always welcome in the Unesco Library as well as in the Documentation Centres for Education, Social Sciences and Mass Communications.

International library co-operation is furthered by various libraries in the UN system which, in their specific subject fields, seek to promote such co-operation as, e.g. the *International Nuclear Information System* of the International Atomic Energy Agency, or the International Information System for Agriculture which is now being worked out by the Food and Agriculture Organisation of the UN.

International co-operation is also being strengthened by closer co-operation between various agencies in the United Nations family. The Inter-Agency Working Party on Indexing, a sub-committee of the UN Administrative Committee for Co-ordination, was established in 1966, and prepared during its existence several suggestions concerning common standards and measures, for instance, the UN Microfiche standard mentioned above.

In general, the Inter-Agency Working Party on Storage and Retrieval of Documentation is concerned with the co-ordination of the efforts of individual UN agencies in the field of documentation and libraries and the promotion of co-operative inter-agency activities, such as the development of an inter-agency thesaurus of economic and social development terms, a standard inter-agency format for the communication of non-numerial data in machine-readable form, etc.

On 23 and 24 August 1971, the Inter-Agency Working Party on Storage and Retrieval of Documentation met at the invitation of the Inter-Organisation Board (IOB) at the International Labour Office in Geneva. From the draft conclusion I cite that a Task Force should be appointed by the IOB to study the feasibility of establishing a computer-based information system for documentation related to economic and social development. The Task Force should formulate a concept for an overall system, comprising documentation of importance to development generated both inside and outside the UN system. A detailed design and programme for implementation of a sub-system to serve as a prototype for the development of the overall system will be prepared by the Task Force. Initially, the prototype sub-system would relate exclusively to documentation of lasting interest, resulting from the technical co-operation programmes of the UN family of organisations. Purely administrative documents and progress reports would be excluded.

In relation to the general subject of the activities of international libraries, I should like to draw your attention to a paper prepared by Dr. G. Rozsa, the Director of the UN Library in Geneva, on *La spécialisation et l'intégration: quelques aspects du travail d'information des bibliothèques internationales.* The complete text figures as Annex II to Newsletter No. 29 of the Association of International Libraries, recently issued. Copies may be obtained from the Editor, Mr. A. E. Johnson, ILO/CLD, CH–1211 Geneva 22.

Although I have dwelt more particularly on Unesco's own programme activities, I in no way intended to neglect the work done by many other international organisations, also active in the promotion of documentation and library development. May I draw your attention in this respect to the recent re-edition of a document prepared by the Directorate for Scientific Affairs of the Organisation for Economic Co-operation and Development.

The Association of International Libraries is a meeting-ground for staff members of various UN agency libraries and of those of other intergovernmental and non-governmental organisations. Representatives of some of the national institutions specialising in the publications and documents of the international agencies participate in its activities.

Twenty-five years of Unesco experience, and especially the close co-operation with IFLA and other international non-governmental organisations, have taught us that the national and international development of library activities is based upon international co-operation of professional organisations and individual institutions.

I believe that you can also profit from your attendance at this Seminar, the forthcoming IFLA Council meeting and other professional contacts that your present travels may bring you. When you will have returned to your home base, the execution of your daily work may well constitute a link in an ever-strengthening international chain, and the recognition of this fact may contribute to open up a wider perspective for all of us.

(b) International Librarianship

P. HAVARD-WILLIAMS

Dean, Library School, University of Ottawa
Vice-President, International Federation of Library Associations

In 1959, in a contribution to *Unesco Bulletin for Libraries.*
I wrote:
> Since 1945, the most urgent problems in the field of international librarianship have been connected with the role of libraries in furthering fundamental education, the building of library systems in those countries formerly without them and the problem of communication at the level of research and documentation.

This simple statement was based on a perusal of publications during the previous 15 years, in particular, the articles published during this period in the *Unesco Bulletin for Libraries* itself. I was later taken by surprise, when consulting the examination papers of the British Library Association, to find the above sentence quoted, and the candidates asked: 'What do you understand by "international librarianship" and what are the principal developments to which reference is made?' I must confess I had given little attention to what I had meant by 'international librarianship', nor could I indeed have answered the rest of the question! (Nor yet could I have imagined myself talking to an international Unesco seminar on the subject.) The first point, then, is that while one often uses the term 'international librarianship', one really has given to it no special connotation, and one is at some difficulty in defining it.

A second experience, I think, illustrates a further point. In 1964, I attended my first IFLA Conference at Rome. I was quite inexperienced in international work of this kind, and the mere mechanism of behaving at an international

---

[1] Op. cit. v.13, 1959, p. 110.

conference, with different languages, different modes of expression, and different ways of thinking was a problem. Dealing with the technique of simultaneous translation even as a consumer needs some experience to get the best out of the system. I am reminded of the way I was taught concepts of religion. Early in my life, I imagined God to be something like an enormous outsize Anglican archbishop—at least three times the size of an ordinary bishop, and, of course, with every faculty to match. My expectations of the librarians I would meet at an international conference were on similar lines: I somehow expected to find a different breed of librarians, three times as large, ten times as imposing. But it is not like that. Somewhat irreverently I am tempted to say that all one finds is 'the same old lot'—and I do not mean that to be contemptuous, but rather to indicate that international work is done, not by some exceptional kind of unknown librarian species from Mars, but by the librarians we all know in our own countries—librarians who have their own job to do in their own various libraries, librarians who contribute on a national level to the development of professional work in their own countries: librarians who after all are one's colleagues—with others like them working in a similar way each in their own country. I am not saying that there is no such thing as international librarianship: what I am saying is that there is no *mystique* about it, and that I define international librarianship as co-operative activity in the field of librarianship done for the benefit of the individual librarian in the whole of the world, and done frequently by the likes of you and me.

In the 12 years since I wrote that article in the *Unesco Bulletin for Libraries,* preoccupations have changed, though they may still be grouped into (a) general preoccupations; and (b) specialised preoccupations—libraries for the people, and libraries for the specialist (as if specialists were not people). As time goes on, the distinction becomes blurred, but it is still valid, though the manifestations on one side or the other are different from what they were 10 or more years ago. With regard to the blurring of the distinction between libraries for the people and those for the specialist, no more excellent example exists than the city library in which the IFLA Seminar was recently held at Liverpool under the auspices of Unesco, where a group of central specialist services is supported not only by central general service, but also by a network of services right throughout the area of the city. Part of this blurring, too, is evident in the current concern with co-operation (an old preoccupation) and with library networks (a more recent concept). Reading the literature, one has the impression that co-operation exists only as a word in the language of librarianship. You might, however, have a look at an article by the Right Honourable Lester B. Pearson, former Prime Minister of Canada and a Nobel Prize winner, on 'A New Strategy for Global Development'. This speech, reported in the *Unesco Courier* for February 1970[2] summarises the findings of the Pearson Commission which has published its full report as *Partners in Development.* Mr. Pearson is not unaware of the difficulties attending co-

[2] Op. cit. pp. 4–12.

operation. While co-operation in the whole world is more important than ever before, the difference in the rate of development among nations over the past 150 years has caused considerable stress:

'The roots of modern progress reach back to the origin of human civilisation, but its acceleration since the industrial revolution has had an uneven impact and has created serious strains' (p. 6).

These strains have become accentuated with the increasing speed and growth and industrial progress. Against this background, 'the nature of international co-operation for development (has) a tentative groping quality'. Mr. Pearson is talking about co-operation primarily on an economic scale, but in fact this embraces all kinds of human activity. There is a world-wide pre-occupation between north and south, east and west, richer and poorer, industrialised and agricultural.

'. . . the paramount, long-term interest of all nations, rich and poor, is in the creation of a world in which all the resources, human and physical, are put to the greatest possible use.'

In the view of Mr. Pearson,

'This is the vision which should inspire all those who look beyond the anxieties of today to the opportunities of tomorrow' (p. 7).

It is in the light of this point of view that we should be looking at the development of international librarianship. Those of us with experience in this field know all too well its groping, tentative nature. In looking back, however, it is to be hoped that it will create in us the will, the desire, to carry on and develop further what has been so arduously achieved to date.

Librarians are well aware of co-operation. This has been a by-word over the past half-century, as librarians have become more and more conscious of the increasing demands of readers, the increasing volume of publication, and the unwillingness of nations and communities to face up to the financial implications of the best bibliographical services. In this connection, you should read the excellent article of Professor F. W. Saunders in the *Journal of Librarianship*.[3] The problem is complicated, indeed, by the fact that it is in the nature of a library not to be complete. There is no librarian, I am sure, who is prepared to say he has enough money for books, staff and services: and, even less likely, is there any librarian who would say that he (or she) has too much money for books or serials, staff or services. Librarians—as librarians— are, from the nature of their task—poor and hard-up. The concept of co-operation has given them relative strength, and they have drawn on wider resources—whether at the local, or regional, national, or international levels— in order to improve their services to their clients. This kind of outlook has led to the establishment of the Farmington Plan in the United States, the Scandia Plan in the Scandinavian countries, the various forms of co-operation between the libraries in the different regions of Africa—a multitude of co-operative

---

[3] V. 1, no. 4, 1969, pp. 195–209.

ventures exist all over the world to try to meet the demands of scholars and scientists (for it is these last who always get the best treatment) requiring an ever wider range of research materials. There have been, too, co-operative purchasing schemes among public libraries—as in the United Kingdom, for instance—where they have been founded in order to achieve a comprehensive coverage of English books throughout the regions of the country.

In many places, co-operation has been seen as inter-library lending—sometimes a case of librarians banding together in order to lend among themselves what they had not got. There has been something of this situation at a certain level in the United Kingdom, where the great copyright libraries have refused to co-operate in inter-lending, even though other libraries have needed their books and journals for the use of scholars. Fortunately the position is improving, in spite of the parochial attitude of the great universities little prepared to share what they have, even with universities nearby. A striking contrast is found in the position of the National Library and the National Science Library in Canada, which under their respective directors, Mr. Guy Sylvestre and Dr. Jack Brown, are giving important leadership to to the libraries of their country. And, of course, there is the example of the 'warehouse on the moor'—the National Lending Library for Science and Technology—the greater availability of scientific and technical literature is of world-wide importance to international as well as national co-operation.

International lending is not unknown, and has existed for many years, particularly among the countries of Europe on the one hand and between those of the British Commonwealth on the other. But international lending is only a beginning—though an important beginning—to library co-operation on an international scale. The present concern of those who are thinking on this particular scale is on the total resources of systems—total resources in this connection include books, information, technical services, including traditional bibliographical and acquisition services, co-operative cataloguing as well as the technological aspect of the same services in terms of data-processing, and the library application of computers. The development of staff training needs also to be included and the modern technology of buildings in so far as these affect modern building planning.

The notion of library networks is a concept which is going the rounds at present. This indicates a welcome change in Western Europe at least, where academic libraries, public libraries, special libraries, school libraries (if any) have not only been separate, with different philosophies and methods of provision, but have also sought to keep separate. The kind of collaborative effort in Birmingham, for instance, between two university libraries (Birmingham and Aston) and the Birmingham Public Library would have been unthinkable 20 years ago, not because it would not have been possible (though at a manual, rather than an automated, level) but because the whole mental outlook of the people concerned would not have permitted it. The impact of the greater use of library and information services, the phenomenal rate of growth of published material and the increase in the kinds of published material (not only books, but reports, microforms, computer soft-ware, programmed learning texts, and so on) has made us think more clearly. We have to face the fact of co-operative effort much more realistically than we did 20 or even 10 years ago, and we have to seek co-operative responses from our colleagues on different scales, from local, through regional to national, continental and international level.

We have been helped in this not only by the immense demand for our services (accompanied by an almost equal unwillingness to pay adequately for the consequent development), but also by the immense urge to keep up with science, and to ingratiate ourselves with the ever influential scientists. The *great* benefit to libraries of computer applications in my view is the clearer view of library operations given by systems analysis, and the concepts of scientific management. These have helped us to pinpoint *more clearly* our strengths and weaknesses. Apart from analysing individual library operations, these new procedures in examining our operations have made us recognise that, with the best will in the world, we cannot hope to give service at any level without integrated library systems which have to be planned at national and/or regional levels and, as far as this is possible, at international level also. In this connection, one must look to the forthcoming publications of the Cambridge University Library Management Research Unit, under E. B. Ceadel and J. L. Schofield.

Politics is the art of the possible: international politics might be described as the art of the possible possible—every achievement must be at least two steps further on than what one may achieve nationally. It is difficult enough to get things done on a national scale, and one should have no illusions about international agreement even in so limited a field as library and information work. (I remind you again of the Right Honourable Mr. Pearson's statement.)

For all that, a great deal is being done in a groping, hesitant way, in international librarianship. The publications of Unesco themselves indicate the range of activity which is being supported by this organisation, itself dependent on the good will and the financial support of its member states. It is limited as to what it can do by what is asked of it by their representatives. Its activities are well documented in the *Unesco Bulletin for Libraries,* in the annual reports of non-governmental organisations such as the International Federation of Library Associations, but for the purpose of this article one must mention some particularly significant activities. First, Unesco has done a great deal for the development of library science and documentation through the numerous grants it has given over the years for specific projects. These have been in the form of contracts to individual libraries, to individuals, or to non-governmental organisations (International Federation of Library Associations, International Federation for Documentation, International Council on Archives, etc.). Publications which have appeared as the result of contracts include Mr. M. Gelfand's *University Libraries for Developing Countries,* Miss J. E. Sabor's *Methods of Teaching Librarianship* and *Bibliographie des répertoires nationaux de périodiques en cours* which has appeared as a joint

M

IFLA/UNESCO publication. In an effort to develop the training of librarians and library assistants where there are no library schools, a course of 60 lectures on tape, with over 500 coloured slides and an accompanying guide and bibliographical material, has been prepared by the Library School of the University of Buenos Aires for Spanish-speaking countries, while the preparation for corresponding material for French-speaking and English-speaking countries is in progress. The importance of training generally has been an important preoccupation of the Unesco Department of Documentation, Libraries and Archives, and contracts have been awarded for studies on minimum standards for the training of librarians and documentalists, and introductory courses in documentation. Unesco has also financed or helped to finance the establishment of library schools in Malaysia, East Africa and most recently, in the West Indies. The non-governmental organisations have been special recipients of subventions from Unesco. Not only have they benefited from numerous contracts, but they have also received substantial grants which have enabled them to organise permanent headquarters and develop their work in their chosen field of activity.

The kind of seminar, organised by IFLA with a subvention from Unesco, and held in Liverpool in August 1971, represents an important contribution to international activity. This seminar for librarians from developing countries brought together the leaders in the profession from a wide range of developing countries and enabled them not only to hear of recent developments in the various kinds of libraries throughout the world, but also enabled them to compare experiences in terms of their own countries. This sort of meeting enables ideas from the most advanced systems to pass via leading experts to their colleagues in their own countries when they return. Another kind of seminar organised under the auspices of Unesco was the International Seminar on University Libraries held at Birmingham in April 1968: this enabled university librarians of countries of Western Europe to exchange experiences and consider the position of university libraries in relation to the organisation of the library systems of their countries. It is hoped that the important proceedings of this seminar will be published before too long. Significant meetings of experts on the national planning of documentation and library services in relation to economic and social development have taken place in Africa, Asia and Latin America. and a further meeting to consider similar problems in Arab States will take place, it is hoped, in 1971–2.

And lastly, the contribution of Unesco to publications of importance in a number of fields including librarianship must be known to all librarians. For many years, *Unesco Bulletin for Libraries* has given librarians all over the world an insight as to what other librarians are thinking about, and insights into important activities on the international plane. The articles which have appeared have always been of a high standard and have ranged widely over topics which affect all types of library and documentation service. There is also *Bibliography, Documentation, Terminology* in which the Department of Documentation Library and Archives Services publishes the results of an annual survey of bibliographical activities. And, of course, there are the various periodical bibliographies published by Unesco.

There are other agencies which give grants to bodies of librarians and documentalists. IFLA, for instance, has recently received considerable support from the American Council on Library Resources, which has made a large grant to enable IFLA to develop its headquarter services over a period of three years, in which time the Federation can increase its membership and hence the financial support it can expect from its member associations and associate members. The Council on Library Resources has also given aid to the Committee on Cataloguing of IFLA to enable it to establish a permanent secretariat to increase its contribution to the important work it has been undertaking over the past 10 years since the Paris Conference of 1959. Another (more unlikely body) which has helped the activity of librarians working at the international level is NATO, which some years ago gave money for the work of the Classification Research Group, which has revolutionised concepts in modern classification theory. OECD (the Organisation for Economic Corporation and Development) has also been active recently in financing the visits of experts to give advice on technical matters. The recent visit of Mr. Graham Mackenzie, Librarian of the University of Lancaster, to a technological university in Greece is an example of this.

With the exception of the Council on Library Resources, all the above are inter-governmental agencies. Much of the international work achieved, however, is done by non-governmental organisations (NGOs) such as FID or IFLA. The programme of FID has recently been revised, and the FID Council have arranged their priorities to include first a Research Referral Centre, related to Unesco's computerised documentation centre. This is another admission of the formidable task facing anyone concerned with the dissemination of information: techniques are required not only to get the information, but to get the information from those who get the information. In other words, it is recognised that it is impossible for any one agency to have all the necessary information at its immediate disposal, so that a central agency to discover who has the appropriate information and where it is becomes essential in the modern scientific world. This is not only an international problem, of course; its existence (if not the proper, definitive way to deal with it) has been faced in most of the countries in Europe and North America—a proposal for a national referral centre in connection with the foundation of the British Library is to be found in the evidence of the Library Association.[4]

FID is also intent on establishing a multi-lingual thesaurus for documentation and information work, and are seeking to develop the Universal Decimal Classification to provide a link with other thesauri and classifications. FID is concerned, too, about training—perhaps more than other agencies. Projects which are in hand or planned include summer schools for advanced documentalist training, the formulation of syllabuses for introductory courses on

[4] Library Association: The National Library Service, in *Libr. Ass. Rec.* 70(6), June 1968, 154–9.

computers in information, publication of training guides, guidelines for the education of documentation users in the efficient use of the results of research and development, etc.

In 1959, when I wrote the article from which I quoted at the beginning of this paper, I was hardly aware of IFLA. Its ways were not mine, and those who were involved moved in a heady atmosphere which was one to which I was unaccustomed. That, I think, would not be true today of someone in a similar position. The growth of IFLA's position of influence in the field of international librarianship in the past six or eight years has been very considerable, though, of course, this development itself has been dependent on much earlier devoted work done in difficult circumstances, and without the kind of financial support which this organisation is now getting from several sources.

General Council each year has dealt with themes of contemporary interest —at Copenhagen in 1969, for instance, 'Library Education and Research in Librarianship'; at Moscow in 1970, 'Libraries as a Force in Education'; at Budapest in 1972, the theme will be connected with International Book Year. The theme 'The Organisation of the Library Profession' is a particularly important one for those from developing countries, but it is, perhaps, equally important to some of the countries, called 'developed' where internecine rivalries have sometimes limited the influence of what might have been a cohesive professional body.

The influence of IFLA discussions have had their effect on almost every field of library development, as indeed have those of FID and ICA on their respective spheres. In the field of national and university libraries, particular attention has been paid to the professional structure of these libraries, their relation to the bodies they serve, and the problems of standards of staffing, service and accommodation. Standards have been promulgated for hospital libraries, and a revision of the 1959 standards for public libraries is under way in the Public Libraries Section. The Hospital Libraries section has also published a list of books suitable for hospital libraries—*Reading Round the World*, by Gardner and Lewis—and an international institute on hospital librarianship took place before the General Council, for which the IFLA Board gave four bursaries to assist the attendance of participants from developing countries. The Public Libraries Section has paid considerable attention to the problems of library legislation, which is an all-embracing subject affecting all forms of public library, and which is of interest to many countries which are establishing, or revising, their library laws.

The Section of Special Libraries, besides publishing *Inspel*, exists in a number of specialised sub-sections (geographical and map libraries, observatory libraries, social science libraries) which are concerned with bibliographical and administrative problems in the various fields. The Special Libraries section at the Liverpool Council paid particular attention to the relations of special libraries with libraries of a more general character.

Perhaps the most influential Committee as regards the life of the individual librarian (you will recall my definition of 'international librarianship' at the beginning of this paper) has been the committee which is now called the 'Committee on Cataloguing'. This is international librarianship at its most realistic—international co-operation resulting in international standards which, if not universally accepted in practice, have had a very real influence on cataloguing practice throughout the world. The recent Anglo-American Code has wide implications for the cataloguing of English language publications everywhere and is the result of a real, though often tense, co-operation across the Atlantic, as well as with other English-speaking countries throughout the world. It arose—or perhaps one had better say, its final completion was achieved—largely through the impetus of the International Conference on Cataloguing Principles held in Paris in 1959, and organised by IFLA with the help of Unesco. Numerous other studies have continued this work, including, for instance, Madame Honoré's work on an *International list of Approved Forms of Catalogue Entries for the Names of States,* and Monsieur Pierrot's *International List of Uniform Headings for Anonymous Classics.* An international list of uniform headings for corporate bodies is being undertaken in the USSR. An International Meeting of Cataloguing Experts was held in Copenhagen in 1968 to update, so to speak, the findings of the Paris Conference.

The Committee on Statistics and Standards is another active committee whose findings will affect librarians the world over before too long. It has held several significant meetings and co-operated with the International Standards Organisation Technical Committee 46 (ISO/TC 46) to produce 'International Standardisation of Library Statistics' in 1968. A further meeting of experts took place in Paris in 1970 with the financial assistance of Unesco, and a publication by Professor Frank Schick will result, produced under a contract between Unesco and IFLA. All countries will shortly be receiving a census form for libraries which it is hoped will be completed next year, and provide a reasonably reliable source of information on libraries on a world-wide scale for the first time.

The Committee on Library Building has also been an active one, and has more recently been paying attention to the question of standards, which at the present time is a recurring theme in many fields of librarianship and documentation service. A committee on standards has been set up under the chairmanship of Herr Werner Mevissen of Bremen: while it was set up to look at standards for library buildings in a general way, its work has in fact concentrated on public library buildings. You will find a paper on problems of university library standards in a forthcoming issue of *Libri* and I hope to do some further work on this in the forthcoming year. The Committee on Library Buildings also organised a Colloquium on University Library Buildings in Lausanne (under my chairmanship) in June, and the proceedings will be published at the end of the present year by La Bibliothèque Cantonale et Universitaire de Lausanne.

At this point, one should mention the various documentation centres which have been set by various sections and committees of IFLA, for the benefit of world librarianship. The 'Centre de documentation de Paris', which has a

177

wealth of material on library buildings of all kinds from all over the world, is one of these. It consists of a world-wide bibliography on library buildings together with brochures on a great many buildings, which Monsieur Bleton, first as secretary and then as chairman of the Library Buildings Committee, has collected over the years. Anyone inexperienced planning a library building would be well advised to consult this invaluable source of information. At present, a great deal of the material is handwritten but, with the collaboration of my secretarial assistants, it is now being gradually typed up and I hope will be suitable in due course for publication by Monsieur Bleton.

Another documentation centre is that at Bremen on new university libraries. This is maintained by Dr. Kluth at the Bremen State and University Library, and is being compiled to shed light on problems of setting up new libraries in institutions of higher education. More recently, a substantial grant from the Council of Library Resources has enabled the Committee on Cataloguing to set up a permanent centre in London. There is also a research centre for the documentation of library theory and research in Moscow, a centre for the bibliography of African official publications at the German State Library in West Berlin, and a documentation centre on the problems of large city systems at the City Library in Liverpool.

One might even say that IFLA has had its MARC in the world made for it. The spurt given to automation (almost the only publicity-worth topic to be found in libraries today) has rested to a great extent on the work done in the Library of Congress and the British National Bibliography on the MARC Projects. IFLA, however, has been the main forum for exchanges of ideas on MARC, including an important series of papers given at the Toronto General Council in 1967, and sponsored by the National and University Libraries Section.

MARC and its works—the computerisation of catalogues and the acceptance from country to country of native-produced bibliographies for native-produced books (i.e. the shared cataloguing project)—has, of course, implications wider than Anglo-American; its consequences are being felt in many countries, and is being developed for libraries in France (Grenoble) and in Germany (Frankfurt). Progress in computerised cataloguing has also been made elsewhere, for instance in Italy and in Eastern Europe. The discussion of mechanisation in libraries has been carried on in the sessions of the Committee on Mechanisation, which has had close ties with the work in the field being done by FID. A number of papers on automation have given news of progress in various countries (e.g. the papers of Lingenberg and Pflug for Germany, and those of R. T. Kimber for the United Kingdom). The Mechanisation Committee also co-operated with the Committee on Cataloguing at Copenhagen, and more recently has co-operated with the German Unesco-Commission in the organisation at Regensburg and Berlin of seminars for automation experts to exchange information and to investigate the possibilities of international co-operation in this important field. The former Chairman of the Committee is preparing a manual of data-processing in libraries under the terms of a

Unesco contract. The danger of a pre-occupation with 'mechanics' in libraries is the danger of forgetting the purpose of techniques—to get the appropriate book or information to the reader who wants it. The work of the Committee on Bibliography will also in due course be of considerable value to us all individually in our libraries. The Committee has undertaken surveys of current bibliographical information in more than 60 countries, and hopes to publish the material with the assistance of Unesco.

I have not, of course, given a complete résumé of all the activities of the various governmental and non-governmental organisations. What I have tried to do is to give examples of fruitful international work whose conception and completion will be of assistance and of real value to all practising librarians in due course. Some, like the work of the Committee on Cataloguing or of FID's survey on the training of librarians and documentalists, have already had their effect on the world practice of librarianship; others are still in progress and will take some time to reach us in our daily work. What is certain is that in the field of international librarianship there is always room for those with ideas and a capacity to work in order to get these ideas accepted and fulfilled. Contributions must start at the local level, regional and national problems are built on what is seen to be of value in individual libraries. International work is built on satisfactory work achieved nationally, in order to provide once more in the individual library the most satisfactory service that we wish to see for the individual client. Libraries, after all, exist, not for international committees, not even for librarians (though one feels somewhat doubtful about this) but for the satisfaction of the individual reader or borrower. It is this which gives point to our work, and makes libraries institutions of importance in the sociology of education, of knowledge and of culture.

There are two further topics which are now in a state of development. The first is the international application of planning to the domain of libraries. This, due to a certain climate of opinion on the question of applying 'planning, programming, budgetary systems' to libraries, derives from an article by Mr. C. V. Penna of the Unesco staff: 'The Planning of Library Services' which appeared in the *Unesco Bulletin for Libraries*[5] and has been developed by Mr. P. H. Sewell and Dr. H. Liebaers as *The Planning of Library and Documentation Services* (Unesco Manuals for libraries) 1970. In an article, 'Libraries and Educational Planning', Mr. D. J. Foskett gives an account of the seminar on library planning which is included in training courses for educational planners organised each year by the International Institute for Educational Planning in Paris.

. . . a few introductory lectures on the nature and planning of library services, a practical exercise, discussion. In 1970, the lectures were based on the systems approach: that the library, information and documentation services of a country must be studied and developed as an integrated whole, in relation to other systems, such as the educational system, the economic and industrial system, the scientific and cultural systems.

[5] Op. cit. v. 21, no 2, 1967, pp. 60–92.

Secondly, there has been a return to the conception of a world coverage system of bibliography—a notion long given up as a 'dead duck' by the founders of the International Institute of Bibliography, but now revived in a somewhat different form with the backing of Unesco. This project is called UNISIST—a made-up word, which means nothing in particular, but which designates a world information science service under the auspices of Unesco and the General Assembly of the International Council of Scientific Unions (ICSU). In the shorter report on a feasibility study it is stated that 'a world scientific information system, considered as a flexible network, which would extend the voluntary co-operation of existing and future information services, is not only feasible; it is desirable and necessary if the information needs of the world scientists are to be met in the future' (p. 20). The practical development of this I hope you will hear more about—it is sufficient at present to draw your attention to it, so that you are aware that the concepts of international librarianship are constantly in a state of evolution. They will evolve further only if each and every one of us in the profession of librarianship and documentation aims in the long run to play a part in the evolution of ideas for improved services which will satisfy our readers, our borrowers, our client-scientists and make libraries more significant institutions in the cultural, artistic, scientific and technological society of our time.

(c)   Report on Seminar on International Librarianship

A. G. T. OFORI
Director of Library Services, Ghana Library Board

Two papers were read by Miss Coops of Unesco and by Mr. Havard-Williams of Canada; both papers discussed 'Co-operation' as the basic element in international librarianship.

Miss Coops gave an outline of the libraries and documentary work for which Unesco is directly responsible or seeks to promote. She began by quoting from the Constitution to emphasise Unesco's fundamental function of promoting collaboration among nations. She described some aspects of the work of the Documentation Libraries and Archives Division and the work of FID as being directly concerned with the promotion of international librarianship. Special mention was made of such studies as 'the draft mode of law on archives' 'standards for library services', project ISORD; international information systems and research in documentation. She made reference to the computerised documentation services of Unesco (CCDS) and the system analysis work which began in 1970. She mentioned that Unesco might organise a workshop for staffs of depository libraries and other information systems with a view to helping them to make greater use of and ensure wider dissemination of Unesco documents and publications.

The papers referred to the work of the following sectors of Unesco as being relative to international librarianship:

(a) Education sector which provides educational information through (IBE) and educational planning through (IIEP). The International Institute of Educational Planning has noted the need for creating national library systems for economic and social development.

(b) Science sector studies lead to the establishment of a world system of science information system (UNISIST).

(c) The work of the sectors for social science, human science and culture contribute to the development of social science information systems.

(d) Communication sector promotes the free flow of books and cited (IBY 1972) as one of the major sponsored projects of the sector in 1971–2.

Miss Coops emphasised that international librarianship was further promoted by the various libraries of the UN system which, though specialised in their own fields, promoted co-operation. There were other agencies such as the Inter Agency Working Party on Indexing and the UN Administrative Committee for Co-ordination. She concluded by referring to the work of the numerous non-governmental organisations including IFLA, whose work was concerned with the development and promotion of international librarianship and co-operation.

Mr. P. Havard-Williams, who read the second paper, stressed 'co-operation' as the key word to international librarianship. He said co-operation had been a by-word for half a century and, as the needs of readers became more complex, co-operation had become the major means of giving relative strength to the drawing upon wider resources to improve the services to library users. He cited the Farmington Plan of USA and such other co-operative exercises as major activities within such other fields as co-operative purchase of books in the United Kingdom. The national and international co-operative interlending schemes among European countries and within the Commonwealth were specific examples. He assumed that thoughts were being directed to co-operation in total resources of systems, i.e. for books, technical services, data processing and library application of computers, the development of training needs, and the technology of modern buildings.

A very lively discussion followed the two papers. Members praised Unesco's effort in the field of international librarianship and unanimously underscored the view that the effort to bring delegates to participate in this pre-seminar and the IFLA meeting in Liverpool was a significant event in international librarianship.

Unesco's efforts in assisting member countries by missions and experts was also discussed. Though the principle was laudable, participants thought some experts lacked adequate expertise in their fields of study and often reports and recommendations were of little use to them. Miss Coops, however, explained the official stand on the issue and emphasised that Unesco would send a mission only at the request of a member state.

There was much discussion on the role of national library associations and the exchange of staff. The seminar accepted the view that strong national associations were a necessary first step to international librarianship. This would promote regional activities which could lead to improved appreciation of the problems and difficulties facing local, regional and international librarianship.

A call was made for a guide to staff exchange possibilities throughout the world. It was stressed, however, that bilateral agreements were means of promoting international librarianship.

(d)   Report on the Consultative Committee Deliberations for the IFLA Pre-Session Seminar for Developing Countries

Mrs. F. A. OGUNSHEYE

Assoc. Professor and Acting Head, Dept. of Library Studies, Ibadan University

The members of the IFLA Pre-session Seminar were in attendance as observers at the Consultative Committee of IFLA held on Monday, 29 August 1971. This was a commendable arrangement as it gave members of the Seminar an opportunity to find out what IFLA Standing Committees' programmes were in general and which IFLA activities were related to the needs in developing countries. The Consultative Committee of IFLA consisted of the Executive Board of IFLA, representatives of sections, sub-sections, chairmen of standing committees and representatives of international members. It is the body which is charged with the responsibility for planning and co-ordinating IFLA's programmes, and can be regarded as the policy-making body of the Federation. This body is also responsible for election, nominations, financial decisions, and programme development, for which it relies on a Programme Development Group for advice and working papers. It was therefore an excellent introduction to the organisation, structure and activities of IFLA.

The decisions of the Consultative Committee have to be presented to the General Council of IFLA for ratification. It therefore functions as a working committee for the IFLA Council.

AGENDA
Apart from the minutes of the previous meetings held in Moscow, there were listed several topics of interest to the Pre-session Seminar.

1.   Communications from the President
(a)   *Grants*
The President reported that the Council on Library Resources (USA) had made a grant of $54,000 to IFLA for three years for the support of a permanent secretariat on cataloguing. This contribution was in addition to the $100,000 already donated for the general support of IFLA Secretariat.

(b) *Publications*
A new Publications Committee has been established, consisting of Mr. P. Havard-Williams in charge of editorial functions and Mr. W. Koops who will negotiate with publishers.

(c) *International Book Year*
It was announced that 1972 has been declared International Book Year by Unesco. IFLA as its contribution has chosen the topic, *Reading in a Changing World*, as general theme for the IFLA General Council which will meet in Budapest from August–September 1972. A contract has been signed with Unesco for the preparation of working papers on the significance of the reading habits and the use of books and the importance of the study of these phenomena for the development of efficient library services. All sections, committees and national organisations are asked to relate their activities to the International Book Year Theme.

(d) *UNISIST*
This is an international scheme for establishing a world-wide information system for science and technology. A meeting of government representatives has been planned to discuss the UNISIST recommendations. IFLA and FID had met to discuss these recommendations and had issued a joint statement, published in IFLA *Newsletter, 37*: July 1971. Briefly the joint statement recommended the inclusion of social sciences and humanities for proposed subject coverage of the International Information Systems. It drew attention to the work of other existing information systems and efforts by international organisations, IFLA, FID, IATUL. It recommended that UNISIST should collaborate with these organisations to set up effective information systems that cannot operate without libraries or 'store houses' of literature. Arising from the UNISIST recommendations were a number of contracts. One of these was concerned with the designing of a questionnaire to procure reliable information for the establishment of a network of information services in (a) advanced countries, and (b) developing countries.

(e) *Procedure for the election of officers for sections and committees*
The President announced that a new procedure and regulations have been designed to control the proliferation of sections and committees. These recommendations were to be referred to the Council.

The President announced that the deadline for receiving papers for the Budapest Council Meeting would be June 1972. All papers were to be submitted before that date.

2. Unesco resolution on apartheid and colonialism
Unesco had passed a resolution regarding policy of non-governmental organisation on South Africa, Rhodesia, and territories under Portuguese rule. The resolution requested that the Director General of Unesco should investigate

183

NGOs that enjoy relations with Unesco, which have branches in the above-named countries. It called upon the Executive Board to take necessary measures to cut off relations, as from 31 December 1971, with NGOs whose branches practise racial discrimination or segregation. This resolution was discussed by the IFLA Board at its Brussels meeting on 11–13 February, and the Board decided to issue the following statement:

(1) IFLA having consultative status, category A, with Unesco, abides *ipso facto* by the Bill of Human Rights.

(2) IFLA is a professional international organisation and not a political one.

(3) IFLA, not being different from other professional NGOs, consulted other organisations, more particularly FID and the Union of International Associations.

(4) IFLA has only requested from its members to be professional bodies and does not feel that it has the right to investigate its members and will not do so in the future (the expression of this opinion was underscored by the Unesco secretariat when it circulated the answers of the NGOs).

(5) The isolation of IFLO members or members of other NGOs in the incriminated territories would lead to a situation where the resolution would defeat its own purposes.

(6) IFLA fails to understand why NGOs with very limited influence are invited to sever their relations with their members in these countries while the much more powerful member states maintain existing relations with these countries.

This IFLA statement has been communicated to NGOs and member organisations. The President reported that there had been no statement of disagreement so far. Members have expressed support for it. The matter was to be discussed again at the Board. In IFLA's letter to the Director General of Unesco, IFLA reiterated its reluctance to investigate its members or get involved in political issues. However 'IFLA, for its part, reasserts its opposition to colonialism in all its forms'. It was surprising that the IFLA statement omitted any mention of apartheid, or segregation policies for condemnation.

3. Elections for the executive board

Two candidates were presented for the vacancy created by the retirement from office of Dr. F. Mohrhardt who had been first vice-president for six years. These were Mr. Erik J. Spicer, Parliamentary Librarian, Library of Parliament, Ottawa, Canada; and Mr. Robert Vosper, Head Librarian and Professor of Library Service at the University of California, Los Angeles.

The Consultative Committee is charged with the responsibility of presenting these two candidates in order of preference to the Council and therefore had to vote to determine that order. The President urged members to vote as professionals not as national members. In the voting that took place, Mr. R. Vosper was given precedence over Mr. E. Spicer.

4. Proposal for new scale of members' dues

The Treasurer's Report, which was tabled, showed that IFLA's income in 1970 was only 125,526 S.frs., while expenditure was 154,785 S.frs. This deficit has been overcome by payments from the capital fund which was rapidly diminishing. It was therefore imperative that IFLA should find ways of increasing its income from members' subscription. The Council of Library Resources had made a grant of $100,000 for three years 'to strengthen IFLA's administrative and staff operations'. The Belgian Government had contributed the equivalent of $23,000 to IFLA, in addition to the rent of the present offices of the IFLA secretariat, for three years.

These generous offers notwithstanding, IFLA will need to increase the subscription of members. The Treasurer has proposed that IFLA National Members should pay 0.1% of each country's contribution to Unesco to IFLA. The contribution of institutions as associate members will form part of the national contribution of each state. This would increase income from subscription from 60,000 to 146,000 S.frs. This suggestion has been communicated to Member Associations. Most of the reactions received have been positive and a few reluctant.

This new increase is of concern to Associations from developing countries who are finding it difficult to get foreign exchange to meet their present financial obligations to IFLA and whose government would definitely not take kindly to these increases in subscription. While some developing countries may be tempted to ask themselves if, in view of priorities of their national governments, they can afford the luxury of becoming full voting members, it is hoped that the opportunities for the fertile exchange of ideas on IFLA's platform will outweigh the misgivings they may hold.

5. Unesco budget 1973–4

Several topics were requested for submission to Unesco for inclusion in its 1973–4 budget. These were:

(a) The role of libraries in adult education with reference to new needs, new media and new methods. A public libraries group is to work out standards for use of audio-visual aids in libraries.

(b) Seminar on subject specialisation. University section to discuss demands of subject departmentation and subject specialisation.

(c) New demands made on libraries from industrial and commercial institutions and the role of university libraries.

(d) Seminar on preservation of books and documents, to include training problems, the experience of Florence, co-operation between libraries and archives and standards for equipment.

(e) Symposium on national libraries—task and function of the national library.

(f) Meeting on Principles of Bibliographic control.

(g) International Library School.

There were suggestions from some members that IFLA should establish priorities in its own programme and base its recommendations to Unesco on these priorities. The President informed the Committee that only Unesco can take the final decision about these programmes. IFLA has only been asked to make suggestions of topics. IFLA could not impose any priorities on Unesco.

6. Report of joint meeting of FID and IFLA officers in Brussels
A meeting of FID and IFLA officers was held in Brussels on 15–16 February 1971. The full report of that meeting is published in the IFLA *Newsletter,* No. 37, July 1971. Group discussions were held on various aspects of librarianship of common interest to both FID and IFLA. These were on research, training, mechanisation, standardisation, and developing countries. Recommendations were made for joint projects and joint activities. The decisions of the FID/DC Developing Countries and the IFLA Project on Developing Countries are of special significance to the Pre-session Seminar.

The group, after establishing areas of common interest, decided that the formation of a joint FID/IFLA Committee for Developing Countries possibly in 1971 would be a desirable thing.

The function of the Committee would be:
(1) To ensure that resources are fully used.
(2) To select projects that would be of general value to developing countries.
(3) To co-operate with Unesco on work for developing countries.
(4) To set up a programme with the assistance of experts from developing countries.
(5) To prepare a programme for IFLA/FID in Budapest 1972.
(6) To see that documentation and library development proceed side by side.

The President urged the sections and sub-sections to discuss these and other recommendations for collaboration with FID. These recommendations for joint action, designed to cope with the problem of developing countries, are laudable. It will enable two international associations to help effectively with library development in these areas. It is hoped, however, that such a committee will only be a temporary measure designed to aid the developing countries to catch up to the point where they can engage in meaningful communication with the professional association through the sections and sub-sections to which they properly belong. It is hoped that the committee will not separate developing countries from the general stream of ideas and cross fertilisation going on through the standing committees, sections and sub-sections.

7. New sections and subgroups
The Consultative Committee discussed new rules for the creation of new sections and subgroups proposed by the Programme Development Group (PDG).

8. A standing advisory committee was also proposed by the PDG for all
sections, committees, etc. The standing committee should consist of 5–10 nominated persons to serve for a period of six years. It was suggested that the

President and Secretary should also be members of the committee. The matter is to be kept on the agenda for further discussions.

9. Formal structure for programme development group

The PDG also proposed measures for regularising its position. These include election procedure—term of office for three years and a scheme for rotation of membership. The recommendations were accepted but terms of reference of the PDG were requested.

10. Under *Any other business,* resolutions were called for. The resolutions were to be handed in before Thursday 2 September, in four languages, to Mr. Havard-Williams. Plans and recommendations were requested for PDG from sections.

The organiser of IFLA Council 1971, Dr. Chandler, briefed the Consultative Committee on arrangements for the Council Meeting. He regretted the fact that some papers which were received after the deadline stipulated were not available for circulation, but these would be available at the sessional meetings of each section. The President thanked Dr. Chandler for the arrangements for IFLA Council and reminded members that June 1972 was the deadline for papers for the Budapest meeting.

Comments from the IFLA Pre-session Seminar

An informal meeting of the Pre-session Seminar group was called after the Consultative Committee. This was to enable members to give their comments on the Consultative Committee deliberations, particularly in respect of those items on the agenda that were of great interest to developing countries. Mr. Campbell and Mrs. D. Anderson were invited to participate as experienced members who could give background information to the Consultative Committee. Mr. Campbell explained that the Consultative Committee was a new body consulting with committees and sections of IFLA through their chairmen or representatives.

After much discussion, the following observations formed the consensus of opinion of the meeting:
(1) That the members appreciated and are grateful for the opportunity offered to them by the IFLA Councils Pre-session Seminar to learn about new achievements in Advanced Librarianship and realised the extent of the gap that exists in library development between the developed countries and themselves. Attendance at the Consultative Committee also afforded members the opportunity to understand the functions of IFLA.
(2) The members, however, noted with concern the complete lack of representation from developing countries on IFLA Committees and hoped IFLA would do all that is constitutionally possible to rectify the situation.
(3) That IFLA might wish to consider reactivating the section on developing countries. The opinion was, however, expressed that this should not be

allowed to segregate developing countries from activities of other sections and groups.

(4) That IFLA might wish to amend the constitution so that there could be regional representation for Asia, Africa and Latin America and the West Indies on IFLA Board as vice-presidents.

(5) As observers, the Pre-session group expressed grave concern that the IFLA resolution omitted any mention of apartheid or segregation policy in its statement condemning colonialism, especially as the term 'apartheid' was specifically mentioned in the Unesco Resolution.

(6) The members hope that problems of developing countries will be listed, and as a priority on the IFLA programme recommendations to Unesco.

In conclusion, this has been a most useful and stimulating experience for members of the IFLA Pre-session Seminar, who urged each other to endeavour to become full voting members and to participate fully on the world professional level on the platform of IFLA.

11   INTERNATIONAL LIBRARY TECHNOLOGY

(a)   Reports on Exhibitions

W. H. SNAPE

Principal Lecturer-in-charge, School of Librarianship, Liverpool Polytechnic

For the first time in its history the International Federation of Library Associations launched a Library Technology and Library Suppliers' Exhibition during its 37th Council held at Liverpool from 30 August–2 September 1971. Of necessity this was what scientists would call a 'small controlled experiment' but there is no doubt it considerably enhanced the 1971 IFLA Pre-session Seminar for Developing Countries, sponsored by Unesco, on 'Recent Developments in Advanced Librarianship'.

Some 24 exhibitors, sponsored by the Library Associations of America, West Germany, Scandinavia and the United Kingdom, exhibited their wares covering the 10 areas listed by Dr. G. Chandler, the local organiser, in Section 5 of the programme sent to all participants. Each area has been dealt with by individual reporters and it is my task to report on the overall impact of the exhibition.

The problem of organising library services in the modern world has never been so complex and so potentially expensive as it is today. In the context of the publication explosion and the advent of multi-media resources, even the so-called most advanced countries falter at the efforts needed to select, acquire, exploit and store the seemingly overwhelming mass of material. This came out very forcibly in the discussions which took place, for example, on the function of the National Library in a developing country. It became obvious that our colleagues in Nigeria, or Ethiopia, or Uganda, or Korea, etc., had a very realistic view of the relative importance of legal deposit and the need to make their National Libraries the very acme of library services in their own countries.

The publishers, booksellers, library suppliers and library system experts who were present, together created an atmosphere of goodwill and expertise which augurs well for any similar venture in the future.

By and large, the exhibits nominated by the various national library associations had a common attribute in that they reflected the universal desire of all librarians—and librarianship is nothing if it is not universal in application—to cut the cost of library operations, whilst at the same time making them more effective. Delegates were undoubtedly impressed by the total impact of the exhibition in such impressive and eminently suitable surroundings. That organisations from Germany, Scandinavia and the United States thought it worth while to exhibit is no doubt flattering, but the attention to detail in the equipment shown was a spur to all who wish to exploit fully their library resources. It was to be expected that British exhibits would be in the majority, but in addition Unesco seminar delegates benefited by the fact that three exhibitors chose the IFLA Council for the first public showing of their equipment and one of these is not likely ever to be shown in public again.

One of the restricting factors in estimating the cost and effectiveness of library operations has been the economic disincentiveness of the manual effort involved in collecting, storing and rendering useful the vital statistics needed for such an operation. Our overseas colleagues quickly grasped the fact that in the mechanical and automatic systems shown lie the means to achieve those goals for libraries everywhere.

Books and other traditional materials will, as Dr. Urquhart realised when planning the National Lending Library of Science and Technology, remain a major mode of communication for many years to come. As a British librarian, however, one cannot but envy the librarian from a developing country who has the opportunity from the outset to weld into a whole communication network composite parts, using the best examples of *all* the communication media necessary if libraries are to fulfil their proper functions. All Unesco seminarians valued the chance to glimpse some of the exciting challenges and possibilities which lie ahead.

(b)   Comments on Exhibits on Mechanisation of Loan and Other Related Procedure

M. E. GILL

The two examples of computer-based loan procedures exhibited showed interesting variations in the technology but both seemed workable alternatives to tedious manual methods. Both were designed for off-line operation but both claimed convertibility to on-line use.

I found that, in addition to the Plessey Company and Automated Library Systems representatives, Mr. N. S. M. Cox of Oriel Computer Services Limited was only too willing to discuss the general problem even though his company had no actual exhibit on display.

I divide my comments into two sections:
A. General
(1) Is not on-line operation with its ability to give a reader an immediate answer to his query about a book not found on the shelf justified in those libraries that receive frequent queries of that sort? The computer industry seems to think that the lower cost of the off-line systems provides a safer commercial approach. We need a librarian's assessment.
(2) If on-line is to be preferred, then the book must be identified by both

reader and computer by the same code. Both systems exhibited use an accession number rather than a call number. I appreciate the problems computers have with alphanumeric numbers but what are we going to change—our classification systems, our cataloguing rules or our computer technology?

(3) The impressive ease with which overdue notices, fines slips and recalls, etc., can be produced, and the promptness with which they can be despatched, must lend an authority to the libraries' demands on their readers which would be difficult to cost.

The use of the day-to-day records which are collected by the computer would also aid in the production of general library statistics, including those in connection with the Public Lending Right should this become necessary.

B. From the point of view of the developing country

(1) Considerations of cost are modified by the fact that the computer would be replacing cheaper labour than in more developed countries.

(2) There is also the added cost of isolation—the equipment, if installed, is likely to be the only one of its kind for miles around and even routine service tends to be an expensive proposition.

(3) The exhibition, for very good reasons, tended to show only the most recent advances. It is possible that others, not quite so recent but still in advance of current practice in less developed countries, would be more appropriate to those countries. It is to be hoped that their existence will not be overlooked by the Unesco group.

On a personal note, may I thank you for organising an exhibition which I found extremely interesting and which brought together many things which I had planned to travel to several spots in order to see.

As far as the more formal section of the seminar is concerned, I am sure that the relatively small size of the group enabled us in the discussions to remove the inevitable bias of authors who live with problems which are not always the same as those we face. There was, therefore, no expert with all the ready-made answers but a group of critical minds searching for solutions. I am sure the conference benefited as a result.

(c) Inter-library Lending Procedures—A Report on the Exhibitions Mounted at the IFLA Conference

S. W. FERGUSON

Inter-Library Lending Procedure was demonstrated at the IFLA conference by the exhibition put on by the National Lending Library for Science and Technology.

At the NNL's exhibition, a demonstration of Telex links with other libraries as well as the NLL's headquarters at Boston Spa was given. Sample requests for publications received at the HQ from other libraries were transmitted to the NLL's exhibition centre. These requests received by Telex were transferred by special equipment to standard request forms used by the NLL.

The demonstration of the Telex operations and other equipment, supplemented by literature on the work of the NLL, as well as sample request forms, etc., which were available illustrated the excellent facilities offered by the NLL.

I was impressed by the speed at which requests could be processed and despatched and even more so by the fact that the NLL photocopying service is available to institutions overseas.

(d)   Report on Exhibition—Micro Publishing

L. Z. CHEELO

The publishing of microforms—microfilms, microfiche, etc.—as revealed or illustrated in the stands at the exhibition, aims at achieving the following:
(a)   Saving in storage space.
(b)   Low costs in the acquisition of library materials.
(c)   Low maintenance costs of these materials.
These aims, which are in fact advantages, are highlighted by the fact that there is so much reading material published that handling it is a physical problem. To my mind this line of argument assumes each library will necessarily need to acquire all these materials, but in fact I do not believe this to be true, except in the case of national libraries.

One aspect which does not come out from the publishers of microforms is how the reader is to fit in all this. There is too much concern with the problems of the librarian, and not the reader for whom all this is done really.

Also, these microforms do not seem to have reached perfection yet. Within a short space of their arrival on the market, different types have been introduced. As one from a developing country which cannot afford something that will be out of date (possibly fairly soon), for reasons of limited resources, I do not admire these materials from the point of view of practicability.

(e)   Report on the Exhibition—Bibliographic Control

SUTHILAK AMBHANWONG

Bibliographical works represented at the exhibition in St. George's Hall and in the foyer of International Library were of various types and subjects, published by outstanding publishers in several countries. Most of them were of high standard and serve as necessary tools for research in the varying fields.

Some publishers of bibliographies included Mansell Information Publishing Limited, André Deutsch Ltd. and Crosby Lockwood and Son Ltd. In addition, the Library Association (London), the American Library Association, and the

National Library of Australia produced a great number of valuable bibliographies of different types. Xerox bibliographics makes available several catalogues of libraries in book form. The only sample of computer generated book catalogue in the exhibition belongs to Enoch Pratt Free Library, Baltimore, Maryland.

Bibliographies on display may be divided into 10 types, namely: general bibliographies; subject bibliographies; national bibliography; author bibliography; library catalogue; union catalogue; current bibliography; list of theses; lists and union lists of serials; periodical indexes.

Although bibliographical control has been done extensively in several countries in the western world, only large academic and research libraries can afford most of these bibliographical works which are expensive. For developing countries, only a few titles can be made available in their libraries; consequently some bibliographies are of little value since only a few items listed in them are acquired and made available to their clientele.

Nevertheless, an effort has been made to record here some outstanding bibliographical works at the exhibition.

General Bibliographies
Hodges, Elizabeth D. comp. and ed. Books for Elementary School libraries: an initial collection. Chicago, American Library Association, 1969.
Prie, James, W. comp. Books for Junior College libraries. Chicago, American Library Association, 1969.
Reference and subscription book reviews 1968–70. Chicago, American Library Association, 1970.
Reference books for small- and medium-sized public libraries. Committee of the Reference Services Division. Chicago, American Library Association.
A Short title catalogue arranged geographically of books printed and distributed by printers, publishers and booksellers in the English provincial towns and in Scotland and Ireland up to and including the year 1900, compiled by E. A. Clough. London, Library Association, 1969.
Short title catalogue of books printed in the British Isles, the British Colonies and the United States of America and of English books printed elsewhere 1701–1800 held in the libraries of the Australian capital territory, edited by William J. Cameron and Diana J. Carroll. Canberra, National Library of Australia, 1966.
Walford, A. J. ed. Guide to reference material. London, Library Association, three vols., 1966, 1968, 1970. Volume 1 Science and Technology; volume 2 Social and Historical Sciences, Philosophy and Religion; volume 3 Generalities, Languages, the Arts and Literature.
Winchell, Constance M. Guide to reference books. Eighth ed. Chicago, American Library Association, 1967.
Subject Bibliographies
1. *Art*
Chamberlin, Mary W. Guide to art reference books. Chicago, American Library Association, 1959.
2. *Asia*
Pearson, J. D. Oriental and Asian bibliography. London, Crosby, 1966. An essay on bibliographical works of Asian countries.
3. *Bank Publications*
Checklist of overseas bank publications. Canberra, February 1971. Arranged alphabetically by country.

4. *Catholic Church*
A bibliography of the Catholic Church from the National Union Catalogue, Pre-1956 Imprints, compiled and edited at the Library of Congress, with the co-operation of the American Library Association. London, Mansell Publications, 1970.
5. *Children's Literature*
Crouch, Marcus. Books about children's literature: a book list prepared by the Committee of the Youth Libraries Group. Rev. ed. London, Library Association, 1966.
Muir, Marcie. A bibliography of Australian children's books. London, André Deutsch, 1970.
6. *Films*
Film acquisitions 1969. Canberra, the National Library of Australia Film Collection, 1970. Annotated list of films acquired in 1969.
Kula, Sam. Bibliography of film librarianship. London, Library Association, 1969.
7. *Government Publications*
Jackson, Ellen. Subject guide to major United States government publications. Chicago, American Library Association, 1965.
Wood, Jennings ed. United States government publications: a partial list of non-GPO imprints. Chicago, American Library Association, 1964.
8. *Medical Science*
Books and periodicals for medical libraries in hospital. London, Library Association, 1966.
Thornton, John L. A select bibliography of medical bibliography, with an introductory essay on medical bibliography. London, Library Association, 1970. Includes books in English published in the nineteenth and twentieth centuries, and a few items relating to persons, truants from medicine, who qualified as doctors but mainly devoted their careers to politics, the arts and other subjects.
9. *Sabah*
Sabah: a bibliography of the dispute between Malaysia and the Philippines. Canberra, National Library of Australia, August 1969.
10. *South Africa*
Musiker, Reuben. South African bibliography. London, Crosby, 1970.
11. *Urban*
Walkley, Gavin ed. Bibliography of urban studies in Australia. Canberra, the National Library of Australia for the Australian Institute of Urban Studies, 1971.

National Bibliographies
Australian National Bibliography. Canberra, National Library of Australia. Issues four times a month and an annual volume.
Ghana National Bibliography. Accra, Ghana Library Board, 1968.

Author Bibliographies
Payne, Waveney R. N. comp. A Shakespeare bibliography: the catalogue of the Birmingham Shakespeare Library. London, Mansell Publications, 1971. Seven vols. Contains every book connected with the life and works of Shakespeare.
Payne, Waveney, R. N. A Shakespeare bibliography. London, Library Association, 1969.

Library Catalogue
City of Liverpool Libraries. Catalogue of the Music Library, 1954.
Enoch Pratt Free Library. Catalogue of books and phonorecords for adults and young adults, October 1969–June 1970. Baltimore, Md., 1971.
Oregon State Library. Book catalogue of adult non-fiction. Salem, Oregon, 1970 (Xerox).

Union Catalogue
Australia National Library. The National Union Catalogue. Canberra, the Library.

Datta, Rajishwari. Union catalogue of the Central Government of India publications held by libraries in London, Oxford and Cambridge. London, Mansell Publications, 1970.

Union catalogues of the government of Pakistan publications held by libraries in London, Oxford and Cambridge. Cambridge, University of Cambridge, 1970.

Macdonald, Teresa. Union catalogue of the Government of Ceyon publications held by libraries in London, Oxford and Cambridge. London, Mansell Publications, 1970.

The National Union Catalogue, Pre-1956 imprints; compiled and edited at the Library of Congress with the co-operation of the American Library Association. London, Mansell. 610 vols., 1969.

Current Bibliographies
ALA book list. Twice a month, and once in August.

Aslib book list; a monthly list of recommended scientific and technical books with annotations.

List of Theses
Swift, Catherine G. Union list of higher degree theses of the universities of New Zealand. Wellington, New Zealand Library Association, 1969. Annotated list of theses in 28 universities.

Lists and Union Lists of Serials (including Abstracts)
Abstracting Services. The Hague, International Federation for Documentation, 1969.
Volume 1 Science, Technology, Medicine, Agriculture.
Volume 2 Social Sciences and Humanities.
Alphabetical list of periodicals and newspapers including official publications in both print and microfilm.

Baker, Anthony, ed. Union list of current commercial periodicals. London, Library Association, 1968.

Checklist of South-east Asian newspapers. 29th ed. Canberra, National Library of Australia, 1970.

Current Australian serials. Seventh ed. Canberra, National Library of Australia, 1971.

Directory of periodicals published by international organisation. Brussels, Union of International Association.

Indian periodicals and newspapers. Canberra, National Library of Australia holdings at 31 December 1969. Canberra, National Library of Australia.

Serials in Australian libraries; social sciences and humanities: a union list. Canberra, National Library of Australia, 1969. (Loose leaf.)

South-east Asian periodicals and official publications. Canberra, National Library of Australia, March 1970.
Part 1 Brunei, Malaysia, Sabah, Sarawak and Singapore.
Part 2 Burma, Cambodia, Laos, Timor and Vietnam.
Part 3 Indonesia.
Part 4 Philippines Islands.
Part 5 Thailand.

Westminster City Libraries. Union list of periodicals. London, the Library, 1970.

Woodworth, David, comp. Guide to current British journals. London, Library Association, 1970.

World list of social science periodicals. Third ed., rev. and enl. Paris, Unesco, 1952.

Periodical Indexes
British Education Index, compiled by the librarians of Institutes and Schools of Education. London, Library Association.

British Humanities Index. London, Library Association.

British Technology Index. London, Library Association.

Index to foreign legal periodicals; published by Institute of Advanced Legal Studies, University of London in co-operation with the Library Association of Law Libraries, 1971.

Index to legal periodicals, September 1968 to August 1969, edited by Mildred Russell; published by H. W. Wilson in co-operation with American Association of Law Libraries, 1969.

(f)   Liverpool-Ohio Computer Link

GUY A. MARCO

The Ohio College Library Centre is composed of about 70 academic libraries and has three primary goals, and several secondary ones. The Centre expects to reach its primary goals during 1971.

The first goal is the preparation of a union catalogue covering the holdings of the 70 member libraries. This catalogue will be a computer-based catalogue rather than a book or card catalogue, and access to the catalogue will be by a cathode ray tube terminal. While the catalogue will probably contain only material added or catalogued by the members from 1971 onwards during the first few years, the Centre hopes eventually to have all holdings of all member libraries in its central data bank.

The second goal of the Centre is to provide cataloguing copy for member libraries at costs considerably below what the libraries pay individually. Co-operation is the key element of this goal. One set of MARC tapes is purchased by the Centre each year instead of 70 sets being purchased, one by each member library. This set of MARC tapes is put into the computer data bank in Columbus, Ohio, and each of the members has access to the cataloguing information via the cathode ray tube terminal. Items in the computer data bank can be found by using a card number index, an author-title index or a title index. If there is no exact catalogue copy in the data bank, copy for a similar item will be displayed on the screen and the member library can alter the material displayed on the screen so that it matches exactly the book in hand.

If similar copy is not available under MARC cataloguing, then the member library can do original cataloguing on the cathode ray tube terminal and transmit the information to Columbus where it will be available, within seconds, to the next library needing copy for that particular title. This means that no title will need to be catalogued more than once whether by the Library of Congress or a member of the Centre. This feature eliminates the current method under which a title not catalogued by the Library of Congress might be purchased by 50 libraries and catalogued 50 times, once by each library.

The third major goal for the year 1971 is the production of catalogue cards for all members. The Centre will produce catalogue cards from the data sent by a member over the cathode ray tube whether the information represents original cataloguing by the library, complete acceptance of the MARC cataloguing, or an adaptation of Library of Congress cataloguing with modification by a local library. The computer will not only print all cards centrally but will, furthermore, put the cards in alphabetical order ready for filing and ship them to the member library. Since both the printing and arranging will be done by computer, the costs to members will be much less than if the work were done manually in the local library.

Secondary, long-range goals include developing a central acquisition file and a system for handling serials. Although no target date has yet been set for these features, the Ohio College Library Centre hopes to see both systems running in the next few years.

This system was demonstrated in Liverpool on 31 August between 3.00 p.m. and 4.00 p.m. Questions may be directed to Guy Marco.

(g)   Telephone-Computer Link to the Libraries of Ohio State

Mrs. R. PANKHURST

The demonstration, so highly successful, proved that the computer had indeed opened vast new opportunities for eliminating the duller repetitive side of cataloguing and for supplying the reader, especially the research worker, with an answer to his dream for instant information.

(h)   Technological Advances and the Library Building

FRANCIS L. KENT

University Librarian, American University of Beirut, Lebanon

The choice, in the title of this paper, of the phrase 'technological advances', rather than 'advanced technology', is deliberate. Paradoxically, it may well turn out that the modern advanced technologies exert less effect on library planning than technological developments have done throughout the centuries.

But first let us consider, in connection with library science, the term 'developing countries', since it is not with the 'advanced' countries that this Seminar is concerned.

It seems to me that we have come to use this word 'developing' a little too widely, in part because of an understandable desire not to offend by designating any country as 'backward'. A certain realistic gradation would appear to be in order.

In library development some countries are, unmistakably, 'backward'. These are they which have not begun to comprehend the importance for their own development of the organisation, storage and communication of knowledge. No country represented at this Seminar can be backward in this sense or it would not be here. I would describe as 'undeveloped' those having some professional awareness of the necessity but lacking official understanding or support. 'Underdeveloped' are those where less has been done than could have been—within the resources available. In this category, by the way, are still to be found all too many so-called 'advanced' countries which do not do as much as they should, and could. 'Developing' are those where—again within the resources available—officialdom is aware and awake and doing its best.

The 'Western' world, by which I mean Europe and North America and places within their spheres of influence, has much less of a monopoly in librarianship than it frequently thinks it has. Ranganathan of India, Sheniti of Egypt, Penna of Latin America, are only a few of the many who have made seminal contributions to modern library science. And where would any of us be without Hammurabi, who accorded public access to his Royal Library in Babylon; without the great library of Alexandria; or, in times which are comparatively recent, without the Benedictines who seem to be the first to have thought of inter-library loans? The Benedictines are, admittedly, of European origin, though the Christian tradition out of which they grew was in the first place Middle Eastern. So also was the Renaissance, that most remarkable period when the flow of scholars from fallen Constantinople to the West coincided with the invention of printing with movable types, which in an embryonic and long-unrealised form seems to have originated in ancient China. And the alphabet itself is first found in Byblos, a few miles from where I write, and visible on a clear day from my window.

Too often the phrase 'advanced technology' is confined in meaning to automation and in particular computerisation. I would say rather that any development facilitating better libraries and library services is—in its place and time—'advanced' in relation to what went before.

Consider some of these developments in our technology. Many have had a profound effect on library construction—the topic of this essay—and many others have had little or none though they have contributed to general improvement.

In the latter category I would include, among others, the following: the typewriter; improved equipment such as tables and chairs, filing cabinets, shelving and all the other details to which the Library Technology Project in the USA has devoted so much attention; studies on improved specifications for durable paper and on the repair and preservation of existing materials; better methods of organisation and management, of theft detection and prevention; photocopying machinery. Nor should we forget Panizzi's British Museum cataloguing rules, without which the International Conference on Cataloguing Principles could not have been conducted by Hugh Chaplin (Panizzi's successor at several removes) in Paris in 1961; or Ranganathan's fundamental work in India on classification, which, whatever one may think of his proposals, gave rise to the studies of Aslib's Classification Research Group and other bodies that look forward to the computerisation of information resources. And, of course, there are many other technical developments, including the whole story of microforms. (These last do not save as much space as one might think: one tends to acquire much material that one would not otherwise have at all, and the reading machines require the allocation of additional space per reader—and more readers' places—since most people cannot use a borrowed microform at home. Perhaps the microform falls within both categories.)

In the former category, what of the following?

When Hammurabi threw open his Royal Library to the public, or such of it as could read, may he not have had to provide for extra seating accommodation in the building?

Scholars in the Alexandrine Library must have had what we now call open access on a considerable scale. An open access library is an entirely different architectural conception from a building with a closed stack, or the medieval library of chained books.

The Benedictine inter-library loan system must have required space for packing, despatch, receiving, unpacking, and additional office space not needed in a static library.

The Renaissance library, of which that of the Escorial in Spain is perhaps the earliest large example, reflected the then 'publication explosion' consequent on the introduction of printing, and the generalisation of knowledge following the influx of Eastern scholars to the West. It bears no comparison in design with the monastic library which it gradually replaced. Our modern carrel system seems to be an attempt to combine the generalisation of the Renaissance library, open access, and a modicum of privacy for the reader.

It may be as well to add that in very modern times the introduction of heating and air-conditioning—conducive to the well-being of readers and books alike—has added up to 20% of the size and cost of a library building.

This rather lengthy historical preamble leads me to the question which is probably in the minds of participants in this Seminar: where are we to go from wherever we are? To get back to the ostensible subject of this paper: how do we plan our buildings in order to accommodate present or foreseeable technological developments? The first question that comes to mind is inevitably that of the use of the computer. I think there are three main aspects of this problem:

(a) Do you, or will you, have access to a computer—on line or off, in your own building or elsewhere?

(b) Are there other non-computer manual or mechanical methods which will give you comparable results at less cost?

(c) Can you, as a librarian trying to serve your clientele, afford the great cost, and possible breakdown, of computerisation? In your country, are there adequate maintenance facilities?

The computer is, to be sure, a fantastic technological development. It can send men to the moon and bring them back, even though something goes wrong. But it is downright stupid—what you want to get out; you have to put in. The machine will do in an incredibly short time what you tell it to do:

but you have to give it its instructions in *its* terms and not *yours*. So you have to have a computer programmer, and he costs you a lot of money. Who pays for this? The salaries of computer people rise faster than do those of librarians. Manual, or non-electronic mechanical, methods may meet your needs adequately at tolerable cost.

Many libraries have attempted computer programmes: for acquisitions, cataloguing, circulation, periodicals, and information retrieval. Some, after much agony and several years' hard work, have succeeded. Some have failed. The classic example of failure is that of Florida Atlantic University, which set out in the mid-60s to be the first 'fully-automated university library in the world'. Within three years it had collapsed: books were not catalogued, booksellers' bills were not paid, reference services had become impossible, the University was at a standstill in its library services, morale had ceased to exist. Dr. H. Axford, University Librarian, Arizona State University at Tempe near Phoenix, was called in as a consultant to sort out the mess. The cost, in terms not only of lost money but also of lost library service, has not been publicised but must have been enormous. Axford has published his work, but there is no assessment of the cost of the disaster and its solution.[1]

A recent caveat against computerisation has been written by Ellsworth Mason.[2] This prominent American librarian and library consultant, Director of Library Services at Hofstra University, Long Island, NY, gives caustic warning against the idea that computerisation in libraries solves everything. It does not. All the implications of landing a man on the moon and getting him back are basically mathematical. They are brilliantly organised and carried out. But in library work we are asking that the computer store and file and retrieve *all* knowledge, past, present and to come, in *all* languages, and in innumerable scripts transliterated or not. (Many have, as yet, no standardised transliteration; in some, such as Arabic, the script does not indicate all the vowels.)

How, then, are we to plan our buildings so as to cope with technological development in general and computerisation in particular? The best answer I know is contained in the report of a conference held in 1967 in New York, under the auspices of Educational Facilities Laboratories, by a specially-convened group of librarians, library architects, computer specialists and communication experts.[3] They demonstrated that although the potentialities of the computer seem limitless, the amount of work still to be done before all knowledge can be stored in and retrieved from it is staggering, and so is the cost. This is, of course, especially true of the humanities and social sciences, where ideas are often more prominent than facts or formulae. They concluded that 'the bulk of a scholar's negotiations in a library will be with books even 30 years from now', and that possibly 'the long-range effect of microfilm technology on the book and library building will be greater than that of the computer'. But while we must attempt to think in long-range terms, we have to plan here and now.

I believe, therefore, that we should start from existing formulae which provide guides to the size of collections, the space occupied by a given number of volumes, the area to be allowed per reader's seat and per staff member, the allowance required for corridors, stair-wells, lifts, toilets, stores and machinery. We should specify that the building be as flexible as possible, using all the advantages of modular construction with a minimum of fixed load-bearing interior walls. The Educational Facilities Laboratories report suggests that some 2,000 square feet be allowed for a possible computer installation. This is a little less than 1% of the floor area of a library designed to contain 1–1.25 million volumes and about 1,200–1,400 readers' places, which is not a great deal in proportion: if used as readers' space, such an area could accommodate no more than about 80 readers. If computerisation never takes place, or if the computer is housed elsewhere than in the library, e.g. in a separate computer centre forming part of the larger unit (university, city, state) to which the library belongs, the space can be held in reserve for some other, perhaps unforeseeable, purpose. A minor point of importance, however, is that at the time the building is constructed adequate allowance should be made for the additional electrical connections, air-conditioning ducts and the like, that the computer, if installed, will require. All the above should be clearly indicated and fully discussed in the librarian's building programme or architect's brief, so that the architect knows what is wanted.

More important, I feel, is planning for technology *other* than that of the computer. If we go in for microfilms on a large scale, we shall need many microfilm readers, so, as was said above, much of the space we save by using microfilm will be claimed by these machines. Facsimile transmission of text by television, which amounts to a sort of improved inter-library loan and is already in use in some places, may slow down the rate of expansion but requires space for the viewing machines. The same goes for all other audio-visual aids.

But we must walk, with at least one foot always on the ground, before we can run. Some who rushed into computerisation have tripped and fallen, as we have seen. We are in the dilemma of not being able to see very far ahead, yet having to plan in terms of hard concrete and harder cash for what we cannot clearly see. So the librarian has to be both visionary and practical: visionary, because without imagination and forethought he will contribute little; practical, because all his ideas will be subjected to an administrative scrutiny which can sometimes be far from sympathetic. Further, if he is to be a successful planner, he must make it clear that as a responsible professional man he is himself convinced of what he says he wants; that is, he should claim, and be seen to claim justly, the authority that should be his. There have been far too many cases, even in large universities, where the librarian has been squeezed out of a construction project by a combination of the President or Vice-Chancellor, the Trustees or Board of Governors, the architect, and sometimes the donor of the money as well. The result is always a disaster. The more complex the organisation, the harder it is for the librarian to be in contact with the top administrators; yet such contact is essential, for without the intimate knowledge of the institution's aims and programmes which it affords, the librarian cannot begin to plan his buildings and services to meet the predictable needs. When these are known to him, it is for him to determine what existing technologies will best serve and how 'advanced' it is practicable for his thinking to be, and to write his building programme accordingly. The true 'developing' situation is one in which sane planning in accordance with circumstances of time and place is inspired by the vision of still better things to come, even if their exact nature is not at present clearly definable.

REFERENCES

1. Axford, H. W., 'Performance budgeting at the Florida Atlantic University Library', *College and Research Libraries,* March 1971, pp. 87–95.
2. Mason, E., 'The great gas bubble prick't; or, computers revealed', *College and Research Libraries,* May 1971, pp. 183–96.
3. Educational Facilities Laboratories, *The impact of technology on the library building,* New York, EFL, 1967.

Library Literature and *Library and Information Science Abstracts* contain many further references.

APPENDIX

BARBADOS	M. E. Gill, Librarian, University of West Indies, Bridgetown, Barbados.
CEYLON	T. G. Piyadasa, Acting Librarian, Vidyalankara University, Kelaniya, Ceylon.
CYPRUS	C. D. Stephanou, Chief Librarian, Library Paedagogical Academy, Nicosia, Cyprus.
ETHIOPIA	Mrs. R. Pankhurst, Haile Selassie I University Library, Addis Ababa, Ethiopia.
GHANA	A. G. T. Ofori, Director of Library Services, Ghana Library Board, Accra, Ghana.
	D. Cornelius, Principal Librarian, Accra Central Library, Ghana.
INDIA	D. R. Kalia, Special Duty Officer, Central Secretariat Library, New Delhi, India.
	J. C. Mehta, Delhi Public Library, S. P. Muckerji Marg, Delhi, 6, India.
	M. N. Nagaraj, Assistant Librarian, National Library, Calcutta, India.
IRAN	Mrs. P. Soltani, Chief of the Cataloguing Dept., Tehran Book Processing Centre, Tehran, Iran.
JAMAICA	Mrs. S. W. Ferguson, Chief Librarian, College of Arts, Science and Technology, Kingston, Jamaica.
	Miss L. T. Thomas, Deputy Director, Jamaica Library Service, Kingston, Jamaica.
	Mrs. S. Lampart, Senior Librarian, St. Thomas Parish Library, Morant Bay, Jamaica.
JORDAN	F. Mo'az, City Librarian of Amman, Municipal Public Library, Amman, Jordan.
KENYA	F. O. Pala, Chief Librarian, Kenya National Library Service, Nairobi, Kenya.
KOREA	K. H. Park, Librarian, Institute of Science and Technology, Seoul, Korea.
	B. M. Rhee, Instructor, Dept. of Library Science, Yonsei University, Seoul, Korea.
LEBANON	F. L. Kent, Librarian, American University of Beirut.
MALAYSIA	Miss P. Ng Soo Ching, Assistant Director, National Library of Malaysia, Kuala Lumpur, Malaysia.
	J. S. Soosai, Librarian, Rubber Research Institute of Malaya Library, Kuala Lumpur, Malaysia.
NIGERIA	K. Okorie, Director of Library Services and Secretary to the Board, East Central State Library Board, Enugu, Nigeria.
	S. B. Aje, Director, National Library of Nigeria, Lagos, Nigeria.
	Mrs. F. A. Ogunsheye, Assoc. Professor and Acting Head, Dept. of Library Studies, Ibadan University, Ibadan, Nigeria.
PAKISTAN	S. J. Haider, Assistant Professor, Department of Library Science, University of Karachi, Pakistan.
SINGAPORE	H. T. Lim, Senior Assistant Librarian, Library, University of Singapore, Singapore.
SUDAN	I. D. Mamoun, Librarian, Shambat Library, University of Khartoum, Khartoum, Sudan.
TAIWAN	Tze-Chung Li, Director, National Central Library, Taiwan.
TANZANIA	F. K. Tawete, Librarian, College of National Education Library, Dar Es Salaam, Tanzania.

THAILAND	Miss S. Ambhanwong, Librarian, Central Library, Chulalongkorn University, Bangkok, Thailand.
TRINIDAD & TOBAGO	Miss L. Hutchinson, Acting Principal Librarian, Central Library of Trinidad & Tobago, Port of Spain, Trinidad & Tobago.
UGANDA	T. K. Lwanga, University Librarian, Makerere University Library, Kampala, Uganda.
ZAMBIA	L. Z. Cheelo, City Librarian, Lusaka City Library, Lusaka, Zambia.

SELECT INDEX

Of participants, countries represented and types of library and themes surveyed at the Seminar